EMBRACING QUEER STUDENTS' DIVERSE
IDENTITIES AT HISTORICALLY BLACK
COLLEGES AND UNIVERSITIES

EMBRACING QUEER STUDENTS' DIVERSE IDENTITIES AT HISTORICALLY BLACK COLLEGES AND UNIVERSITIES

A Primer for Presidents, Administrators, and Faculty

EDITED BY
STEVE D. MOBLEY, JR.,
NADREA R. NJOKU, JENNIFER M. JOHNSON, AND LORI D. PATTON

FOREWORD BY
BEVERLY GUY-SHEFTALL

RUTGERS UNIVERSITY PRESS
New Brunswick, Camden, and Newark, New Jersey,
London and Oxford

Rutgers University Press is a department of Rutgers, The State University of New Jersey, one of the leading public research universities in the nation. By publishing worldwide, it furthers the University's mission of dedication to excellence in teaching, scholarship, research, and clinical care.

Library of Congress Cataloging-in-Publication Data

Names: Mobley, Steve D., editor. | Njoku, Nadréa R., editor. | Johnson, Jennifer M., 1970- editor. | Patton, Lori D., editor.
Title: Embracing queer students' diverse identities at historically Black colleges and universities : a primer for presidents, administrators, and faculty / edited by Steve D. Mobley, Jr., Nadrea R. Njoku, Jennifer M. Johnson, and Lori D. Patton ; foreword by Beverly Guy-Sheftall.
Description: New Brunswick : Rutgers University Press, [2025] | Includes bibliographical references and index.
Identifiers: LCCN 2024003470 | ISBN 9781978816091 (paperback ; acid-free paper) | ISBN 9781978816138 (cloth ; acid-free paper) | ISBN 9781978816107 (epub) | ISBN 9781978816121 (pdf)
Subjects: LCSH: African American universities and colleges—Administration. | Sexual minority students—Education (Higher) | Sexual minority college students—Identity. | Belonging (Social psychology)
Classification: LCC LC2781 .E55 2025 | DDC 378.1/982660973—dc23/eng/20240531
LC record available at https://lccn.loc.gov/2024003470

A British Cataloging-in-Publication record for this book is available from the British Library.

This collection copyright © 2025 by Rutgers, The State University of New Jersey
Individual chapters copyright © 2025 in the names of their authors
All rights reserved

No part of this book may be reproduced or utilized in any form or by any means, electronic or mechanical, or by any information storage and retrieval system, without written permission from the publisher. Please contact Rutgers University Press, 106 Somerset Street, New Brunswick, NJ 08901. The only exception to this prohibition is "fair use" as defined by U.S. copyright law.

References to internet websites (URLs) were accurate at the time of writing. Neither the author nor Rutgers University Press is responsible for URLs that may have expired or changed since the manuscript was prepared.

∞ The paper used in this publication meets the requirements of the American National Standard for Information Sciences—Permanence of Paper for Printed Library Materials, ANSI Z39.48-1992.

rutgersuniversitypress.org

To all the students who have called for this book by crossing our paths and bravely telling their stories.

CONTENTS

Foreword by Beverly Guy-Sheftall   ix

Introduction: (Re)Calling the Past and Present   1
STEVE D. MOBLEY JR.

PART I: ESSENTIAL QUEER AND TRANS* VOICES FROM WITH/IN HISTORICALLY BLACK COLLEGES AND UNIVERSITIES

1   And Some of Us Are Queer: An HBCU Sankofa Story   15
K. T. EWING

2   The (Mis)Education of Yémaya: Fostering Togetherness with Black Trans* Womx[x]yn Students at Historically Black Colleges and Universities through Policy Reformation and (Re)Education   32
YÉMAYA DIAVIAN POPE

3   Intersectionality in Theory and Praxis: The Role of Student Organizing as Preparation for Fostering Inclusive Spaces as an HBCU Administrator   49
TRINICE MCNALLY

PART II: ACKNOWLEDGING THE URGENT AND NECESSARY: ORGANIZATIONAL ACCOUNTS OF CULTURAL TRANSFORMATION AT HBCUS

4   Inclusion Flows from the Top: The Role of Boards in Building Inclusive Campuses at HBCUs   67
FELECIA COMMODORE AND ASHLEY GRAY

5   Blazing the Trail: Creating an LGBTQIA-Inclusive Campus   84
CHEVELLE MOSS-SAVAGE, LETIZIA GAMBRELL-BOONE, AND MAKOLA M. ABDULLAH

6   When HBCUs Speak OUT: Navigating HBCU Culture and Queer Student Expectations as Student Affairs Professionals   95
DARRYL B. HOLLOMAN, DARYL LOWE, BONNIE TAYLOR, AND LESLIE HALL

7	Understanding the Engagement and Politics of Quare HBCU Student Leaders	109
	TOBIAS RAPHAEL MORGAN	
8	Creating Inclusive Academic Spaces for Queer Students at HBCUs	124
	KATHRYN C. WYMER, JENNIFER M. WILLIAMS, AND W. RUSSELL ROBINSON	
9	The Lavender Fund, the First Officially Recognized University-Wide LGBT Fundraiser in HBCU History: How It Came to Be and How It Continues	139
	CHRISTOPHER N. CROSS AND DIANA LU	

PART III: DELIBERATE AND INTENTIONAL QUEER AND TRANS* SCHOLARLY HBCU EXPLORATIONS

10	A Manifesto for Black Quare Liberation and Inclusion at HBCUs	157
	JARREL T. JOHNSON	
11	Outsider Within: The Experiences of Queer Black Women College Athletes at Historically Black Colleges and Universities	170
	CHRISTA J. PORTER AND AKILAH R. CARTER-FRANCIQUE	
12	Queering the Yard: LGBTQ Advocacy, Experiences, and Socialization at Two Public HBCUs	184
	MICHELE K. LEWIS AND ISIAH MARSHALL JR.	
13	Researching Alongside, For, and By Black, Gay, Lesbian, Bisexual, Transgender, and Queer Communities at HBCUs: A Reflection	196
	LORI D. PATTON, NADREA R. NJOKU, AND JENNIFER M. JOHNSON	

Acknowledgments	203
Notes on Contributors	205
Index	213

FOREWORD
BEVERLY GUY-SHEFTALL

HBCUs must be advocates for and support *all* Black identities—especially those that lie in the margins (e.g. social class, sexuality, gender, gender identity, religion, etc). *Embracing Queer Students' Diverse Identities at Historically Black Colleges and Universities* is groundbreaking, and I am pleased to offer a praise song. For over four decades as founding director of the Women's Research & Resource Center at Spelman College and a women's studies professor, I have been committed to institutional and curricular transformation around lesbian, gay, bisexual, trans*, and queer (LGBTQ) issues at HBCUs.[1] This pioneering anthology fulfills all my wishes as they relate to the publication of rigorous, candid, data-driven, visionary essays from the perspectives of HBCU stakeholders, including senior-level administrators, faculty, student affairs practitioners, and HBCU researchers who have a deep and vested interest in these distinct and formidable institutions. While their analyses and solutions are powerful and consistent with my own observations and scholarship about Black queer and trans* matters at HBCUs, I was especially compelled by their careful and thorough case studies in various contexts, particularly public universities. This volume deliberately underscores that neither Black colleges nor their stakeholders are a monolith (see the introduction, this volume).

We have come a long way since I began my teaching career in 1971 at Alabama State University. LGBTQ centers now exist at eight HBCUs, as well as queer studies courses and queer student organizations, Safe Zone trainings, queer-inclusive presidential advisory boards, gender-neutral bathrooms, Lavender Graduation ceremonies, more visible out queer professors, and collaborations with boards of trustees and alumni. However, "for many Black queer HBCU students, their institutional status remains ambiguous" (chapter 1, p. 16). Spelman College has been cited for its cutting-edge and pioneering queer-friendly efforts—especially where academic matters are concerned. We are the only HBCU that has attained the following:

1. A women's studies major that includes a queer studies concentration,
2. A dedicated tenure line in queer studies,
3. An endowed professorship in queer studies, and
4. Substantial external funding over several decades, including from the Ford, Arcus and Mellon Foundations, for a variety of gender and sexuality projects.

Spelman College also has a supportive Student Affairs Division with leadership that has ushered in significant change in recent years (see chapter 6).

What makes this anthology a pioneering contribution to scholarship surrounding LGBTQ inclusion on HBCU campuses are the portraits of those universities that have tackled issues around queer friendliness; the meticulous attention to diagnoses of what ails us; the articulation of carefully crafted solutions that have worked on various campuses, especially when senior leadership, Boards of Trustees, alumni, student development professionals, faculty, and student organizations are committed to institutional change; and the candor with which the contributors approach the barriers, including conservative heteronormative cultures that have characterized HBCUs historically.

It is certainly the case that HBCUs, which were founded in the nineteenth century for formerly enslaved African Americans, are well known for empowering students to become leaders and change agents. And yet too many of our queer and trans* students experience chilly and unwelcoming environments on many of our campuses. This first-of-its kind collection provides a useful blueprint for how HBCUs can become queer-inclusive and queer-affirming with respect to its LGBTQ students and curricula. We know that the cultures of racial justice that HBCUs have intentionally and admirably cultivated are in large measure responsible for our success in educating high-quality undergraduates. We are now at a critical juncture where a new challenge awaits us—that of crafting cultures on our campuses in which academic excellence, inclusion, and equity are at the forefront of our institutional imperatives. *Embracing Queer Students' Diverse Identities* makes our task easier. Let's get to work!

NOTE

1. See especially *Facilitating Campus Climates of Pluralism, Inclusivity, and Progressive Change at HBCUs*, coedited by M. Jacqui Alexander and Beverly Guy-Sheftall. This project resource book, which the Arcus Foundation funded, circulated at the culminating event of The Audre Lorde Project, Phase II, Conference at Spelman College.

EMBRACING QUEER STUDENTS' DIVERSE
IDENTITIES AT HISTORICALLY BLACK
COLLEGES AND UNIVERSITIES

INTRODUCTION
(Re)Calling the Past and Present
STEVE D. MOBLEY JR.

Embracing Queer Students' Diverse Identities at Historically Black Colleges and Universities: A Primer for Presidents, Administrators, and Faculty has been a long time in the making. This book began as an idea in 2017 and has now come to fruition in 2024. This book is both a call to action and a passion project—imbued in Black love. This communal anthology summons a protective care for Black queer and trans* folx, Black communities, and historically Black colleges and universities (HBCUs). The volume is a "for us, by us" (FUBU) project. It does not talk at or down to HBCUs with voices from the "outside." Further, this volume is the *first* of its kind. It is indeed a shift changer. While there have been several edited volumes within the fields of higher education and student affairs that focus exclusively on queer and trans* issues and *may* feature HBCU perspectives, these works have not focused exclusively on HBCU contexts.

It is also important to note that historically and contemporarily, HBCU communities have been misrepresented and exploited not only in the broader societal context, but in education research as well (Milner, 2007; Mobley & Johnson, 2019). As editors, we understand that HBCUs have been victims of anti-Black *and* ill-intended research that has gravely impacted how the public perceives them (Williams et al., 2019). As such, this book features the much-needed perspectives of HBCU scholars, presidents, faculty, administrators, and alumni that have been and are invested in the work of ensuring that these distinct institutions are champions for their queer and trans* stakeholders. This is vital to consider because mainstream HBCU narratives are often sanitized and would lead one to believe that these unique postsecondary contexts have been devoid of queer and trans* communities (Mobley et al., 2019).

Any discussion about the presence of HBCU queer and trans* cultures has to make clear that these particular communities have always attended, graduated, led, and taught at these schools (Sales, 2011). This is not a contemporary discussion or phenomena. Black queer and trans* HBCU stakeholders have shaped and transformed the U.S. societal context to effectuate change not only for Black queer and trans* individuals but for society writ large. There have been countless prominent Black queer and trans* HBCU alumni, faculty, and administrators. Zora Neale Hurston, Langston Hughes, Audre Lorde, Bayard Rustin, Pauli Murray, Alain Locke, Barbara Jordan, Andre Leon Talley, Wanda Sykes, Lucy Diggs Slowe, Alice Walker, and countless others have various ties to HBCUs. However, when they are heralded in the mainstream or within HBCU discourses, their queer or trans* identities are often erased or their HBCU affiliations are left out of dialogues surrounding their lives. This is negligent and conveys that Blackness, queerness, or transness cannot be one with HBCU experiences.

(RE)ADDRESSING A PALPABLE VOID IN HBCU SCHOLARSHIP

Several decades of HBCU research have enhanced our scholarly perspectives of the histories of these institutions, the challenges they have and continue to face, and how their students, faculty, and administrators experience these contexts. Much of the extant HBCU research has also sought to affirm their legacies and (re)assert their relevancy among higher education landscapes that are often white supremacist and anti-Black. As Williams et al. (2019) note, "Broader narratives about HBCUs—not unlike the narratives attached to Black Americans in general—too often depict them from a deficit perspective, without balanced or nuanced consideration of their assets" (p. 558).

HBCUs should be celebrated for how they unabashedly provide Black students with culturally affirming academic and social environments (see Fleming, 1984; Fries-Britt & Turner, 2002; Johnson & McGowan, 2017; Njoku et al., 2017; Williams et al., 2022). Also of note, although HBCUs make up just 3% of U.S. postsecondary contexts, in 2020, "Black students earned 44% of the associate's degrees, 79% percent of the bachelor's degrees, 72% of the master's degrees, and 59 percent of the doctoral degrees conferred by HBCUs during the 2019–2020 academic year" (National Center for Education Statistics, 2020, para. 6). This must be commended, especially considering that HBCUs have been intentionally underfunded since their inceptions compared to historically white institutions (HWIs) and *still* outperform HWIs regarding Black student success.

However, while it is vital to mention these facts, it is also important to note some nuances. Most scholars, to date, have treated HBCUs and their students as a monolith. As a result, many facets of these institutions are understudied. For example, research exploring the intraracial differences among Black communities on HBCU campuses is still scant. Specifically, although there is a bourgeoning research lineage that deliberately underscores the experiences of lesbian, gay, bisexual, and queer (LGBQ) HBCU stakeholders, this scholarship has significant gaps. The majority of this scholarship features the experiences of LGBQ students—with most featuring the lived experiences of gay HBCU students (e.g. Carter, 2013; Ford, 2015; Means & Jaeger, 2013; Patton, 2011; Squire & Mobley, 2015). Very few studies in the literature on LGBQ HBCU students feature the experiences of lesbian-identified students (e.g., De la Cruz et al., 2022; Patton et al., 2020; Patton & Simmons, 2008). In addition, work on the experiences of trans* HBCU students does not exist. We also still know very little about how LGBQ and trans* HBCU faculty, staff, or administrators navigate their HBCU campuses.

Thus, as editors, we were driven by one question that we grappled with constantly as we conceived and thought about what *Embracing Queer Students' Diverse Identities at Historically Black Colleges and Universities* should contribute and then address: Are the experiences of Black LGBQ and trans* HBCU stakeholders overlooked in previous scholarship or have these perspectives been included and presented as *just* Black, thus dismissing the unique and diverse sexual and gender identities that are abundant in HBCU communities (Mobley et al., 2020; Stewart, 2015)? It is sobering to contend with the reality that the queer and trans* identities of LGBQ and trans* students, faculty, staff, and administrators have been minimized or erased in previous studies simply for the sake of including Black voices in previous research. Conversely, it was not lost on us that due to the conservative cultures that HBCUs often engender, their LGBQ and trans* stakeholders may have been reluctant to be "out" even in research realms. Even in books, book chapters, and journal articles, LGBQ and trans* folx have not been safe. So what we as editors and the contributors in this volume sought to do was to make clear how various LGBQ and trans* HBCU stakeholders have stood and do stand at the forefront of ensuring that these educational contexts are among the sites where Blackness can be and has been everlastingly (re)imagined and given space to be (re)presented in its infinite possibilities (Mobley & Hall, 2020).

ORGANIZATION OF THE BOOK

Part One

This book consists of thirteen chapters and is organized around three parts that encompass diverse perspectives on how to best engage LGBQ and trans* communities at HBCUs. The first section—Essential Queer and Trans* Voices from with/in Historically Black Colleges and Universities—is uniquely powerful. These contributors travel across space and time and (re)tell their stories in the form of scholarly personal narratives. In *Liberating Scholarly Writing*, Nash (2004) wrote, "scholarly personal narratives . . . are about giving yourself permission to express your own voice in your own language; your own take on your own story in your own inimitable manner" (p. 24). Each narrative is bold and candid and invites HBCUs to learn and liberate themselves in a particular manner.

In chapter 1, Dr. K. T. Ewing sets the tone of the entire volume with their work titled "And Some of Us Are Queer: An HBCU Sankofa Story." Dr. Ewing shares their lived experiences of being Black and queer at an HBCU and how they navigated these particular identities as an HBCU faculty member. In the Ghanaian Twi language, Sankofa means "go back and get it." In its simplest rendering, Sankofa conjures what it means to look to the past to gain what you need for the future. HBCUs remain appealing to Black students because they can provide an environment that values the histories and lived experiences of Black people. However, what Ewing underscores is that despite how HBCUs have stood at the forefront of historical movements for Black liberation and equality, they are subtly and sometimes strikingly conservative environments. Dr. Ewing beautifully conveys the beauty and tensions of their HBCU experiences. In particular, this chapter examines what support systems and self-care for queer students can look like from the perspective of a Black, queer HBCU alum and faculty member. They also offer recommendations for how HBCU faculty members can fully support their queer students.

The author of chapter 2, Yémaya Diavian Pope, provides an intimate look at how trans* HBCU students navigate their institutional context. In her chapter, "The (Mis)Education of Yémaya: Fostering Togetherness with Black Trans* Womx[x]yn Students at Historically Black Colleges & Universities through Policy Reformation and (Re)Education," you will observe a theme woven throughout: Black womx[x]yn. Her (re)telling is especially compelling because she is the first trans* female on record to graduate from Morehouse College in the school's over 150-year history. Also, Yémaya was the first full-time female student on the Morehouse student record since the 1930s, which, as a graduate, makes her the first institutionally documented Morehouse woman in over eighty years. She even shifts language in her chapter. Her spelling of "womx[x]yn" when referring to Black womx[x]yn (cisgender and trans*) in plural form is meant to create a visual distinction (with the use of brackets) that acknowledges biologically constructed notions of gender and highlights both the pluralistic and specious nature of womanhood. Yémaya's contribution focuses on Black trans* HBCU womx[x]yn in higher education and the nature of their (mis)education at HBCUs—a miseducation rooted in a lack of togetherness. She makes clear that she does not emphasize Black trans* womx[x]yn students in order to negate or erase Black trans* men and other trans* and queer identities. Yémaya's choice to underscore the experiences of Black trans* womx[x]yn is because they are and have been relegated to the margins and erased in broader societal discourses, in HBCU scholarship, and on college and university campuses.

With chapter 3, Trinice McNally rounds out this portion of the work and provides a rich journey. Her contribution, "Intersectionality in Theory and

Praxis: The Role of Student Organizing as Preparation for Fostering Inclusive Spaces as an HBCU Administrator," highlights her journey as a Black, queer immigrant woman who began her journey of activism, from founding the first Gay-Straight Alliance at an HBCU in Florida to becoming the founding director of the first Center for Diversity, Inclusion and Multicultural Affairs at the University of the District of Columbia. In addition, her work provides recommendations about ways HBCUs can foster both intersectional and inclusive learning environments that are committed to centering the experiences of historically marginalized students in order to bring about the transformation required to shift the learning environments and culture for queer HBCU students.

Part Two

In the second part—Acknowledging the Urgent and Necessary: Organizational Accounts of Cultural Transformation at HBCUs—the contributors delve deeply into how HBCU organizational structures, including HBCU boards of trustees, presidents, faculty, and administrators, can best engage their GLBQ and trans* communities. In chapter 4, titled "Inclusion Flows from the Top: The Role of Boards in Building Inclusive Campuses at HBCUs," Drs. Felecia Commodore and Ashley Gray, highlight how institutional leadership at HBCUs can intentionally and strategically support LGBTQ students, faculty, and staff. Focusing specifically on the board of trustees, the chapter explores how board composition can impact the decision-making processes and ultimately the decisions that shape strategic planning and culture of an institution. With a special focus on private institutions, they discuss board diversity, board member values, ideologies, and external relationships and the ways boards can collectively work to address the needs of LGBTQ students. They also make recommendations for future research and practice.

Chapter 5, "Blazing the Trail: Creating an LGBTQIA-Inclusive Campus," is especially unique because it features a blueprint of how an HBCU president and their cabinet can and should endeavor to support queer and trans* inclusivity on their campus. Chevelle Moss-Savage and Drs. Letizia Gambrell-Boone and Makola M. Abdullah highlight how Virginia State University (VSU) has worked to best support their lesbian, gay, bisexual, transgender, queer/questioning, intersex and asexual/agender+ (LGBTQIA+) students. Under the leadership of President Abdullah, VSU has been at the forefront of conveying a model of how presidential buy-in is especially important for engaging queer and trans* HBCU stakeholders. This chapter also provides commentary for future research and action steps for HBCU presidents interested in creating a more visibly inclusive campus for HBCU LGBTQIA+ community members who are navigating multiple intersecting identities.

Chapter 6 features a dynamic scholar-practitioner team. With Dr. Darryl B. Holloman at the helm, this contribution, "When HBCUs Speak OUT: Navigating

HBCU Culture and Queer Student Expectations as Student Affairs Professionals," documents how the vice-president of student affairs and his cabinet at Spelman College have engaged this work. His narrative is distinct because he is the first openly gay man to serve as vice-president of student affairs at his traditionally all-women HBCU. In this chapter, Dr. Holloman, Daryl Lowe, Dr. Bonnie Taylor, and Dr. Leslie Hall affirm that queer and trans* communities have always contributed to HBCU cultures. The chapter also underscores how it is imperative for HBCU vice-presidents of student affairs to lead the charge to ensure that their campus environments promote student success for *all* of their students. This chapter also highlights the innovative initiatives occurring at Spelman and provides recommendations to help to guide HBCU vice-presidents of student affairs as they advocate for and provide programming and services for their queer and trans* students.

In chapter 7, "Understanding the Engagement and Politics of Quare HBCU Student Leaders," Dr. Tobias Raphael Morgan foregrounds his experiences as a queer and questioning HBCU student leader and places them in conversation with his time as a student affairs administrator to convey how HBCUs can best serve their LGBQ and trans* HBCU student leaders.[1] This chapter provides rich insights into how HBCU student affairs stakeholders should challenge tradition and make room for queer and trans* students who aspire to or currently are involved in HBCU royal courts or student government and even those who may pursue membership in Black Greek letter organizations.

Chapter 8, "Creating Inclusive Academic Spaces for Queer Students at HBCUs," is based on major developments that have occurred at North Carolina Central University (NCCU) to increase academic inclusivity and advocacy for its queer students. In this chapter, Dr. Kathryn Wymer, Jennifer Williams, and Dr. W. Russell Robinson offer valuable insights into how HBCU faculty can create inclusive academic environments and offer specific strategies for engaging HBCU communities inside and outside the classroom. NCCU has also had to grapple with legal challenges, such as North Carolina's HB2, which many at the time deemed the most anti-LGBT law in the United States. Faculty and administrators responded by creating academic spaces to facilitate productive conversations and action. Together these three authors highlight the academic programming that has been developed and show models for how HBCU faculty and administrators can actively support their LGBQ and trans* communities.

In the final chapter of this section, Drs. Christopher N. Cross and Diana Lu provide guidance about how HBCU advancement offices can engage their LGBQ and trans*stakeholders. Chapter 9, "The Lavender Fund, the First Officially Recognized University-Wide LGBT Fundraiser in HBCU History: How It Came to Be, and How It Continues," describes the establishment of the Lavender Fund at Howard University. This initiative is the first university-sponsored HBCU platform for actively engaging current queer and trans* students and alumni. The authors discuss how this initiative was championed using a top-down administrative approach that began with the Board of Trustees and the university president to establish key infrastructures coupled with fund-raising to engage queer and trans* students, alumni, and allies. This work also offers thoughtful recommendations for how this type of work can be replicated in other HBCU communities.

Part Three

The final part of the book, Deliberate and Intentional Queer and Trans* Scholarly HBCU Explorations shows how researchers can and should engage LGBQ and trans* HBCU communities with an ethic of care. In chapter 10, "A Manifesto for Black Quare Liberation and Inclusion at HBCUs," Dr. Jarrel T. Johnson outlines four tenets for HBCU administrators to consider as they seek to create inclusive environments for their quare and trans* collegians: (1) quaring student identities, (2) quaring HBCU organizational structures, (3) quaring student policies and practices, and (4) quaring for co-conspirators. The basis for these tenets is a quare theory framework (Ferguson, 2004; Johnson, 2001; Johnson & Henderson, 2005) that highlights the lived experiences of Black queer and trans* identities, illuminates the relationship between theory and practice, and dismantles forces of power and oppression that relegate quare and trans* collegians to the margins of HBCUs. Dr. Johnson also used the quare theory framework to empower HBCU administrators to understand the roles they can play in affirming the emancipation of Black identities at multiple intersections and in systematically mobilizing queer and trans* student inclusion efforts on their respective campuses. At the conclusion of this manifesto, Dr. Johnson provides recommendations for future institutional practices and policies at HBCUs.

Chapter 11, "Outsider Within: The Experiences of Queer Black Women College Athletes at Historically Black Colleges and Universities," provides insights into a topic that has rarely been discussed. The content of this chapter will benefit professionals in higher education and student affairs and members of HBCU communities. In this chapter, Drs. Christa J. Porter and Akilah R. Carter-Francique illuminate the experiential realities of Black queer women college athletes at HBCUs. Research on this topic has found that Black women college athletes live at the intersections of marginalization based on their race, their gender, and their social class and are consequently rendered silent and invisible. Only a tiny portion of that literature has highlighted the multiplicative identity intersections that queerness creates. Acknowledging HBCUs and their cultural climate, Drs. Porter and Carter-Francique employ intersectionality and the concept of "outsider within" status to unpack the contemporary structural, political, and representational effects that occur within athletic HBCU realms.

In chapter 12, Drs. Michele K. Lewis and Isiah Marshall Jr. provide insight and guidance about how HBCU administrations can use financial and relational resources to address and support queer issues within the context of the HBCU experience. In their study, "Queering the Yard: LGBTQ Advocacy, Experiences, and Socialization at Two Public HBCUs," the authors focus on Winston-Salem State University and Jackson State University. Their work illustrates a continuing need for the expansion of policies that foster inclusivity and sensitivity, including policies for transgender students on campus. The chapter concludes with a discussion of current and planned social activities and advocacy efforts and the curricular and co-curricular changes HBCU stakeholders in North Carolina and Mississippi identified as necessary for the support of queer and trans* students.

The final chapter of this book offers critical insights from my co-editors, Drs. Nadrea Njoku, Jennifer M. Johnson, and Lori D. Patton. In chapter 13, "Researching, Alongside, for, and by Black, Gay, Lesbian, Bisexual, Transgender, and Queer Communities at HBCUs: A Reflection," they provide guidance and offer reflections on their experiences researching alongside and for LGBQ HBCU communities. Each of the chapter authors has contributed to the current research pertaining to the central nature of this volume. Each also has an insider/outsider status which is quite captivating to see them unpack in their contribution to this work. Each coauthor has individually and collectively worked to amplify the experiences of LGBQ and trans* HBCU communities through their research, scholarship, and practice. This chapter makes space, asks and answers questions, and provides room for the next phase of HBCU queer and trans* work in a particular manner.

The dearth of research pertaining to LGBQ and trans* HBCU stakeholders has resulted in a myopic view of HBCU experiences that begs for more nuance. Here is where essential queer and trans* voices from with/in HBCUs enter scholarly and practical education spaces. HBCU communities are now at a vital junction and must rise to the occasion. It is morally necessary for HBCUs to (re)examine their positions on how they choose to engage their LGBQ and trans* stakeholders. *Now* is the time. It has *been* time!

A CALL TO ACTION

Not only is there a critical need for more research exploring LGBQ and trans* HBCUs communities, but acknowledging, understanding, and ultimately supporting these distinct communities is also necessary. Given the central role HBCUs play in providing leadership within their institutions and education that centers Black communities, these schools are uniquely positioned to grapple with how to best engage their LGBQ and trans* stakeholders. This book seeks to open an opportunity for HBCU presidents, administrators, and faculty to model and facilitate conversations regarding these folx on their campuses, in surrounding communities, and in society writ large.

A major strength of this edited volume are the perspectives of the contributors, who include HBCU presidents, faculty members, administrators, alumni, and HBCU researchers. These individuals are uniquely positioned to offer practice- and policy-oriented recommendations to ensure that HBCUs are accessible and welcoming spaces for diverse learning and development. Each author shares specific challenges and considerations related to serving LGBQ and trans* populations within these distinct college and university settings. The ultimate goal of this book is to summon HBCU communities, higher education scholars, and scholar-practitioners to take thoughtful and urgent action to support and recognize these individuals. With this book as a primary resource, HBCUs can work toward becoming fully inclusive campus communities for their queer and trans* stakeholders.

The goal of this book is to serve as a guide for HBCU communities about how they seek to best engage and create environments that inculcate success that includes holistic identities of Blackness, queerness, and transness. *Embracing Queer Students' Diverse Identities at Historically Black Colleges and Universities: A Primer for Presidents, Administrators, and Faculty* contains scholarship that can serve as a major resource for HBCU constituents as they begin and sustain transformative dialogues that challenge their students, faculty, and administrators to extend conversations surrounding LGBQ and trans* issues. The ways HBCUs provide support for these populations will undoubtedly impact higher education, Black communities, and the larger society (Lenning, 2017; Lewis & Ericksen, 2016). Our hope is that this work will prompt HBCU communities, higher education scholars, and scholar-practitioners to take action so that HBCUs can more intentionally engage in the necessary work of becoming inclusive campus communities for all of their LGBQ and trans* stakeholders.

NOTE

1. In this book, two authors use quare theory and use the term "quare" in their chapters to describe Black LGBQ and trans* communities at HBCUs. This is done because quare theory is useful in making sense of Black queer and trans* students' identities. Unlike queer theory, quare theory contests white Western queer and trans* liberation norms and the notion that a person's identities can be understood as detached constructs (Johnson, 2001).

REFERENCES

Carter, B. A. (2013). "Nothing better or worse than being Black, gay, and in the band": A qualitative examination of gay undergraduates participating in historically Black college or university marching bands. *Journal of Research in Music Education*, 61(1), 26–43.

De la Cruz, J., Winfrey, A., & Solomon, S. (2022). Navigating the network: An exploratory study of LGBTQIA+ information practices at two single-sex HBCUs. *College & Research Libraries*, 83(2), 278–295.

Ferguson, R. A. (2004). *Aberrations in Black: Toward a queer of color of critique*. University of Minnesota Press.

Fleming, J. (1984). *Blacks in college: A comparative study of students' success in Black and in white institutions*. Jossey-Bass.

Ford, O., III. (2015). From navigation to negotiation: An examination of the lived experiences of Black gay male alumni of historically Black colleges and universities. *Journal of Homosexuality, 62*(3), 353–373.

Fries-Britt, S., & Turner, B. (2002). Uneven stories: Successful Black collegians at a Black and a white campus. *The Review of Higher Education, 25*(3), 315–330.

Johnson, E. P. (2001). "Quare" studies, or (almost) everything I know about queer studies I learned from my grandmother. *Text and Performance Quarterly, 21*(1), 1–25. doi:10.1080/10462930128119

Johnson, E. P., & Henderson, M. G. (2005). Introduction: Queering Black studies/ "quaring" queer studies. In E. P. Johnson & M. G. Henderson (Eds.), *Black queer studies* (pp. 1–17). Duke University Press.

Johnson, J. M., & McGowan, B. L. (2017). Untold stories: The gendered experiences of high achieving African American male alumni of historically Black colleges and universities. *Journal of African American Males in Education, 8*(1), 23–44.

Lenning, E. (2017). Unapologetically queer in unapologetically Black spaces: Creating an inclusive HBCU campus. *Humboldt Journal of Social Relations, 39*, 283–293.

Lewis, M. W., & Ericksen, K. S. (2016). Improving the climate for LGBTQ students at an historically Black university. *Journal of LGBT Youth, 13*(3), 249–269.

Means, D. R., & Jaeger, A. J. (2013). Black in the rainbow: "Quaring" the Black gay male student experience at historically Black universities. *Journal of African American Males in Education, 4*(2), 124–140.

Milner, H. R. (2007). Race, culture, and researcher positionality: Working through dangers seen, unseen, and unforeseen. *Educational Researcher, 36*(7), 388–400. doi:10.3102/0013189X07309471

Mobley, S. D., Jr., & Hall, L. (2020). (Re)Defining queer and trans* student retention and success at historically Black colleges and universities. *Journal of College Student Retention: Research, Theory & Practice, 21*(4), 497–519.

Mobley, S. D., Jr., & Johnson, J. M. (2019). "No pumps allowed": The "problem" with gender expression and the Morehouse College "Appropriate Attire Policy." *Journal of Homosexuality, 66*(7), 867–895.

Mobley, S. D., Jr., McNally, T., & Moore, G. (2019). Revealing the potential for HBCUs to be liberatory environments for queer students. In E. M. Zamani-Gallaher, D. D. Choudhuri, & J. L. Taylor (Eds.), *Rethinking LGBTQIA students and collegiate contexts: Identity, policies, and campus climate* (pp. 99–119). Routledge.

Mobley, S. D., Jr., Taylor, L. D., Jr., & Haynes, C. (2020). (Un)seen work: The pedagogical experiences of Black queer men in faculty roles. *International Journal of Qualitative Studies in Education, 33*, 604–620. https://doi.org/10.1080/09518398.2020.1747659

Nash, R. J. (2004). *Liberating scholarly writing: The power of personal narrative*. Teachers College Press.

National Center for Education Statistics. (2020). *Historically Black colleges and universities*. https://nces.ed.gov/fastfacts/display.asp?id=667

Njoku, N., Butler, M., & Beatty, C. C. (2017). Reimagining the historically Black college and university (HBCU) environment: Exposing race secrets and the binding chains of respectability and othermothering. *International Journal of Qualitative Studies in Education, 30*(8), 783–799.

Patton, L. D. (2011). Perspectives on identity, disclosure, and the campus environment among African American gay and bisexual men at one historically Black college. *Journal of College Student Development, 52*(1), 77–100.

Patton, L. D., Blockett, R. A., & McGowan, B. L. (2020). Complexities and contradictions: Black lesbian, gay, bisexual, and queer students' lived realities across three urban HBCU contexts. *Urban Education, 58*(6), 1355–1382, 1–28.

Patton, L. D. & Simmons, S. L. (2008). Exploring complexities of multiple identities in a Black college environment. *The Negro Educational Review, 59*(3–4), 197–215.

Sales, R. N. (2011). Their goodness followed their horizon's rim: Lesbians in HBCUs. In M. J. Alexander & B. Guy-Sheftall (Eds.), *Facilitating campus climates of pluralism, inclusivity, and progressive change at HBCUs* (pp. 113–180). Women's Research & Resource Center at Spelman College.

Squire, D. D., & Mobley, S. D., Jr. (2015). Negotiating race and sexual orientation in the college choice process of Black gay males. *The Urban Review, 47*(3), 466–491.

Williams, K. L., Burt, B. A., Clay, K. L., & Bridges, B. K. (2019). Stories untold: Counter-narratives to anti-Blackness and deficit-oriented discourse concerning HBCUs. *American Educational Research Journal, 56*(2), 556–599.

Williams, K. L., Mobley, S. D., Jr., Campbell, E., & Jowers, R. (2022). Meeting at the margins: Culturally relevant and sustaining practices at HBCUs for underserved populations. *Higher Education, 84*, 1067–1087.

PART 1 ESSENTIAL QUEER AND TRANS* VOICES FROM WITH/IN HISTORICALLY BLACK COLLEGES AND UNIVERSITIES

1 · AND SOME OF US ARE QUEER
An HBCU Sankofa Story
K. T. EWING

> When someone asks, "Why do you have to bring it up? Why can't you do whatever you want in the privacy of your own home?" they are ignoring our oppression. They are, in fact, suggesting that we not exist.
> —Smith, 1983/2000, p. xlix

Louisiana in June is akin to a romance novel. It is lush, humid, and blooming with life at the beginning of hurricane season. The summer I moved to New Orleans to attend Xavier University of Louisiana, like many young people, I began a college journey that would shape my future in ways I had dreamed of for years. My alma mater sits in one of the most enchanting cities in the country, and it was the perfect place to conjure a more authentic life. As a descendant of three generations of HBCU alumni, it was almost inevitable that I would choose one of those legacy-filled campuses to start my life anew. The first time I set foot in the Emerald City, I knew I was home. Once I arrived, I was determined to do more than survive. I wanted to thrive.

What does it mean to be Black and queer on an HBCU campus? Historically Black colleges and universities (HBCUs) were originally designed as welcoming learning environments for Black students. Beginning with the establishment of Cheyney University in 1837 and quickly rising in number after the demise of chattel slavery in the United States, HBCUs have excelled and continue to excel at fulfilling their missions of educating millions of Black students and preparing them to thrive in a landscape pockmarked by white supremacy. More students are enrolling in HBCUs since the rise of the Black Lives Matter movement and other campus movements for diversity and equity such as the Human Rights Campaign's HBCU initiative.

However, for many Black queer HBCU students, their institutional status remains ambiguous. They are visible enough to present a challenge to an assumed homogeneity, yet they are invisible enough to not warrant organizational and institutional support. For American-born students, their tripartite nature—American, Black, and queer—gives additional depth and nuance to W.E.B. Du Bois's (1903) theory of double consciousness. While they can take solace in a space that loudly affirms the inherent worth of Black people, they often must work harder to find or create spaces that affirm their queer identities. In order to fully live up to their mission of serving marginalized communities, HBCUs must continue moving in the direction of inclusivity for queer students. We are in the midst of the most openly affirming movement for Black lives ever (while still significantly failing trans women and trans men). From the release of *Bessie*, a film highlighting the life of a queer blues icon played by another queer musical icon, to Janelle Monae's public assertion of pansexuality, Generation Z comes to campus today with far more diverse images of themselves on television than Generation X or Millennials. This public affirmation matters pedagogically and from a student affairs perspective.

To explore the unique status of Black queer students in our institutions, the wisdom of our ancestors is useful. In the Ghanaian Twi language, Sankofa means "go back and get it." The word is reflected in the symbol of a bird with its head turned backward and an egg in its beak. In its simplest rendering, Sankofa conjures what it means to look to the past in order to gain what you need for the future. Historically Black colleges and universities remain appealing to Black students because they can provide an environment that values the histories and lived experiences of Black people. However, despite their presence at the forefront of historical movements for liberation and equality, HBCUs are subtly and sometimes strikingly conservative environments (Mobley et al., 2021; Njoku et al., 2017). For queer Black students, HBCUs can be as isolating as they are inviting. In order to continue fulfilling their missions of providing a quality education and a safe harbor to Black students, it is necessary to examine what support systems and self-care for queer Black students can entail, particularly when they are supported by faculty, staff, and administration (Johnson, 2021; Mobley & Hall, 2020).

HBCUs cannot fully support queer students if they are not accustomed to seeing them, recognizing the fullness of their humanity, and embracing them as equal members of the Black community. I was a queer Black student on an HBCU campus. I also have served as an associate professor of history at an HBCU. What follows is an examination of how I moved through my undergraduate institution and gathered the tools I would use to eventually become for others what I needed when I was most vulnerable. I offer this essay in the hope that HBCU faculty and administrators will use it as a lens into the journey of a young Black queer student who hoped to thrive on campus but had to do so with minimal institutional support. I found my way, and it is my duty to be a light and a compass.

The year 1982 marked the publication of *All the Women Are White, All the Blacks Are Men, But Some of Us Are Brave*. This collection of works was an embodiment of intersectionality years before legal scholar Kimberlé Crenshaw coined the term and gave a name to the theoretical framework that had shaped decades of Black women's scholarship and praxis (see Crenshaw, 1989; 1991). Hull et al. (1982) collected writings from a diverse range of Black women's experiences and academic disciplines to provide a road map for analyzing Black women's lives within a white supremacist framework. Although the impact of oppression factors highly in many of the works, Black liberation is a unifying theme. The women in *But Some of Us Are Brave* did not yield to systemic inequality. They carried a torch of freedom that revealed the nuances of their inner lives and lit a path for future generations of Black women scholars.

In 1983, immediately on the heels of *But Some of Us Are Brave*, Barbara Smith published *Home Girls: A Black Feminist Anthology*. As a Black lesbian feminist scholar, she paid particular attention to representing many types of Black women, including those who are typically unacknowledged in compilations of Black writings. While lovingly holding Black communities accountable for their role in perpetuating harm, Smith (1983/2000) clearly states that the "homophobia among Black people in America is largely reflective of the homophobic culture in which we live" (p. 190). *Home Girls* directly addresses the problems of racism, sexism, homophobia, and classism in a way that gives light to the overlapping, structural nature of these oppressions. This anthology, along with *But Some of Us Are Brave*, provides a critical window into understanding intersectionality, particularly now as younger scholars are interested in studying, transforming, and dismantling harmful structures in today's society.

The presence of Black, visibly queer scholars in the academy is a fulfillment and a call to action. I was born the year *Home Girls* was published. We came of age together. In some ways, my presence in academia is a manifestation of the book's dreams. However, my cohort and I are not the culmination of our ancestors' dreams. We are recipients of their legacy and have an obligation to continue smoothing the path for our descendants. In order to do this, particularly at HBCUs, it is necessary to go back and bring our queer pasts to the present. Our work is to make space for futures yet to manifest, for theory to become and remain praxis, for ideas to become flesh. With this understanding, my essay is part reflection, part literature review, and part instruction on what is necessary to create nurturing environments for Black queer students on HBCU campuses.

FINDING WHAT I NEEDED: THE COLLEGE YEARS

Someone should have told me I looked a mess. In a misguided attempt to grow into my adult self, I ended up looking like an early 2000s tragedy. My T-shirts were two sizes too large. My pants and shorts were equally ill fitting. High-top

Air Force 1s and Timberland boots were my favorite footwear. Whenever possible, I wore sweat suits. I did it so often that one of my professors called it my uniform. Even he, a middle-aged white man, knew I needed a fashion intervention. Worst of all, I kept my hair in straight-back cornrows with a bandana around the edges because I could not find any energy to care about styling it.

Twenty years into the future, many of us look back on that era and laugh at how very few people of any gender presentation pulled off a look that has not aged well. I was not in that number, not because I was a young queer Black woman, but because I was one without a sense of personal style. I was not freely participating in the latest fashion trend; I was trying to discover what my adult style could be when I had not had an opportunity to explore it before college.

I had spent the entirety of my preteen and teenage years rebelling against the traditionally feminine attire my perfumed princess of a mother bought for me. Much to her stylish chagrin, I inherited neither her sense of fashion nor her love of dresses, lace, and anything sparkly. She loves me dearly, but she did not understand me. Perhaps if I had been a more confident and stylish tomboy, we would have had an opportunity to bond over fashion and what it means to carefully adorn the body, even if we disagreed on the details. The moment I moved to Louisiana, securely beyond the loving tyranny of her wardrobe choices, I wrapped myself in androgynous clothing and attempted to blend into every wall I could find. Being a masculine queer woman comes with a heightened visibility that is intensely uncomfortable for people with loner tendencies. College was an opportunity for me to fade into the background and, like my cis-hetero counterparts, to fashion an adult identity largely on my own terms.

HBCUs have a useful practice of holding sessions that teach young people how to dress themselves professionally. Men from the campus community volunteer their time teaching young men how to tie a tie, select an appropriate business suit, match their belts and shoes, and so forth. Young women have access to a similar grooming process, although theirs tends to be more informal, on a one-on-one basis, or via an event hosted by any number of women's groups on campus. I noticed during my time as a professor at an HBCU that the university had a wonderful program that bussed students to local department stores that reserved several hours solely for the students. They were given special attention by the staff, taught the basics of professional dress, and given a large discount on purchases.

Although I recognize the white supremacist implications of teaching young Black students that their worth is determined by their attire, it is a genuine attempt on behalf of HBCU faculty and administrators to help ease the students' transition into adulthood. For many students, particularly first-generation college students, this grooming process is a necessary lifeline and introduction to the professional world that will help them accrue many career opportunities. An unfortunate flaw in this process is that because it reinforces traditional ideas of gendered dress, many queer students can find themselves left out.

I do not desire a queer version of this training. Rather, my point is to note that the absence is indicative of a lack of attention paid to this community. Providing the training while creating a more inclusive environment for queer students would ultimately reinforce a hierarchy of dress that reified a notion that in order to be taken seriously, queer students must emulate the restrictive standards that seemingly emphasize appearance over substance. While this would undoubtedly be personally affirming for many, ultimately it would not lead to the kind of structural transformation necessary for fully including Black queer students into an expanded vision of HBCU futures.

With regard to professional aesthetics, who are the models for queer, trans, and nonbinary students? Although there were several noticeable masculine women among my campus peers who had undeniable style, my loner tendencies generally kept me out of their orbit. The rest dressed almost as badly as I did. In our defense, the late 1990s and early 2000s was the era of tall tees and shorts that looked like cutoff wide-legged pants. Women who dress in traditionally feminine manners have a wide range of professionally dressed Black women on campus to observe as they develop their own style. Androgynous and masculine women generally lack similar models. Men who challenge and confront norms and mores surrounding what is masculine or who may choose to dress in gender-nonconforming manners also lack models, and an increased likelihood of physical violence also stunts their ability to fully express themselves via their attire (Mobley & Johnson, 2019). Trans women also experience the threat of violence for adorning themselves in accordance with their gender. On conservative campuses, the likelihood of queer students "seeing" an older authentic version of themselves was almost nonexistent. Unfortunately, this remains a problem.

I never figured out how to "properly" dress in college. I was also never taught the symbolic meaning of dress outside the importance of adorning myself respectably, whatever that was supposed to mean. We were taught that in order to be respected, we had to present ourselves as our elders in the Black Freedom Struggle did when they were our age. Interestingly enough, the emphasis was placed on their church clothes and *not* on their overalls. Sadly enough, this is often still true. Until more faculty employ a pedagogical approach that embraces working-class aesthetics beyond rhetoric, we will continue missing an opportunity to help students see themselves and the fullness of their communities reflected in history. For example, *Liberated Threads: Black Women, Style, and the Global Politics of Soul* shows us that "in substance and symbolically, soul and style politics writ large are more critical to the Black liberation and women's liberation struggles than we have previously recognized" (Ford, 2015, p. 3). When style is positioned as a liberatory ethic, it becomes easier to see how Black queer students' attire, even when they dress as shabbily as I did, is inextricable from a politics of visibility that stakes a claim on HBCU campuses (Ford, 2015). Being visible is often a first step toward claiming space and being recognized. Rather than policing or shunning their clothing and visible markers of queerness, this is an opportunity for faculty and administrators to recognize some of the most vulnerable students and ensure that they feel confident and welcome on campus. What might my college style have been if I had someone on campus who could teach me to adorn myself not in service to cisgender markers of adulthood and professionalism but rather with a nod to who I was becoming as an openly queer adolescent? In retrospect, I might have navigated campus life with the enhanced confidence that could have come from knowing I was dressed well and in alignment with how I saw myself in the world.

Fortunately, dressing poorly did not prevent me from cultivating romantic partnerships. Although I have always been generally even-tempered, like many of my peers, I experienced my first love and subsequent heartbreak all in the first few dizzying months of freshman year. When love was at its most exciting, I had no older adult to share it with. When I felt the pieces of my heart turn from pebbles to ash, I had no older adult to walk me through the pain. So I turned inward. In hindsight, the isolation might have been useful because it gave me the final push I needed to dedicate myself to finding queer foremothers to comfort me in a way my biological mother was unprepared to handle. In fairness to her, I never gave her an opportunity. That is one of the many ways that homoantagonism robs queer youth and their parents of opportunities to grow through benchmark moments with each other. The structural nature of homophobia crystallized my fear of disrupting the static dreams my mother was conditioned to have of her only daughter. That is a theft no one can repay. Mercifully, we have an opportunity to keep making deposits toward a future in which queer HBCU students can love and be loved beyond institutional barriers to their wholeness.

Then there was Dr. Gaudin. She was neither Black nor masculine presenting, but she saw me in spite of my half-hearted attempt to be invisible. She allowed her office to serve as a bridge between my student self and my inner self. She opened her door and simply let me exist. We chatted almost every day I was on campus. If there was nothing to say, she simply let me sit. I even took my lunches in there when I was not sunning myself on the grand steps at the entrance to the administration building. I felt as free in her office as I did under the New Orleans sun. Her quiet, steady embrace was liberating. She was a safe harbor, and I try to pass her gift on by pouring my time into my students. I have grown accustomed to queer students coming by simply to chat or grab a snack before heading to class or home. Even when they are not enrolled in my class, they are *my* students because we share a campus home.

Although I had many great instructors, there was only one who was equipped and willing to see me. I did not hide my inner life from my peers or faculty, but I also was not very forthcoming. The combination of my natural tendency toward solitude and a fear of open hostility ensured that I remained quiet and relatively isolated beyond my roommate, Zenobia Gaither, and my intimate circle of friends. This isolation increased after I moved off campus into a studio apartment the summer before my sophomore year. Along with stretches of sustained silence, I enjoyed having space to cultivate a queer, young adult self, free of the constant reminders of how I did not fit in with most of the other young women. Like any young scholar, I filled the silences with books and the soul-warming scent of Nag Champa mixed with Super Hit incense. Although I had a wonderful first-year roommate who loved and fully included me in her life, moving off campus literally gave me more space and uninterrupted time to think. It gave me the comfort of curating a personal library without concern for anyone entering our room, browsing the titles, and asking unwanted questions.

I found a world when I read my first Audre Lorde poems in the public library. The simply titled "Love Poem" in *The Collected Poems of Audre Lorde* (Lorde, 2000) was the first poem I had ever read by a woman to a woman that was not in a composition notebook shared by friends. This was "official" poetry to me. It was the kind of validation that said we could exist freely in life and in print. After devouring her poetry, I moved to her other writings. For me, none were more powerful than *Zami: A New Spelling of My Name* (Lorde, 1982/1998). Her biomythography, like her poetry and essays, explores the meaning of being a Black lesbian in America. Unlike her poems and essays, however, *Zami* gave me a fuller picture of how Lorde developed as a woman and a writer.

Lorde's genre-bending account of her life is ultimately about a search for community. She wrote, "I remember how being young and Black and gay and lonely felt," and I was rocked to my core (Lorde, 1982/1998, p. 176). Even now, reading those words takes me back to the emotional isolation of college. As a Black lesbian woman, Lorde felt the tension between two parts of herself that society sought to pit against the other—her race and her sexuality. This is a tension many Black lesbians feel and one that is frequently written about, as evidenced by the works of Jewelle Gomez, Pat Parker, Cheryl Clarke, Barbara Smith, and others. With notable exceptions, many of Lorde's early, close relationships were with white women. When she was finally able to cultivate new, greatly sought-after friendships with other Black lesbians, she realized that she was not alone in experiencing conflicting feelings. In this regard, *Zami* is a coming-of-age story that particularly appeals to queer readers in search of their place, and therefore it still appeals to new generations of readers in the digital age. Lorde's story situates her firmly in the center of a growing community of conscious Black lesbians seeking to understand and define their place in society. She was a part of a thriving community of thinkers and activists who used writing as a powerful tool against oppression. Her work still holds the distinction of being some of the most well-known and influential writing on what it means to be a Black lesbian in twentieth century America.

Although many young people first encounter Lorde through quote-laden memes on social media, their curiosity sends them down a path that leads to

Zami (Lorde, 1982/1998), *Sister Outsider* (Lorde, 1984/2007), and her other influential writings. In the essay "The Transformation of Silence into Language and Action," Lorde explains why speaking out against injustice is essential to survival, saying, "Your silence will not protect you" (Lorde, 1984/2007, p. 41). Ever since she offered this piece of advice to Black women, it has been passed down like a mantra, repeated over and over again among people in need of strength in a society that demands their silent invisibility. Because of her ubiquity in popular culture, I have learned that assigning her texts is a useful method for helping students parse social media dialogues about racism, sexism, homophobia, and the need for an intersectional analysis of how oppression operates. When she writes: "I have come to believe over and over again that what is most important to me must be spoken, made verbal and shared, even at the risk of having it bruised or misunderstood" (Lorde, 1984/2007, p. 40), she is expressing a sentiment that translates across sex, orientation, and gender identity. When faculty harness the power of Lorde's message, they have the ability to help generations of queer HBCU students liberate themselves.

Fragmenting and compartmentalizing oneself can be a deadly enterprise. For queer students who are constantly asked to choose among and prioritize the various components of their being, this is an important and often costly lesson. With the increasing focus on defining Blackness and using it as the measure of who is authentic enough to be considered part of the struggle, many people realize the futility of dividing themselves into parts. For example, Lorde understood that she could not separate her sex, her race, her sexuality, her socioeconomic status, and everything else that made her who she was. She observed: "As a Black lesbian mother in an interracial marriage, there was usually some part of me guaranteed to offend everybody's comfortable prejudices of who I should be. That is how I learned that if I didn't define myself for myself, I would be crunched into other people's fantasies for me and eaten alive" (Lorde, 1984/2007, p. 137). Even the fact that the last half of the quote is better known than the former is indicative of how we have fragmented pieces of Lorde's identity to more neatly fit her into a pro-Black narrative, as if her marriage in any way negates the legitimacy of her race advocacy.

I think of that passage often, particularly when I teach Martin Luther King Jr.'s (1964/2000) *Why We Can't Wait*. An implicit instruction happens when educators teach King and never mention Bayard Rustin, a key architect of the modern Civil Rights Movement and the 1963 March on Washington for Jobs and Freedom. Queer students learn that they are expected to wait for the right time to have their issues heard, that they must crunch themselves into a monolithic vision of Blackness in order to survive. The implicit training happens when educators allow the idea that racism is more important than homophobia to remain unchecked instead of using the modern Civil Rights

Movement as an opportunity to teach intersectionality. This happened to me as an undergraduate history major. I was not taught that the racism that King fought was inextricably tied to the homoantagonism that sidelined Bayard Rustin from a movement he co-organized. The historians who trained me are not, to my knowledge, homophobic. What I realize is that they were not trained to recognize and reach out to queer students by integrating queer history into the course content. This was a systemic failure, not a personal one, but the impact remains the same. When HBCUs hold Black History Month celebrations without a mention of our queer trailblazers, we are complicit in historical erasure and the further silencing of our queer students. When English and history departments teach the magnificent contours of Lorraine Hansberry's life and neglect her body of writing in *The Ladder*, we are complicit in erasing the fullness of her narrative and its liberatory possibilities for queer creative writers on our campuses (see Perry, 2019).

Film was another lifeline. I spent hours in my apartment with Aja Owens, another masculine queer student, watching any queer-themed film we could get our hands on. Aja was a mass communications major, and she is still one thousand times more social and resourceful than I am. If something existed in the world, she knew someone who could get it for us. We watched the classic film *Paris Is Burning* (Livingston, 1990) and witnessed the beauty of queer Black men and trans women who lived openly, inviting the rest of the city to catch up to the future. We also watched *Black Is . . . Black Ain't* (Riggs, 1995), an inclusive documentary released in 1994 about a range of Black queer identities. Watching Marlon Riggs's exploration of Blackness while eating endless boxes of strawberry shortcake ice cream bars taught Aja and I that our queer family was no secret and that our erasure was a decision to sacrifice us on an altar of respectability. We became more determined to live. Most importantly for us, Black lesbian filmmaker Cheryl Dunye's *The Watermelon Woman* (1996) and *Stranger Inside* (2001) gave us fictionalized portrayals of Black queer women that we devoured like hungry children. Although the women's experiences differed from our own, they were spiritually kindred. Lastly, the documentary film *Brother Outsider: The Life of Bayard Rustin* (Kates & Singer, 2003) was released the year before I graduated. There was no announcement or screening on campus. However, I now teach this film as part of my regular instruction on the Black Freedom Struggle.

The people, books, and films I encountered in college provided a foundation for me to build a healthy sense of Black queer identity, even though I was on a relatively conservative campus. When I realized that people like me existed openly before I was born, I knew I could survive anything, even if statistics sometimes indicated otherwise. I knew that if I survived, I had an obligation to be for younger people what I needed to see when I felt alone.

WHAT I DO: FULFILLING A PROMISE

> Just as I cannot leave part of myself—Black, female, raised-poor, or lesbian—at home on any march, no one of us should feel we can leave someone behind in the struggle for liberation.
>
> —Gomez, 1993, pp. 97–98

Dr. James Conway, a friend in my graduate school cohort, sent me the job advertisement for my immediate-past position at Tennessee State University, and I saw it as an opportunity to return to an HBCU and continue the work that I love. It was a call to home. As soon as the elation of getting a campus interview settled, the fear of how to present myself threatened to emerge. The only thing preventing mild anxiety from blossoming into a full-blown panic were years of practice with bringing my full self into professional spaces. Without the annual exposure to academic conferences like the Graduate Association for African American History, the Association for the Study of African American Life and History, and the National Women's Studies Association, I would have been much more concerned about how to dress my body for the most important interview of my life. Fortunately, each of these conferences provided an affirming space for me to tacitly announce and grow into my public self as a masculine-presenting woman. At these gatherings, I was consistently in contact with women who provided models of how to bend business and business casual attire to my professional needs. I had also by then been blessed with romantic partners who enjoyed the challenge of upgrading my wardrobe. For the first time in my life, my exterior presentation seamlessly matched my inner sense of self. Therefore, when I walked through the main corridor on the second floor of my new academic home, I felt confident in my outfit because I had come a long way from the poorly fitting outfits of my youth. My liberated threads were the least of my worries. I knew I belonged at Tennessee State University, so my task was to make that indisputable fact known to everyone else.

When I decided to return to academia, I knew I had to be what I needed to see as a queer undergrad. By that time, I was equipped with years of study and the scars of self-discovery. Graduate school had provided an opportunity to study under the direction of a lesbian scholar, Dr. Margaret Caffrey. As a white senior citizen and full professor, there was a chasm between us, but we shared the bridge of being lesbians in the academy. I stood on the bridge unsure if I was able to cross, because although I saw hope in her, I did not see myself. Therefore, I did not come out to her. She saw me and invited me in.

Dr. Caffrey introduced me to *Forty-Three Septembers*, Jewelle Gomez's (1993) collection of essays exploring how her varied experiences have impacted her philosophy of life. Written from the perspective of a Black lesbian author and activist, much of her material stresses how the various parts of who she is have collectively impacted her life experiences and that one part cannot be separated from the rest and given primacy. Like Lorde's writings and the Combahee River Collective Statement (1977), Gomez offers another intellectual companion to Crenshaw's theory of intersectionality. Now when I teach the modern Civil Rights Movement, I draw their attention to Gomez's (1993) analysis of marches as a tool of liberation: "Every movement wants to be the center; every march wants to be The March. But the reality is that no one movement knows enough to be the center of change. And each march is simply one part of the grand march towards social equality" (p. 97). In teaching them that all social justice marches and movements are interconnected, I can show the clear links between the March on Washington for Jobs and Freedom in 1963 and the Stonewall demonstrations in 1969. This pedagogical approach allows students to then more fully recognize the people who existed as part of the Black Freedom Struggle and the women's rights and gay rights movements and fought for the right to render themselves whole in the public eye.

The stories in *Forty-Three Septembers*, like *Zami* and many other writings by Black lesbians, are explorations of family dynamics alongside a search for queer community. By writing about her relationships with relatives, Gomez connects herself to a family of strong Black women and men. Because her unofficial coming out was received warmly and matter-of-factly by her family, her writing takes a slight departure from those by women who experienced familial upheaval after becoming open about their sexuality. Her essays reflect this seamless transition in her life, thus emphasizing the fact that all parts of her being are connected. No portion of her identity takes primacy over the others. This is a model for HBCUs, particularly because we envision ourselves as a family. Black families are inclusive, and when we are at our best, we endeavor to retain an expansive, loving definition of Blackness.

So how do we create more inclusive classrooms? The first step is remembering that we are one of many resources for all of our students. My classroom performance is a text akin to their books (see Alexander, 2005; Haynes et al., 2020; Mobley et al., 2020). I observe them reading me. They casually take in my attire, posture, gestures, and voice. At times it is clear that their gaze is intentional. They want me to see them observing me, trying to figure out what kind of woman I am. Likewise, sometimes they want me to see them. Although I always intend to spend less than an hour on first-day introductions, sometimes the creative ways students introduce themselves leaves us with only a few minutes to spare in the class. Those initial classes are often my best indication of how a group of students will get along with each other for the following fifteen weeks. Amid the nervous smiles and jokes, I catch some quizzical looks at a particular question on the slide I use to guide them through the introductory exercise. Some of them have never been invited to provide their pronouns, nor have they considered that it might be a relevant question. This small but powerful addition to the first-day routine normalizes the practice, especially for cisgender students, of sharing their pronouns as opposed to assuming that gender is evident. It also signals to queer students that the classroom is welcoming and affirming. This matters particularly in spaces that sometimes remain adamant about depicting a monolithic sort of Blackness and an even narrower idea of Black excellence. Sometimes there is fear where there should be freedom. My ultimate task is to free my students from that fear so they can liberate themselves intellectually.

The books we incorporate and suggest for further reading have an impact beyond our time together in the classroom. For example, *Beyond Respectability: The Intellectual Thought of Race Women* (Cooper, 2017) is an excellent model of how Black scholars elevate the way we teach Black women's histories by seamlessly including queer and non-normative sex and gender identities in their research. Cooper does not segregate the identities of the prominent Black women featured in her work when she highlights their achievements and where they stumble in their race advocacy. She allows them to remain intact and thereby teaches readers to view subjects as whole beings. By resisting the urge to fragment the identities of complex Black historical figures, HBCU educators can adopt an inclusive pedagogy that tells a more truthful narrative and empowers future generations of graduates to go forth into their communities to continue the work of Black liberation (see Lindsey, 2017).

Each semester I choose a day to ask a simple question of the Black women in class. Are they Black or are they women? The answer is always that they are both at the same time. I ask if they ever choose to leave their womanhood at home and exist as Black men or if they leave their Blackness at home and exist as white women. They usually have a good laugh about this, but my point becomes clear. I love this exercise, but sometimes it leaves me wanting to take the next step for my queer students. Unfortunately, I fear that the next step might not be safe for them, so I keep my feet planted on the firm ground we have all traveled together. This rudimentary introduction to intersectionality (Crenshaw, 1989, 1991)—which actually references interlocking systems of oppression, not merely overlapping identities—opens more students to the understanding that queer students can no more choose to leave their orientations and gender identities at home than they can choose to leave their racial classifications at home. When they enter a room, they should be able to bring their entire, beautiful selves.

The tide has been turning for years. Every time a student casually allows us to look into their private lives, I count it as a victory for the queer Black students who preceded us in these spaces. I have a practice of starting each class period by greeting them collectively and then saying, "Tell me something good." This usually follows a general inquiry of how they have been in the time since we last met. I do this to reinforce the idea that I see them as whole beings with lives outside our classroom and that I am invested in them as people beyond the four walls we share. I am deeply invested in them being whole. In 2019, a young Black woman shared that her girlfriend was taking her out to dinner for Valentine's Day. The students received her statement with the same enthusiasm with which they had embraced the young woman who spoke before her, mentioning her two dates with a new potential boyfriend. Our students are already embracing change. We must follow their affirming and inclusive example if we are to lead them.

Popular culture is another useful arena for reaching students. Sociologists Zandria F. Robinson and Marcus Hunter's Chocolate Cities Symposium in Memphis is an example of how scholars are bridging the gap between popular culture and the academy (see Hunter & Robinson, 2018). As part of their Chocolate Cities book tour, they invited New Orleans bounce music ambassador Big Freedia to participate in an afternoon symposium at which she discussed the liberatory theory embedded in her art. Big Freedia (2018) proclaimed, "I bring something totally different through the power of ass" and seamlessly illustrated the connection between theory and praxis. As professors discuss Black liberation in classrooms, Big Freedia liberates herself and her city by twerking in the streets, claiming space for her queer self and other marginalized people being pushed to the periphery of a rapidly gentrifying city (see Big Freedia, 2013). I do not label Big Freedia during classroom activities. I examine what she allows us to see and teach students how to analyze and accept her presentation. When students can hold Freddie Ross and Big Freedia at the same time, I know they are much closer to liberation—theoretical and personal—than I was as an undergraduate.

What happens outside the classroom matters as much as the pedagogy we employ inside it. There are some steps that educators and administrators at HBCUs can take to ensure that queer students are seen, welcomed, affirmed, and integrated without having to pass as cisgender/heterosexual or to commit the fashion crimes of my past. For example, does your campus offer Safe Zone or a similar training to equip faculty and administrators with the tools to be effective allies to queer students? Is there a queer student association or a gay-straight alliance? Does such a group enjoy equal support from the administration? None of these things, alone or collectively, can alleviate all of the structural and cultural challenges queer students face at HBCUs, but they are affirming and welcoming steps in the right direction. It is our responsibility to identify and make the changes necessary to fully include queer students in the life of our campuses.

I recognize the value in living boldly, even though it remains contrary to my nature. The Ubuntu Biography Project, a website dedicated to highlighting biographies of "distinguished LGBTQ/SGL people of color/African descent," did not exist when I was an undergraduate student (Maglott, 2017). Perhaps if it had, I would have seen a reflection of my future self sooner. Maybe I could have imagined more possibilities if I had had models within reach. I remain committed to being who I needed to see in my late teens and early twenties, because at that time, there was not a single faculty member who looked like me. Although I was comforted by the presence of so many Black faculty, staff, and administrators, none of them were visibly queer. No androgynous or masculine women were represented on campus outside the student body. So whereas I had plenty of options for peer socialization, I had no one to professionally develop me outside heteronormative frameworks. I was told I had to work twice as hard to get half as far—a sentiment long engrained in me by my parents. However, no one who looked like me could testify to working at least three times as hard to get half as far.

The academy knows we are here. Forty years in the wake of *But Some of Us Are Brave*, I am writing at a time when there are more visible Black queer scholars than ever before. A little more than a generation since its first printing, I am struck by how much and how little has changed. Yes, we now have the popular hashtag #citeblackwomen (see Cite Black Women, n.d.). Sadly, we need the hashtag. We also need to cite Black queer scholars. To quickly name a few, I am thinking of Dionne Bailey, Derrais Carter, T. J. Chester, Ashon T. Crawley, Qiana Cutts Givens, Dominique C. Hill, Vanessa Holden, Jenn M. Jackson, E. Patrick Johnson, Bettina Judd, Nikki Lane, Bettina Love, Sekhmet Maat, McKinley E. Melton, Kevin Mumford, Shelby Ray Pumphrey, C. Riley Snorton, LaMonda H. Stallings, and Kaila A. Story. There are more I have left unnamed because of the lingering danger of being "out" in the academy, particularly for colleagues on the job market, in untenured positions, or on conservative campuses.

Heightened visibility for a relative few across multiple disciplines does not equate to protections for everyone because it does not change the structural nature of inequality. The fact that I cannot comfortably name more people is indicative of the perils that Black queer faculty face in academia. If we are not safe, then our students are not safe. Cheryl Clarke (1983/2000) warned that "homophobia divides black people as political allies, it cuts off political growth, stifles revolution, and perpetuates patriarchal domination. . . . The more homophobic we are as a people the further removed we are from any kind of revolution" (pp. 200–201). Again, Black people and institutions are not inherently more homophobic or transphobic than others. As Mobley and Johnson (2015) have noted, homophobia is embedded in societal structures in ways that are replicated at HBCUs, and our campuses tend to be conservative as a reflection of their founding conditions and as a coping mechanism in a world where they remain financially vulnerable. If HBCUs are to live up to their missions of providing educational and professional opportunities to marginalized populations, then they must ensure that queer students have an equal chance to thrive within their halls. This is more than possible. It is necessary.

SANKOFA AND THE FUTURE

Many histories of HBCUs are conspicuously silent on the issue of queer students and faculty. However, HBCU faculty and administrators cannot afford to assume that the status of Black queer students will passively get better as middle-class and wealthy white men gain more acceptance in society. A quick peek at initial reader comments to an excerpt from Bettina Love's book featured in the *Advocate* clearly serves to underscore her point that the dominant thrust of queer studies and mainstream LGBTQ advocacy continues to marginalize Black queer people. The short excerpt is a critique of the narrow range and limited effectiveness of the widely disseminated It Gets Better campaign. Shared from the perspective of two financially comfortable, cisgender white men, the inspirational video campaign does little to combat the persistent inequality low-income, disabled, trans, or femme queer youth of color face. As Love (2019) notes, "There was not much queer about It Gets Better other than sexuality, and queer is much more than who you love, marry, or have sex with" (para. 3). In advocating for E. Patrick Johnson's (2000) use of "quare," Love reminds us that it is necessary to prioritize theories and practices that center Black queer/quare youth if we intend to fully love and liberate them. We are capable of an expansive love, and it is the only way we can thrive.

I do not believe that Black people, Black communities, and HBCUs are more heterosexist than their white counterparts. There is nothing inherently Black about hating queer people. The homophobia institutionalized at HBCUs is little more than a manifestation of the bias we are all socialized to hold. But many of us choose to unlearn and reject paradigms of oppression. Our students are already heeding the lessons of the past, embracing change, and taking their place as the vanguard of this loving revolution. Are we?

REFERENCES

Alexander, B. K. (2005). Embracing the teachable moment: The Black gay body in the classroom as embodied text. In E. P. Johnson and M. G. Henderson (Eds.), *Black queer studies: A critical anthology* (pp. 249–265). Duke University Press.

Big Freedia. (2018, Mar. 24). Conversation with Big Freedia [Live interview]. Chocolate Cities Symposium, Crosstown Concourse, Memphis, TN.

———. (2013). *Big Freedia—Duffy (Official music video)*. YouTube. https://www.youtube.com/watch?v=HJBnNziI5wk

Cite black women. (n.d.). Retrieved December 2, 2020. https://www.citeblackwomencollective.org/

Clarke, C. (2000). The failure to transform: Homophobia in the black community. In B. Smith (Ed.), *Home girls: A Black feminist anthology* (pp. 190–201). Rutgers University Press. (Original work published 1983)

Combahee River Collective. (1977). The Combahee River Collective statement. https://www.loc.gov/item/lcwaN0028151/

Cooper, B. C. (2017). *Beyond respectability: The intellectual thought of race women*. University of Illinois Press.

Crenshaw, K. (1989). Demarginalizing the intersection of race and sex: A Black feminist critique of antidiscrimination doctrine, feminist theory, and antiracist politics. *The University of Chicago Legal Forum*, 1989(1), 139–168.

———. (1991). Mapping the margins: Intersectionality, identity politics, and violence against women of color. *Stanford Law Review, 43*(6), 1241. https://doi.org/10.2307/1229039

Du Bois, W. E. B. (2016). *The souls of black folk: Essays and sketches.* Dover Publications. (Original work published 1903)

Dunye, C. (Director). (1996). *The watermelon woman* [Film]. Dancing Girl.

———. (Director). (2001). *Stranger inside* [Film]. C-Hundred Film Corporation.

Ford, T. C. (2015). *Liberated threads: Black women, style, and the global politics of soul.* University of North Carolina Press.

Gomez, J. (1993). *Forty-three Septembers: Essays.* Firebrand Books.

Haynes, C., Taylor, L., Jr., Mobley, S. D., Jr., & Haywood, J. (2020). Existing and resisting: The pedagogical realities of Black, critical men and women faculty. *The Journal of Higher Education, 91*(5), 698–721.

Hull, G. T., Bell-Scott, P., & Smith, B. (Eds.). (1982). *All the women are White, all the Blacks are men, but some of us are brave: Black women's studies.* Feminist Press.

Hunter, M. A., & Robinson, Z. F. (2018). *Chocolate cities: The black map of American life.* University of California Press.

Johnson, E. P. (2000). *From* black quare studies or almost everything I know about queer studies I learned from my grandmother. *Callaloo, 23*(1), 120–121. https://doi.org/10.1353/cal.2000.0036

Johnson, J. T. (2021). The category is . . . transformational inclusion: A conceptual framework for (re)imagining the inclusion of Black queer and trans* students attending HBCUs. In G. B. Crosby, K. A. White, M. A. Chanay, & A. Hilton (Eds.), *Reimagining historically Black colleges and universities.* Emerald Publishing Limited.

Kates, N. & Singer, B. (Directors). (2003). *Brother outsider: The life of Bayard Rustin* [Film]. The American Documentary.

King, M. L. (2000). *Why we can't wait.* Signet. (Original work published 1964)

Lindsey, T. B. (2017). *Colored no more: Reinventing Black womanhood in Washington, D.C.* University of Illinois Press.

Livingston, J. (Director). (1990). *Paris is burning* [Film]. Off White Productions Inc.

Lorde, A. (1998). *Zami: A new spelling of my name.* Crossing Press. (Original work published 1982)

———. (2000). *The collected poems of Audre Lorde.* W. W. Norton & Company.

———. (2007). *Sister outsider: Essays and speeches.* Crossing Press. (Original work published 1984)

Love, B. (2019, February 15). A queer Black educator on the shortcomings of "it gets better." *Advocate.* https://www.advocate.com/books/2019/2/15/queer-black-educator-shortcomings-it-gets-better

Maglott, S. (2017, August 13). Stephen Maglott: Legacy. https://ubuntubiographyproject.wordpress.com/legacy/

Mobley, S. D., Jr., & Hall, L. (2020). (Re)defining queer and trans* student retention and success at historically Black colleges and universities. *Journal of College Student Retention: Research, Theory & Practice, 21*(4), 497–519.

Mobley, S. D., Jr., & Johnson, J. M. (2015). The role of HBCUs in addressing the unique needs of LGBT students. *New Directions for Higher Education, 2015*(170), 79–89. https://doi.org/10.1002/he.20133

Mobley, S. D., Jr., & Johnson, J. M. (2019). "No pumps allowed": The "problem" with gender expression and the Morehouse College "Appropriate Attire Policy." *Journal of Homosexuality, 66*(7), 867–895.

Mobley, S. D., Jr., Johnson, R. W., Sewell, J. P., Johnson, J. M., & Neely, A. J. (2021). "We are not victims": Unmasking Black queer and trans* student activism at HBCUs. *About Campus, 26*(3), 24–28.

Mobley, S. D., Jr., Taylor, L., Jr., & Davison, C. H. (2020). (Un)seen work: The pedagogical experiences of Black queer men in faculty roles. *International Journal of Qualitative Studies in Education, 33*(6), 604–620.

Njoku, N., Butler, M., & Beatty, C. C. (2017). Reimagining the historically Black college and university (HBCU) environment: Exposing race secrets and the binding chains of respectability and othermothering. *International Journal of Qualitative Studies in Education, 30*(8), 783–799.

Perry, I. (2019). *Looking for Lorraine: The radiant and radical life of Lorraine Hansberry*. Beacon.

Riggs, M. (Director). (1995). *Black is . . . Black ain't* [Film]. Signifyin' Works.

Smith, B. (Ed.). (2000). *Home girls: A Black feminist anthology*. Rutgers University Press. (Original work published 1983)

2 · THE (MIS)EDUCATION OF YÉMAYA

Fostering Togetherness with Black Trans* Womx[x]yn Students at Historically Black Colleges and Universities through Policy Reformation and (Re)Education

YÉMAYA DIAVIAN POPE

Speaking on the subject of education, the iconic speaker and writer James Baldwin (1985) once stated, "The paradox of education is precisely this—that as one begins to become conscious one begins to examine the society in which he is being educated" (p. 326). This paradox that Baldwin speaks of is precisely the kind of examination I began to engage in throughout my time as an undergraduate student. During my time in college, I quickly learned that my HBCU campus was a microcosm of the broader societal context. My peers and I were involved in constant social interactions, we encountered distinct campus cultures/expectations, and we were subject to constant administrative authority—all while attempting to reach the goal of graduation and degree conferment. In hindsight, I can see that my undergraduate years were a time when I tapped into a higher level of consciousness through (mis)education.

In this chapter you will observe a theme woven throughout: Black womx[x]yn. Specifically, I am focusing on Black trans* womx[x]yn[1] in higher education and the nature of their (mis)education at historically Black colleges and universities (HBCUs). This miseducation is rooted in a lack of togetherness. My emphasis on Black trans* womx[x]yn students is not intended to negate or erase Black trans* men and other trans* and queer identities. I choose to underscore the experiences of Black trans* womx[x]yn because we are and have been relegated to the margins and erased in broader societal discourses, in higher education scholarship, and on college and university campuses.

While there is a clear absence of Black trans* womx[x]yn among HBCU discourses, one context where Black trans* womx[x]yn have been celebrated and acknowledged is in ballroom culture due to their legendary and iconic statuses as members of renowned houses and their participation in ballroom competitions (e.g., in the FX series POSE). Another context where Black trans* womx[x]yn can be "seen" is among the numerous new sources reporting their homicides and their subjection to violent hate crimes. Because Black trans* womx[x]yn are recognized far less often in postsecondary contexts and within HBCU communities in particular. Mobley and Hall (2020) note that "queer and trans* students can be, at times overlooked, neglected, and rendered invisible within HBCU communities" (p. 503). Moreover, often, studies that discuss trans* HBCU students never focus exclusively on Black trans* womx[x]yn, and when discussed, Black trans* HBCU students are sometimes conflated with lesbian, bisexual, and gay communities as though they are not distinct. Thus, this essay adds to the HBCU scholarship surrounding trans* students through featuring my experiences as a Black woman of trans* experience and the journey to reclaiming my womanhood while at Morehouse, reflecting on the history of Black womx[x]yn's education at HBCUs (including the history of the Morehouse women), and offering recommendations to HBCUs so that they may provide culturally engaging contexts for their trans* students.

THE BEST KEPT SECRET: WHO IS YÉMAYA?

One of my favorite films is *Hidden Figures*. Admittedly, I am likely biased because the film was largely shot on the campus of my alma mater, Morehouse College, and because the film's central figure, Katherine Johnson, was an alumna of the same HBCU I attended for the first half of my undergraduate career, West Virginia State University. Beyond my biases, I found *Hidden Figures* fascinating not only because of the sheer mathematical genius of Katherine Johnson and her peers Dorothy Vaughn and Mary Jackson but also because educated Black womx[x]yn were behind the engineering and computations of some of NASA's most complex explorations of the universe. If there is one thing both Katherine Johnson and educated Black trans* womx[x]yn hold in common it is that to be Black and trans* at an HBCU is essentially to be a hidden figure—at least, that has been the case in the past. Even though trans* and queer communities have inextricable presences at HBCUs, our existences, contributions, and stories have been marginalized within or wholly erased from HBCU cultures. This is critical to note because trans* HBCU stakeholders have perpetually had to navigate tensions and conflict while demanding to be recognized and gain necessary resources.

One of the most ancient social institutions is the family. Generally, family is understood as the human relationships resulting from shared DNA and marital ties or those resulting from adoption (Williams, 2020). Often with this concept of family come ideas of community and/or togetherness. People in Black communities are known for electing themselves into families of their choosing and forging kinship between individuals who do not share common ancestry. HBCUs are breeding grounds for strong familial bonds of different sorts, especially when you consider the fact that two core ideas at the inception of HBCUs were racialized group membership, namely Black identity, and serving the educational needs of Black individuals who were excluded from historically white institutions. Primary examples of this type of kinship at HBCUs can be found in Black Greek-letter organizations or even HBCU alumni associations.

Chosen familial ties can be salient for the lived experiences of Black trans* womx[x]yn and queer and trans* students at HBCUs. The kinship ties of trans* and queer students (and really of Black people in general), though not always born from blood, are far from the *fictive* kinship bonds that are often touted within Black communities and even HBCU contexts. Blockett (2017) critiques the concept of "fictive kin," specifically concerning Black trans* and queer people: "Classifying kinship bonds as fictive ignores the worldmaking practices queer and trans* people undertake as they produce familial ties with other queer and trans* comrades. In this case, the kinship networks created by Black queers may not be fictive or imaginary at all" (p. 802). Sadly, for many Black trans* students at HBCUs, their transness is viewed as being at odds with their Blackness. This can often make having rich familial ties with their non-trans* HBCU peers difficult to actualize. Ecologically speaking, the reasons for inharmonious relationships between trans* students and their cisgender peers at HBCUs can be rooted in several factors, including: (1) strongly held transphobic beliefs, (2) a lack of emotional maturity and interpersonal etiquette on part of cisgender individuals when interacting with trans* students, and (3) insufficient resources, including a lack of trans*-inclusive policies and curricula. All of these influences foster a distinctly anti-trans* and, by extension, an anti-Black HBCU ecosystem.

Additionally, it should be noted that "The Miseducation of Yémaya"[2] is not just about my (mis)education. It can represent and speak to the miseducation of people like me at HBCUs. Yémaya could be the Black trans* man who feels invisible at his HBCU because he never sees any representations of himself in the material he is taught or in the professors who teach him. Yémaya could be the Black trans* woman who feels unsafe using the womx[x]yn's restroom on her HBCU campus because current policies do not explicitly protect her right to bathroom choice. Yémaya can represent every Black trans* student at an HBCU who has ever experienced the isolation, frustration, and trauma of miseducation. In order for HBCUs to avoid the further miseducation of its Black trans* students and to foster togetherness with the Black trans* student, they must reform their policies and support (re)education.

MISS EDUCATION: A REVIEW OF BLACK WOMX[X]YN'S EDUCATION AT HBCUS

Some of you may have heard how some womx[x]yn used to go to college to get their Mrs. degree (that is, to find a husband), but that is not what I mean by "miss education." Rather, this is an examination of Black womx[x]yn in higher education—particularly Black womx[x]yn students. As one of the most educated race-gender groups in the United States, Black womx[x]yn have an irrefutable, voracious appetite for learning, and they have contributed and continue to contribute much to the entirety of Black higher education. But what exactly is known of this herstory?

Dr. Marybeth Gasman's (2007) article "Swept Under the Rug? A Historiography of Gender and Black Colleges" treats race and gender as mutually interconnected as it explores and analyzes the erasure of womx[x]yn and gender affairs from HBCU histories and in various texts that discuss Black colleges. Collins (2001) asserts that Black women have been participants in higher education for more than a century but are almost totally absent from research literature on HBCUs and that their experiences with racism and sexism in academe are rarely explored. What are the roots of this history of Black colleges that obscures the experiences of Black womx[x]yn and the histories of gender affairs?

During the inception of HBCUs, one of the major motivating factors for educating Black womx[x]yn was an increasing need for Black teachers (Anderson, 1988). Black womx[x]yn were considered ideal educators for their race and ideal conduits for racial uplift. For this reason, much of the early curricula for Black womx[x]yn students centered on teaching and missionary work as a means of "saving" or "improving" their race (Brazzell, 1992). These Black institutions were not merely an outgrowth of the newly emancipated slaves' need for education but were forged in the contexts of philanthropic capitalism, as many of their establishers and presidents were economically privileged white philanthropists.

The Hampton model is a good example of the role of capitalism in the creation of HBCUs. Hampton University's founder, Samuel Chapman Armstrong, is credited with originating this model, which was based on industrial politics meant to limit Black people to agricultural work and manual and service labor (Buchanan & Hutcheson, 1999). The curriculum of the Hampton model was designed to prepare Black womx[x]yn for domestic labor; it primarily provided training in domestic skillsets that included washing, ironing, sewing, and so forth. Essentially, immediately following emancipation, Black womx[x]yn were expected to fulfill a double responsibility as both homemakers and breadwinners (Brazzell, 1992). Evans (2007) contends that "for Black coeducational colleges admitting women, administrative efforts to match student populations with course offerings were tumultuous at best" (p. 46). There was also an early belief at HBCUs that Black womx[x]yn were a distraction to male students, so administrators put strict behavioral codes in place to police their interactions with males on campus (Mobley et al., 2021; Njoku et al., 2017).

Noble (1956) also provided insights into how Black womx[x]yn HBCU students have been controlled historically: "It appears that many of the Negro woman's rules and regulations may possibly have been predicated on reasons relating to her foremother's sex role as a slave. Overnight she was to so live that by her ideal behavior the sins of her foremother's might be blotted out. Her education in many instances appears to have been based on a philosophy which implied that she was weak and immoral and that at best she should be made fit to rear her children and keep house for her husband" (p. 24). Black womx[x]yn HBCU students have had complex relationships with their respective institutions since their inceptions. There has been an air of needing to keep Black womx[x]yn students chaste, and much of the onus for achieving that goal has been placed upon them.

THE WOMX[X]YN OF MOREHOUSE

Tucked inside the archives of the Woodruff Library in the Atlanta University Center is a curious photo titled "Morehouse-James Hall, circa 1930." Not much information is made known about this image other than the brief description: "View of women sweeping steps and sidewalk in front of Morehouse-James Hall" (Spelman College, n.d.).

I was intrigued by this image. I could not help but wonder why this was important to photograph. Since clearly the photographer thought enough of this moment to immortalize it, I decided that maybe I should mull over it for a while longer. It presented an all-too-familiar visual of Black womx[x]yn doing nothing other than work, being "mules of the earth," as Zora Neale Hurston (1937) suggested. It also harked back to a time in Black college history when Black womx[x]yn students were trained chiefly in domestic skills to serve in an oppressive economic system. I inferred several themes of Black womx[x]yn's labor at HBCUs: Black womx[x]yn who labored at Black institutions in which they were not always welcome and Black womx[x]yn who play their part but are often under recognized like the unnamed womx[x]yn in this photo (fig. 2.1).

As I reflected on the photo, I also noticed the act of *clearing*. When someone sweeps, they are clearing an area (e.g., clearing dust from a pathway). This act of clearing relates to the history of the first thirty-three womx[x]yn students at Morehouse College, known as the "Morehouse Women," who were admitted during the Great Depression to ease the economic burden created during the Depression by lower enrollment. All thirty-three graduated, and the last surviving graduate of their group, Mary Spivey, passed in 2014 at age 99 (Suggs, 2019). Suggs hails Mary Spivey as "the last Morehouse Woman," but **this is not so because we live**. Figuratively speaking, the Morehouse Women took the meta-

FIGURE 2.1. Morehouse-James Hall, circa 1930. (Courtesy of the Spellman College Archives.)

phorical broom that is so often used in Black academia to sweep Black womx[x]yn students under the rug and cleared the way for future Black womx[x]yn students to attend and graduate from their school—womx[x]yn like me.

The androcentric history typically shared about Black colleges communicates spurious notions about Black womx[x]yn student's lack of involvement and perpetuates the sexism and misogyny enacted by men in HBCU spaces who disregarded Black womx[x]yn students. As Gasman (2007) notes, "There are few histories that are explicitly dedicated to the experiences of Black womx[x]yn at HBCUs; in fact most accounts of their lives appear in wide-ranging works in the field of African American Studies" (pp. 777–778). Without question, more academic literature on Black womx[x]yn, especially Black trans* womx[x]yn at HBCUs, is needed going forward in order to depict a more inclusive and whole reality.

HBCU TRANS* STORIES

Scholarship that deliberately centers trans* HBCU students and their experiences has been virtually nonexistent (Mobley & Hall, 2020). However, despite the absence of robust HBCU trans* stories (histories and other documentation about trans* persons), recent HBCU policy changes and efforts to collect the names and stories of Black trans* womx[x]yn are providing some form of documentation that has not previously existed. Two relatively recent HBCU stories of Black trans* womx[x]yn students include the trans*-inclusive policies developed and adopted by traditionally [cisgender] womx[x]yn's HBCUs: Spelman College in Atlanta, Georgia, and Bennett College in Greensboro, North Carolina. Both schools will now consider students for admission who consistently live and self-identify as women, regardless of their gender assignment at birth. These policies are promising because they set important precedents for other HBCUs to follow in creating trans*-inclusive policies.

Another widely noted story of Black trans* womx[x]yn at HBCUs centers on the Morehouse College appropriate attire policy. In 2009, Morehouse College instituted a dress code policy that targeted the college's queer population, specifically a group known as The Plastics that consisted of queer and nonbinary gay men and those who identified as trans* (Mobley & Johnson, 2019; Patton, 2014). The Plastics were known for ornamenting themselves in a style traditionally associated with cisgender womx[x]yn, including wearing dresses and pumps, carrying purses, and wearing makeup. The appropriate attire policy stated that there should be "no wearing of clothing usually worn by women (dresses, tops, tunics, purses, pumps, etc.) on the Morehouse campus or at college-sponsored events." Today, the clause of this policy that forbade feminine attire has been repealed; however, one year after the policy was instituted, Aliya S. King published a major article in *Vibe* magazine in response to the dress code titled "The Mean Girls of Morehouse" (2010). In the article, King got close to the students directly targeted by the appropriate attire policy, and they shared their experiences as gender-queer students at Morehouse. What makes this a part of broader HBCU trans* stories is that Chanel Hudson was one of the Black womx[x]yn students who became central in the story "The Mean Girls of Morehouse." Although Hudson ended up transferring to another school to finish her undergraduate degree, her presence at Morehouse represents the role of Black trans* womx[x]yn at historically Black colleges as nonconformists and emissaries of change.

"MISSED EDUCATION": THE MISEDUCATION OF YÉMAYA

On January 19, 2021, I found myself leaving my beloved home, Atlanta, Georgia, for Huntington, West Virginia, where I would attend Marshall University as a graduate student. From the moment I left Atlanta, I began excitedly counting down the months until I could move back to my home in the Deep South. Atlanta is a "chocolate city," but Huntington is quite small and a far cry from a chocolate city. When I arrived in Huntington, a statue of a man along Hal Greer

Blvd. caught my attention. I later learned that the statue was a likeness of Dr. Carter G. Woodson, known as the father of Black history. Woodson has a significant history in Huntington not only as a student who once attended the city's school for Black students, Douglass School, but later as an educator and principal of the high school he had attended. He founded the Association for the Study of Negro Life and History in 1915 and he established Negro History Week in 1926, which President Ford expanded to Black History Month in 1976 (NAACP.org, n.d.). Although the title of this section is, indeed, a nod to Lauryn Hill, it is Woodson's 1933 publication *The Mis-Education of the Negro* that has inspired the title of this chapter and lays the foundation for my story of miseducation.

Decolonization, liberation, vindicationism, Black culture, and Black humanity are key terms at the center of Woodson's educational philosophy in *The Mis-Education of the Negro*. A quote from Woodson's book that has often been used to capture the whole of his principal theory and argument in *Mis-Education*: "When you control a man's thinking you don't have to worry about his actions" (Woodson, 1933/1972, p. 21). Woodson contended that the miseducation of Black persons is not the absence of an education but rather Black people's subjugation to a politicized educational system based on a hegemonic curriculum that centers and preserves white supremacist ideology. For Woodson, the anti-Black nature of the Black learner's miseducation chiseled away at the self-esteem of Black students, marginalized and erased Black people, and gave license to racialized violence (Givens, 2016).

The Mis-Education of the Negro also reproved Black scholars in the Ebony Tower. According to Woodson, their miseducation followed them from K–12 educational spaces well into higher education. He believed that Black intellectuals in higher education were detached from the reality of the Black masses, and further voiced his concern with the talented tenth stating "These men and women, who were perceived to be the leaders of the race by virtue of their educational training, were miseducated" (quoted in Givens, 2016, p. 44). That is why Woodson (1933/1972) said that "the more 'education' the Negro gets the worse off he is," (p. 84). In Woodson's view, members of the Black community who trusted the educated Black elite to find a solution for the miseducation of the Black student would be disappointed (Givens, 2016).

My miseducation was a "missed education" in many respects. Family is very central to who I am, so much so that familial symbols were purposefully built into my rebirth name. *Yémaya* essentially means "mother" (mother whose children are like the fish), and *Pope* means "father." Given how deeply I cherish the presence of family in my life, the lack of kinship and togetherness I felt at my HBCU left me feeling incredibly isolated and disillusioned. Morehouse was supposed to be a family. The reason I attribute this lack of togetherness to my missed education is because it touched more than my emotional and mental well-being It touched the curriculum I was taught. It touched the pedagogies I experienced

TABLE 2.1 Enrollment and Persistence at Morehouse College, Fall 2018

	Full-Time		Part-Time	
	Men	Women	Men	Women
Undergraduates				
Degree-seeking, first-time freshmen	604		1	
Other first-year, degree-seeking	43			
All other degree-seeking	1,497	1	59	
Total degree-seeking	2,144	1	60	0
All other undergraduates enrolled in credit courses	1			
Total undergraduate	2,145	1	60	0
Graduate				
Degree-seeking, first-time				
All other degree-seeking				
All other graduates enrolled in credit courses				
Total graduate	0	0	0	0
Total all undergraduates				2,206
Total all graduate				0
GRAND TOTAL ALL STUDENTS				2,206

SOURCE: Morehouse College (2018–2019, p. 1).

in the classroom and my primary learning modalities. It touched my participation and inclusion in student life. It touched the type of transphobic attitudes I encountered among administrators and people in other leadership roles. This caused me to miss out on the high-caliber education I could have received had togetherness been fostered.

Although I began my undergraduate studies at West Virginia State University, the bulk of my undergraduate years were spent at Morehouse—a traditionally all-male institution. When I began my tenure at Morehouse in January 2017, I was still masquerading as a man and had not embraced my true self. When I finally came to terms with my need to embody my womanhood in the fall of 2017 it was not about transitioning or becoming, but it was about *returning* to the woman I am—the part of myself that had been forgotten and lost. And so, I embarked on a *Sankofa* journey to retrieve my womanhood and this is when my story became interesting. In a nutshell, as a consequence of reclaiming my womanhood, I became the only full-time woman student who was documented on the enrollment and persistence record among a population of 2,205 male students (see Table 2.1). My place at Morehouse became significant for three primary reasons: (1) I was the first full-time female student on record since the Morehouse Women of the 1930s, (2) I became the first recorded Black woman graduate of trans* experience, and (3) my attendance directly impacted the formation and implementation of Morehouse's 2019 Trans* admission gender policy. Concerning reason three, in *Natural Woman: A Memoir Anthology*, Dr. Jonathan Wesley, who specializes in educational policy studies and examined Morehouse's queer history, attests "Based on what I was researching, it does seem that this policy was put into place because of your [Yémaya's] transition" (Pope, 2023, p. 117).

More to the point, though, the retrieval of my womanhood was accompanied by miseducation. I missed out on learning from a curriculum that intentionally centered Black womx[x]yn like me. In addition, although the largely androcentric education I received in the classroom did prepare me to be successful as a Black person in general, it lacked the intersections of transness and womanism and therefore did not prepare me to be a successful Black woman of trans* experience in the campus society I existed in and in the wider society beyond the campus that I had to navigate daily. As well, I frequently found myself making calculations about my safety, being hypervigilant, and feeling afraid while walking through campus (given how public the reclamation of my womanhood had been at Morehouse). When I was not purposely absent from school, my primary modes of taking in lesson material in class (auditory/visual) were sometimes interfered with by the acute anxiety I felt. As I examined the campus society I was being educated in, I could not help but recognize how it wholly excluded representations of Black people of trans* experience. For example, Morehouse lacked Black trans* professors and other leadership. And while Morehouse had banners around campus showcasing the model image for their male students (e.g., banners depicting male students that read, "Men of Morehouse Are Well Dressed") and graphics lining the walls of buildings honoring the postgraduate achievements of their successful male alumni, no such visuals were prominently displayed for its womx[x]yn students and alumnae—trans* or cisgender. This lack of representation, for me, reinforced the necessity of self-definition as a reality of Black womx[x]yn of trans* experience.

In my campus environment, trans*-inclusionary spaces were virtually nonexistent save for Adodi, the Morehouse safe space organization. The various challenges I endured throughout my collegiate experience contributed to my miseducation. Truthfully, as much as I longed for inclusion and visibility as a woman of Morehouse, sometimes, sharing in the sentiment of James Baldwin, I asked myself, "Do I really want to be integrated into a burning house; that is, an institution that prides itself on its iconic civil rights history and forsakes this reputation by reifying male privilege and the adoption of inequitable policies that disenfranchise Black trans* womx[x]yn's access to a Morehouse education?" Nevertheless, I am of the mind that every fire must extinguish at some point and the gender-based discrimination and prejudice that has set so many HBCUs ablaze can be neutralized only through (re)education and reformational policies that lead to radical and progressive institutional changes, especially for Black trans* students.

RECOMMENDATIONS FOR POLICY AND (RE)EDUCATION

HBCUs have largely been ill equipped to best engage their trans* stakeholders. In particular, Black trans womx[x]yn students have had to piece together their academic and social experiences amid a largely heteronormative and cisnormative Black-centered education. Because of this, many trans* womx[x]yn like myself often have to fill in the gaps of our HBCU experiences that are characterized by the absence of pro-trans* ideologies. As Black womx[x]yn of trans* experience navigate HBCU life, we face unique brands of oppression, sexism, misogyny, microaggressions, the complexities of physical privileges (pretty privilege, passing privilege), and capitalism (body capital, social capital) that accompany our intersectional identities of Black, trans*, and womx[x]yn.

Carter G. Woodson's educational philosophy was largely extracted from his lived experiences, and he strongly believed in centering the lived experiences of Black people in his education model. Woodson's focus on his lived experiences in his philosophy could be attributed to the fact that the literature on Black person's education at that time was virtually absent. Likewise, the content below is mostly derived from my lived experiences because the literature on Black trans* womx[x]yn students in higher education—including on the topics of policies and forms of education that advantage them—does not exist to extrapolate recommendations from. The recommendations posed below seek to foster togetherness through a holistic pro-trans* HBCU experience as well as a (re)imagining of educational alternatives. It is chiefly focused on Black trans* womx[x]yn students (but does not exclude other Black queer and trans* learners) in three main categories: student life, curriculum and instruction, and institutional leadership.

Student Life

Black trans* womx[x]yn do not merely need "friendly" spaces; they need empowering spaces. In general, the entire campus (e.g., campus grounds, classrooms, restrooms, locker rooms, on-campus housing) should be a safe, empowering space for Black trans* womx[x]yn. But along with that, it is absolutely essential that there be pro-trans* organizations and centers on campus that provide community and resources for Black trans* womx[x]yn. In addition, Byrd (2020) suggests the "building of a central online HBCU LGBTQ resource center to service and connect all HBCU students (p. 178)." Byrd also states that "particular attention to the needs of transgender and closeted students should occur in designing the hub (p. 179)." For Byrd, the purpose of an online center is not to be a substitute for on-campus centers but to provide a 24/7 space that is accessible off-campus to provide resources like personal narrative blogs/vlogs from their HBCU peers, virtual chats, forums, links to YouTube channels, referrals for resources in the local area, and links to library databases and archives for relevant research materials. Of course, online (trans*-conscious) user policies for the center would need to be developed along with proactive measures to prohibit cyberbullying (Byrd, 2020, p. 179).

Enrollment and Trans* Intentionality

Mobley and Hall (2020) state that "queer and trans* HBCU student engagement should start during the admissions and recruitment phases" (p. 508). It is very important that enrollment management offices at HBCUs recruit and employ trans* students for campus visit days, open houses, and new student orientation to give tours and offer peer advising support and participate in college fairs geared directly toward queer and trans* high school students (Mobley & Hall, 2020). However, more can be done. Trans* students encounter significant barriers when they are completing the Free Application for Federal Student Aid (FAFSA). Because the information for the FAFSA must match the applicant's Social Security record, trans* applicants are forced to report their sex at birth. Thus, a trans* applicant is essentially outed to administrators who may discriminate against trans* applicants (Center for American Progress and Movement Advancement Project, 2015). Also, when a trans* student completes their FAFSA with their lived gender as opposed to their sex at birth, the inconsistencies in identification can result in application rejection, delays in processing, and reductions in aid or not receiving any aid at all (Center for American Progress and Movement Advancement Project, 2015). In order to combat this, HBCUs should create institutional need-based scholarships and grants specifically to aid Black trans* womx[x]yn students as an underserved HBCU population. These forms of aid should be automatically considered during the admissions process for those who self-identify as Black and trans* on their applications. This automatic consideration would also require that HBCUs routinely include trans* identity markers on their applications and codify admissions policies that include non-discrimination based on gender identity in order to protect trans* applicants throughout the admissions process.

Gender Diversity and Inclusion Liaison

HBCU communities would also be served well by a division of student affairs with practitioners whose primary purpose is to amplify the voices of trans* students. A small team could be assembled with an appointed liaison to handle matters pertaining to gender diversity and inclusion. The idea is that this small team could facilitate communications between queer students (including but not limited to Black trans* womx[x]yn) to the proper administrative officials in order to resolve problems and better include, represent, and accommodate the gender-based needs of queer and trans* students.

Biannual Campus-Wide Gender Identity Seminar

Although the topic of gender can be covered at the classroom level through a restructuring of curriculum, seminars hosted by student affairs for the student body would provide an opportunity to discuss the topic of gender on a mass scale. HBCUs could hold these seminars once in the fall semester and once in the spring semester. These campus-wide seminars should center the voices of educators and professionals who specialize in trans* subject matters, as well as students of various gender identities (including trans* identity) who could provide information and narratives that can help to increase understanding about gender identity. These forums could also be opportune times to discuss health issues related to gender identities like those of Black trans* womx[x]yn and to allow students to submit any questions they might have around trans* and queer identities.

Addressing Mental Health and Wellness

Mobley and Hall (2020) specify that "access to quality gender[-] and sexuality[-]affirming health care is critical for the safety, well-being, and on-going academic progress for queer and trans* students" (p. 511). Investing in mental health and well-being efforts for trans* students would be pivotal in the retention of these students. Trans* students and Black trans* womx[x]yn in particular should have access to trans*-informed physical and mental health practitioners to enrich their HBCU experiences.

Curriculum & Instruction

While Dr. Carter G. Woodson's *Mis-Education of the Negro* did not contain "one footnote or academic citation" (Givens, 2016, p. 35) and was criticized for being contradictory and rife with generalizations and vague remedies for the miseducation of Black people, he offered commentary about Black education that is worth gleaning. In this section, I will revisit the teachings and philosophies of Carter G. Woodson as I recommend reformational policies and (re)education at HBCUs.

Woodson (1933/1972) staunchly believed that Black education should unapologetically feature Black teachers, Black pedagogy, and Black texts. Smith (2019) supports this educational philosophy and contends that "no pedagogy which is truly liberating can remain distant from the oppressed by treating them as unfortunates.... The oppressed must be their own example in the struggle for their redemption" (p. 2). In agreement with this "for us, by us" educational method, I recommend that given the presence of Black trans* womx[x]yn students and other Black trans* identities on HBCU campuses, professors like us should be hired *and* retained through the tenure process and be involved in (re)constructing HBCU curricula in order to truly attain culturally relevant pedagogy inside and outside the classroom. And given the scholarship that is emerging from within Black trans* communities, academic texts written by Black trans* folks should be used across curricula.

Racial-Gender Vindicationism

Givens (2016) explains Woodson's emphasis on race vindicationism, which is focused on instilling Black pride in Black persons through correcting distorted depictions of Black history. Based on this concept of vindicationism, I recommend curricula informed by racial-gender vindicationism that seeks to correct ill-informed perspectives of Black trans* identities and history and to instill pride in the souls of Black trans* womx[x]yn students. This is needed to combat didactic pedagogies that have been used at HBCUs that are in direct contradistinction to constructing trans*ness as a historical and integral part of Black culture throughout the Black diaspora.

Pro-Trans* General Education Requirement and Service Learning

It is not just Black trans* womx[x]yn and other Black queer and trans* students who would benefit from a pro-trans* curriculum at HBCUs. Cisgender students would also benefit. All HBCU students, regardless of their major, should be required to take a race, gender, and sexuality general education course. Such a class would provide an intersectional approach to addressing and informing students about gender identity and how it overlaps with Black identity and various sexualities. This kind of general education course would also improve inclusion in a student body of diverse gender identities and expressions. Smith (2019) contends that "there is a consensus that a good service-learning initiative includes the following: the furthering of academic learning, service to a community, and a reflective process that consists of bettering engagement practices among practicing scholars, students, and community members" (p. 14). Drawing from this consensus, incorporating service learning in a course like race, gender, and sexuality (e.g., by partnering with a LGTBQ organization to have a clothing receptacle in the classroom or somewhere on campus to collect new/lightly used gender-affirming clothing for Black trans* womx[x]yn and other trans* students via student donations) would reinforce students' learning through engagement in a real-world context.

Institutional Leadership

Leaders provide vital representation and help show what is possible. My chief recommendation in this section is for HBCUs to intentionally vet Black trans* womx[x]yn, and others with trans* identities for leadership positions such as college/university presidents, provosts, and deans. These Black trans* leaders could be effective diplomats of liberation engagement a type of engagement that "borrows from the Black Liberation Movement in that its focus . . . is direct and indirect community and campus efforts that can produce social progress and full freedom for Black people" (Smith, 2017, p. 12). In this case, liberation engagement within the democratic systems of HBCUs would involve the social progress of Black trans* womx[x]yn students and their trans* and queer kin on campus.

FINAL THOUGHTS

As I conclude this chapter, I want to emphasize the concept of integration. Integration stems from the Latin word *integratus*, the past participle of *integrare*, which means "to make whole, renew." HBCU ecosystems cannot be made whole and will always lack equilibrium until they foster togetherness with Black trans* womx[x]yn students through a spirit of integration. This togetherness must be actualized on multiple levels (e.g., in student life, in curriculum and instruction, and in leadership). For Black colleges to accomplish this togetherness, there must be a translation of policy into praxis. This could potentially include the revamping of student affairs divisions, pro-trans* (re)education in the curriculum, pedagogy objectives motivated by service, liberation, and inclusion, and pedagogical strategies that reflect a renewed commitment to recognizing the fullness of Black humanity as expressed through the lived experiences, culture, and contributions of Black trans* folk. The presence of Black trans* leadership who act as advocates for the needs, rights, and privileges of Black trans* and queer students will also be critical. Translating these recommendations for campus policies and for restructuring HBCU education into praxis can effectively counteract the miseducation of Black trans* womx[x]yn students and their trans* and queer kin at HBCUs so that my "missed education" will not be theirs.

NOTES

1. My spelling of womx[x]yn when referring to Black womx[x]yn (cisgender and trans*) in plural form is meant to create a visual distinction with the use of brackets that acknowledges biologically constructed notions of gender and highlights both the pluralistic and specious nature of womanhood. Black cisgender and trans* womx[x]yn deviate from, blur, and nuance biological constructions so that such womx[x]yn are defined not by their chromosomal pairings (XX or XY) but by their inherent identities, their performances of gender, and their consequential and empirical gendered realities.

2. In a historical-cultural context, "Yemaya" (a Creolized variant; also spelled "Yemoja," "Yemonja," "Yemaja," or "Yemanja") is a revered deity in the Yoruban tradition. Mami Wata (Mother Water), as Yemaya is sometimes called, is the goddess of the seas, often portrayed as a queenly ebony mermaid, and is celebrated as the mother of all (Canson, 2014). Interestingly, Yemaya is transitive in nature. One specific evidence of this can be found in oral accounts that say in one of the life paths of Yemaya she dressed as a man and sometimes became so masculine that she morphed into a man. Based on the example of Yemaya's transitional nature and her ability to relate to the derision that some trans* people experience, she is an appropriate Black sacred figure to use in the broader discussion of Black trans* persons at HBCUs.

REFERENCES

Anderson, J. D. (1988). *The education of Blacks in the South*. University of North Carolina Press.

Baldwin, J. (1985). *The price of the ticket: Collected nonfiction, 1948–1985*. St. Martin's Press.

Blockett, R. A. (2017). 'I think it's very much placed on us': Black queer men laboring to forge community at a predominantly white and (hetero) cisnormative research institution. *International Journal of Qualitative Studies in Education, 30*(8), 800–816. http://dx.doi.org/10.1080/09518398.2017.1350296

Brazzell, J. C. (1992). Bricks without straw: Missionary-sponsored Black higher education in the post-emancipation era. *The Journal of Higher Education, 63*(1), 26–49.

Buchanan, L., & Hutcheson, P. (1999). Reconsidering the Washington-Du Bois debate: Two Black colleges in 1910–1911. In W. Urban (Ed.), *Essays in 20th century southern education: Exceptionalism and its limits* (pp. 77–100). Garland Press.

Byrd, K. (2020). *LGBTQ student experiences on historically Black college and university campuses.* [Unpublished doctoral dissertation]. College of William & Mary. http://dx.doi.org/10.25774/w4-rqhk-oyo3

Canson, P. E. (2014, August 15). Yemonja. In *Encyclopedia Britannica*. Retrieved July 16, 2021, from https://www.britannica.com/topic/Yemonja

Center for American Progress & Movement Advancement Project. (2015). *Paying an unfair price: The financial penalty for being transgender in America.* Movement Advancement Project. https://www.lgbtmap.org/file/paying-an-unfair-price-transgender.pdf

Collins, A. C. (2001). Black women in the academy: An historical overview. In R. O. Mabokela & A. L. Green (Eds.), *Sisters of the academy: Emergent Black women scholars in higher education* (pp. 29–41). Stylus Publishing.

Evans, S. Y. (2007). *Black women in the ivory tower, 1850–1954.* University Press of Florida.

Gasman, M. (2007). Swept under the rug? A historiography of gender and Black colleges. *American Educational Research Journal, 44*(4), 760–805.

Givens, J. R. (2016). *Culture, curriculum, and consciousness: Resurrecting the educational praxis of Dr. Carter G. Woodson, 1875–1950* [Unpublished doctoral dissertation]. University of Virginia.

Hurston, Z. N. (1937). *Their eyes were watching God.* J. B. Lippincott & Co.

King. A. S. (2010, October 11). The mean girls of Morehouse. *Vibe.* https://www.vibe.com/features/editorial/mean-girls-morehouse-40456/

Mobley, S. D., Jr., & Hall, L. (2020). (Re)defining queer and trans* student retention and success at historically Black colleges and universities. *Journal of College Student Retention, 21*(4), 497–519. doi/10.1177/1521025119895512

Mobley, S. D., Jr., & Johnson, J. M. (2019). "No pumps allowed": The "problem" with gender expression and the Morehouse College "appropriate attire policy." *Journal of Homosexuality, 66*(7), 867–895.

Mobley, S. D., Jr., Solomon, S. L., II, Johnson, A. C., & Reynolds, P. (2021). "Troubling the waters": Unpacking and (re)imagining the historical and contemporary complexity of historically Black college and university cultural politics. In B. C. Williams, F. Tuitt, & D. Squire (Eds.), *Campus rebellions and plantation politics: Power, privilege, and the emancipatory struggle in higher education* (pp. 77–97). State University of New York Press.

Morehouse College. (2018–2019). *Enrollment and Persistence.* Common Data Set. https://morehouse.edu/wp-content/uploads/2022/04/enrollment_and_persistence_1819.pdf

NAACP.org. (n.d.). *Carter G. Woodson.* https://naacp.org/find-resources/history-explained/civil-rights-leaders/carter-g-woodson#:~:text=Woodson's%20devotion%20to%20showcasing%20the,expanded%20into%20Black%20History%20Month

Njoku, N., Butler, M., & Beatty, C. C. (2017). Reimagining the historically Black college and university (HBCU) environment: Exposing race secrets and the binding chains of respectability and othermothering. *International Journal of Qualitative Studies in Education, 30*(8), 783–799.

Noble, J. L. (1956). *The Negro woman's college education.* Columbia University Press.

Patton, L. D. (2014). Preserving respectability or blatant disrespect? A critical discourse analysis of the Morehouse appropriate attire policy and implications for intersectional approaches to examining campus policies. *International Journal of Qualitative Studies, 27*(6), 724–746.

Pope, Y. D. (2023). *Natural Woman: A Memoir Anthology* (p. 117). Kindle Direct Publishing.

Smith, M.P. (2017, October 2). *The mis-engagement of higher education: A case for liberation engagement at historically Black colleges and universities.* Center for Minority Serving Institutions at the University of Pennsylvania. CSMI Research Brief. https://cmsi.gse.rutgers.edu/sites/default/files/The%20Mis-Engagement%20of%20Higher%20Education-%20A%20Case%20for%20Liberation%20Engagement%20at%20Historically%20Black%20Colleges%20and%20Universities.pdf

Smith, S. (2019). *What does a marginalized community say about its experiences in a two-year, service-learning project?* West Virginia University, Graduate Theses, Dissertations, and Problem Reports. 3839. https://researchrepository.wvu.edu/etd/3839

Spelman College. (2017). *Applying to Spelman.* Retrieved July 06, 2021. https://www.spelman.edu/admissions/applying-to-spelman

———. (n.d.). *Morehouse-James Hall, circa 1930* [Photograph]. Spelman College Photographs Collection. https://radar.auctr.edu/islandora/object/sc.002%3A0135

Suggs, E. (2019, February 19). Mary Spivey: The Morehouse woman. *The Atlanta Journal-Constitution.* https://www.ajc.com/lifestyles/mary-spivey-the-morehouse-woman/akqaJZ7DQzmMPp4708MZsJ/

Williams, H. V. (2020, February 23). Black women's fictive kin networks and the sisters in the house. *Medium.* https://hettie-williams.medium.com/black-womens-fictive-kin-networks-and-the-sisters-in-the-house-26291cc1b5a3#:~:text=Black%20Women's%20Fictive%20Kin%20Networks%20and%20the%20Sisters%20in%20the%20House,-Dr.&text=This%20phrase%20fictive%20kinship%20refers,connotes%20blood%20or%20marital%20ties

Woodson, C. G. (1972). *The mis-education of the Negro.* Africa World Press. (Original work published 1933)

3 · INTERSECTIONALITY IN THEORY AND PRAXIS

The Role of Student Organizing as Preparation for Fostering Inclusive Spaces as an HBCU Administrator

TRINICE McNALLY

WATERSHED MOMENTS: NAVIGATING DEAR OL' BC-U

In the summer of 2007, I had just come back from London, England, after spending a summer with family and what felt like a lifetime of learning and understanding Black British culture. I had just been through the arduous process of getting a visa so I could access higher education in the United States. I arrived at my residence hall at Bethune-Cookman University (B-CU) as a first-generation immigrant student. I was excited and worried, and I was anticipating who I would become, how I would change, and what it would feel like to determine for myself who and how I was meant to be and where the journey would take me. Although my dreams of freedom and autonomy soon faded away it was the beginning of some of the greatest and most impactful times in my life.

Dr. Mary McLeod Bethune founded the great Bethune-Cookman University in Daytona Beach, Florida. She established this school for Black girls in 1904, almost four decades after the end of slavery in the United States. B-CU is a sacred place, a place where we are called to *enter to learn and depart to serve*, as the school's motto instructs its students. The university is a testament to Black resilience and excellence personified. However, some of the most painful experiences for queer and trans* students have occurred at my beloved alma mater. Those experiences invoked my commitment to serve.

As some of the oldest institutions for African Americans in the United States, HBCUs are inextricably linked to the Black Church. B-CU is affiliated with the

United Methodist Church, and that foundation of Christianity is still very much part of the experience of every student there. From freshman seminar to consecration ceremonies, the doctrine is conveyed in ways that inspires some, drives fear in others, and creates guilt and despair for those who sit on the margins of mainstream sexual orientation and gender identity. This is not an unusual experience for students at HBCUs. The conservative nature of many HBCU campus cultures has made these environments challenging for their queer constituencies (Harper & Gasman, 2008; Kirby 2011).

As a God-fearing first-year student entering B-CU, I had always questioned my attraction to women and gender-nonconforming individuals. By the time of my sophomore year in 2008, I had finally come to terms with my sexuality and publicly identified as a lesbian. However, that felt less than authentic to my queer experience given that I was attracted to and dated both men and women. During that time, university clergy and chaplains, residence life coordinators, and upperclassmen in band routinely shared with incoming freshmen the dangers of getting "turned out". That belief that people could be turned gay disrupted my holistic development and that of others who were grappling with both sexual orientation and gender identity as some type of accident or crime. B-CU was an environment where students were encouraged in implicit and explicit ways to conceal their queerness because these identities are often deemed inconsistent with the mission and culture of HBCUs (Ford, 2015; Patton et al., 2020).

What I find interesting about my time as an undergrad is that I still managed to find ways to explore my queerness. I frequented Black LGBTQ+ (lesbian, gay, bisexual, trans*, and queer-plus) nightclubs and recognized a substantial number of my peers in those dark, fluorescent rooms. The phenomenon of the "down-low" became an insidious norm for the people I would dance with, people who in public or on campus would not dare to speak to or acknowledge me. Surprisingly, the marching band, the dance troupe, and the chorale became places of solace for me because so many members of those groups were queer identified and/or supportive because of our shared love of the arts. It was during this time that I learned the vital importance of community and camaraderie. My queer kin on campus and I created our own spaces, families, houses, and support systems because our institution did not have venues for us. During my time at B-CU, many LGBTQ+ students were involved in co-curricular activities that we dedicated our lives to not only in order to claim our HBCU experiences but also in order to survive. Campus groups were spaces where I and my queer classmates could be in leadership and galvanize respect.

My dear B-CU served as a source of both strength and strife in my life. I was navigating a conservative Christian liberal arts college as an immigrant (formerly undocumented) bisexual woman who was struggling financially. I remember a visit to the counseling services department as I was grappling with my sexual orientation and learning how to navigate being comfortable and supported. The counselor told me that I was experiencing so much stress because of the lifestyle I chose and offered to pray for me and anoint me with oil. After sharing this with a couple of classmates, I learned that I was not the only student who had been told this. I became extremely disconnected from the institution and its faculty and staff. I am positive that finding community was a key factor that helped me survive and eventually thrive during my years at B-CU.

SAVING GRACES AND A CALL TO ACTION

HBCU administrators often consider themselves to be surrogate family members for their students and not simply just administrators (Hirt et al., 2006). The historic missions that deeply influence HBCU cultures also influence the professional practices of their student affairs professionals, who are committed not only to student success but also to Black student success (Hirt et al., 2008). I was lucky to have administrators at B-CU who provided support to me and my peers who felt isolated, underrepresented, and marginalized. These individuals challenged me to turn my demands, complaints, and/or experiences into action. Dr. Joi Niles, the director of counseling services, and Dr. Dwaun Warmack, the vice-president of student affairs, became my saving graces.

Dr. Niles also served as the principal investigator for Project S.T.E.P.S. (Survival Through Education, Prevention, and Services), which I became involved in. This program, which was funded by the Substance Abuse and Mental Health Services Administration (SAMHSA), was a suicide prevention initiative that trained key stakeholders, including health care providers, mental health care providers, residence hall and security staff, faculty, administrators, student government leaders, and community behavioral health partners to design and implement a strategic plan that served to diminish and eliminate risk factors that increase the vulnerability of marginalized students to suicidal ideation and other behavioral health issues (Suicide Prevention Resource Center, 2011). It was through this initiative and through the encouragement of Dr. Warmack that I was able to establish the first Gay-Straight Alliance at B-CU in 2012. This organization was the first of its kind at an HBCU in the state of Florida.

Immediately after completing my undergraduate studies at B-CU, I took a yearlong hiatus to serve as the lead peer educator for Project S.T.E.P.S. and as the advisor to the Gay-Straight Alliance. The first year of Project S.T.E.P.S. was pivotal for its survival as an organization today. After collecting fifty signatures from supportive peers, we were officially deemed a university-recognized organization. The first year was the most challenging we faced. A large number of LGBTQ+ students refused to join publicly. Yet a solid ten to fifteen pledged their commitment, their time, and their effort to developing what we understood was the first step in ensuring that our campus would provide an inclusive environment for LGBTQ+ students. We realized that other than the Counseling Services department (which had been revamped and run with a new staff) and this new initiative, we were all we had.

Over the next two years, the Gay-Straight Alliance gained close to 100 members. We worked closely with B-CU's Counseling Services department to provide support and access to therapy for LGBTQ+ students. I was later accepted in the master's degree program in transformative leadership at B-CU, where I wrote a thesis titled "Best Practices for Social and Cultural Networks Necessary to Foster Safe Learning Environments for LGBTQ Students at HBCUs" (McNally, 2014). The master's program selected cooperative inquiry action research as its model for graduate research. Reason (1999) notes that "in Cooperative inquiry, all those involved in the research endeavor are both the co-researchers, whose thinking and decision-making contributes to generating ideas, designing and managing the project, and drawing conclusions from the experience; and also co-subjects participating in the activity that is being researched" (p. 207). During my time in the program, I learned that the outcome of critical inquiry is not just the compiled data and research but what you do with it to move it into action. Working on my thesis allowed me to facilitate a case study for which I conducted interviews and collected data on both the perceived and actual experiences of LGBTQ+ students at B-CU. This work propelled my transition to my first professional position in the field of student affairs. However, a critical incident happened that will forever color my time as an administrator: the untimely death of one of my students at the outset of my career.

INTEGRATING RESEARCH INTO PRAXIS: A CASE STUDY

Before I completed my master's degree, President Edison O. Jackson appointed me as the university's first coordinator of diversity initiatives. In that role, I was responsible for initiatives to develop new policies that would foster an inclusive environment for LGBTQ+ students on the B-CU campus. I also continued to advise the Gay-Straight Alliance. Under my advisement, the alliance became active in local social justice movements in central Florida and nationally. It spearheaded several initiatives and programs, including Pride Week, during which it hosted several panels designed to increase dialogues about the needs and experiences of LGBTQ+ students at HBCUs. Programs such as Gay & Greek, transgender awareness forums, National Coming-Out Day events, and Allies against Bullying became staples that raised awareness of LGBTQ+ students at B-CU, affirmed their presence on campus, and set a precedent for administrators. My students and I were putting the campus on notice that if it did not develop programs and support for us, we would do it ourselves.

Even though I had been appointed to this position, B-CU was not committed to ensuring that LGBTQ+ students were protected and supported. In April 2015,

Damian Parks, an openly gay Black student, drowned at a local beach during what some rumored was a hazing ritual for joining a step team. Damian, like many other Gay-Straight Alliance members, was heavily involved in dance and modeling troupes at B-CU and was one of the most talented dancers the university had ever had. He became involved with the Gay-Straight Alliance and served in leadership during his time at B-CU. I was his advisor, and he shared with me his goals of moving to California and dancing with companies like the Alvin Ailey American Dance Theater. After his body was found, B-CU held a memorial for him in our chapel. There, an esteemed clergy member publicly disrespected him by sharing homophobic sentiments that "parents don't send their children to school to be gay" and insinuating that Damian's sexuality was the reason he died. This moment incited a spirit of both retaliation and resistance among active Gay-Straight Alliance members. My students were deeply insulted and hurt by the insensitive and homophobic comments that were allowed to be given by a local clergy member and then delivered on our campus less than forty-eight hours after Damian's death. While students were upset, they also felt helpless. I held meetings to help them process what had occurred and was tasked with explaining to administrators why this was unacceptable. Fortunately, the Vice-President of Student Affairs Dr. Michelle Thompson understood and helped me urge the university to issue an apology after students held a silent protest and made complaints to the university. Later that year, B-CU formally recognized the Gay-Straight Alliance as an established LGBTQ+ student organization. The group was further recognized as a social justice change agent when it received the Silent Impact of the Year Award from the institution for championing change and fighting against bigotry.

Unfortunately, B-CU did not keep its promise to fund a sustainable infrastructure that would develop into institutional funding for an adequate position, department, and budget that could foster an LGBTQ-inclusive campus. This story is far too common in places where student organizations are tasked with the responsibility of leading and providing resources and education for HBCU campuses instead of institutions doing the work they proclaim to be doing in their mission statements and strategic plans (Mobley et. al., 2021). HBCUs should be committed to ensuring that all their students are thriving and have the resources and education they need.

In the "Transformation of Silence into Language and Action" speech from *Sister Outsider*, Audre Lorde (1984b) wrote, "I have come to believe over and over again that what is most important to me must be spoken, made verbal and shared, even at the risk of having it bruised or misunderstood" (p. 28). This essay seeks to share ugly truths about the experiences of LGBTQ students at HBCUs, not to tear down or bash those institutions. If HBCUs are truly to be places where Blackness is centered, then the experiences of LGBTQ and nonbinary students must be prioritized through funding, policy, and resources instead of relying on their student organizations to do that work.

Among the many things Dr. Mary McLeod Bethune left us in her last will and testament were these words: "Respect for the uses of power. We live in a world that respects power above all things. Power, intelligently directed, can lead to more freedom. Unwisely directed, it can be a dreadful, destructive force" (Bethune Cookman University, 2022, para. 10). What I want administrators and members of boards of trustees at HBCUs to know is that they have the power to improve the experiences of their LGBTQ+ and gender-expansive students by creating policies, financial support, and resources for them. If HBCUs aspire to truly be committed to missions, values, and theories that are grounded in providing student-centered services, then they must prioritize these students. Ultimately, HBCUs have the power to be incubators that create policy and evoke change that supports *all* their students so that they can have the opportunity to experience an intersectional and liberatory educational environment (Mobley et al., 2019).

MY TIME AT NORTH CAROLINA CENTRAL UNIVERSITY AND THE SECOND HBCU LGBTQ RESOURCE CENTER IN THE NATION

In April 2013, North Carolina Central University (NCCU) became the second HBCU in the United States and the first in North Carolina to open a center dedicated to LGBTQ issues. Founded under the leadership of the Director of Student Life Assessment Tia Marie Doxey, it has served as the flagship HBCU institution in the Deep South that is intentional about serving LGBTQ+ HBCU students. While in general HBCUs have been reluctant to fully engage with their queer and trans* students, significant strides have been made to ensure that their LGBTQ+ students truly feel welcome (Mobley & Johnson, 2015). The advancements at NCCU are a testament to this.

NCCU's LGBTA Resource Center was created to provide programming and education to the NCCU community and to serve as a safe space for students, staff, and faculty. The center also provides programming and events that educate about and celebrate the LGBTQ community. I began my role as the coordinator for the resource center in August 2016. Prior to my arrival, it was under the leadership of Lakesha Winley, a Black lesbian from Wilmington, North Carolina, and a two-time NCCU alumnus. She initially served in her role as a graduate student and later transitioned to the role of a coordinator. She made a significant impact on the ability of students to trust and connect with the university community. I have found that it is extremely important that young Black people feel represented by and can find connections to employees who mirror their identities. Visibility matters, especially on HBCU campuses. Mobley and Hall (2020) argue that "representation is key. Actively engaging queer and trans* HBCU alumni to come back to their respective campuses to be 'present' and engage would not only show that they care and are committed, but this type of engagement would also provide 'possibility models' for their students as well" (p. 513).

While NCCU is recognized as the second HBCU in the nation and the first in North Carolina to open a center dedicated to LGBTQ+ issues, it should also be recognized as a model of both institutional commitment and infrastructural support. Although Bowie State University in Maryland may have been the first to establish a resource center, it has encountered budgetary and staffing issues. That has impacted how they have been able to lead efforts to ensure that LGBTQ+ students are affirmed and supported. NCCU has followed in the footsteps of HBCUs like Spelman College, which is the first and still the only HBCU with a Women's Research & Resource Center and a women's studies major. NCCU has made significant co-curricular and academic advancements that deliberately center Black LGBTQ issues in the midst of state sanctions against these communities.

HBCUs must be intentional about developing institutional and infrastructural support systems in order to sustain the high regard in which they are held for the diversity that is "inherent among their students, faculty and administrations" (Mobley et al., 2019, p. 109). For at least two years, NCCU was the only HBCU with policy, programming, and a fully funded position and department for LGBTQ-inclusive efforts. Fayetteville State University established a center and a position in 2015. Although the mission statements, core values, and strategic plans of HBCUs emphasize diversity and inclusion, how diverse or inclusive are they if they are not intentional about funding or infrastructure? My hope is that HBCUs will not continue to perpetuate the efforts made at predominantly white institutions to create inclusive environments for students of color without any real strategy or commitment to ensuring that they thrive. HBCUs must fully champion policies and interventions that will best engage all of their queer and trans* stakeholders (Lewis & Eriksen, 2016; Mobley & Johnson, 2015).

Being afforded the opportunity to follow in the footsteps of Black women who pioneered historic work at NCCU gave me the inspiration I needed to fight the battle that Black women often face in both the academy and the student affairs profession. As an HBCU alumnus and Black queer woman, I was able to build and connect with LGBTQ+ and non-binary students immediately. Fortunately, NCCU was and still is a part of the 32 percent of HBCUs that have recognized LGBTQ/ally student organizations on their campuses (Mobley & Johnson, 2019). During my time at NCCU, four organizations served both LGBTQ students and faculty/staff:

- Creating Open Lives Organizing for Real Success (COLORS): This student-led organization for LGBTQ+ students was founded in the early 2000s and is still active.

- Polychromes: An organization for LGBTQ+ faculty and staff that is still operating.
- Dominant Overly Motivated Studs (DOMS): This group is geared toward masculine-identified lesbian students. It is not currently active.
- OutLAW: An organization for LGBTQ+ faculty, staff, and students in the school of law that encourages allies to attend. This organization is still active.

During my time at NCCU, I sustained the work that had been created before my arrival and was able to establish several programmatic, experiential learning, and leadership opportunities for LGBTQ+ and ally students that have since grown and transitioned into benchmark LGBTQ efforts for the center. I established a Black LGBTQ Health & Wellness Day, an LGBTQ Pride Day, an LGBTQ Black Hollywood Prom, and a film series titled Queering Film: Screening of Eden's Garden. Several of these programs were the first of their kind, and they truly changed the campus because they engaged not only our LGBTQ+ students but also administrators, staff, and faculty. Although my time at NCCU greatly shaped my practice and praxis, I needed to evolve further. It soon became time for me to leave the traditional campus space for a little while and enter the community partnership arena for this work.

THE POWER OF PARTNERSHIP, COLLABORATIONS, AND ORGANIZING: FROM ADVOCACY TO THE BLACK RADICAL TRADITION

A key aspect of my practice in student affairs has been my exposure to and engagement with nonprofits and community partnerships that center Black LGBTQ+ communities such as the National Black Justice Coalition and the Human Rights Campaign's HBCU Initiative. Community partnerships with Black LGBTQ+ enterprises have been vital collaborations for HBCUs and have ensured that many of these campuses center and are able to serve their queer and trans* communities (Mobley & Hall, 2020; Mobley & Johnson, 2015). Since 2003, the National Black Justice Coalition has been America's leading national civil rights organization dedicated to the empowerment of Black lesbian, gay, bisexual, transgender, queer+, and same-gender-loving (SGL) people, including people living with HIV/AIDS, through coalition building, advocating for changes in federal policies, research, and education. In addition, the Human Rights Campaign's HBCU Initiative mobilizes and provides needed support to HBCUs and their LGBTQ+ students in the areas of inclusion, equity, and engagement (Human Rights Campaign, 2022).

I came across the National Black Justice Coalition when I was a graduate student intern at the Human Rights Campaign in 2014 after I founded the

Gay-Straight Alliance at B-CU. In 2012, I had been accepted to attend the Human Rights Campaign's HBCU Summit, where I met fifteen other Black LGBTQ+ HBCU student leaders. Even though the Human Rights Campaign was largely led by white organizers, they got something right in their support of the leadership of Black LGBTQ+ students at HBCUs. Many of us had never met or thought it possible to be in community with others who shared similar experiences. That summit, where I met some of the extraordinary people who would become my lifelong friends and colleagues, changed my life. This initiative helped us explore strategies and tools for effectively organizing our campuses toward inclusion. The sessions, which included workshops, conversations with administrators, and opportunities to build community, equipped us to better organize and create change on our campuses. To this day, the Human Rights Campaign HBCU Leadership Summit is curating much-needed spaces to ensure that our students can thrive. Every HBCU administrator should be aware of this program and encourage students to attend.

I later learned that the National Black Justice Coalition, an organization with an extensive history of advocacy at HBCUs, had worked with the Human Rights Campaign to make this happen and that some of the facilitators at the summit were National Black Justice Coalition staff members. After the summit ended, my cohort and I stayed in touch throughout our studies and I felt equipped and clear about the changes I would make on my campus and what my action reach would focus on. I was in the process of doing research to support my thesis, and learning about a Black-led LGBTQ+/SGL organization felt like I had hit the jackpot. After weeks of trying, I was able to schedule a meeting with the executive director and alumnus of Florida Agricultural & Mechanical University, Sharon Lettman-Hicks, and a relationship that served as a cornerstone in my leadership began. The support, resources, and knowledge from Hicks helped me finalize my thesis and move B-CU to create its first-ever coordinator of diversity initiatives. After I had navigated both undergraduate and graduate schooling, it was the advocacy, mentorship, and leadership of the National Black Justice Coalition that shaped my ability to be professional and foster inclusive, affirming, and supportive campus climates.

Learning from Black queer women like Victoria Kirby (a Howard University alumnus) and Jeshawn Wholley (a Spelman College alumnus) gave me the extra fuel I needed to defend my thesis and take on the grueling work of navigating my new role as an administrator. Organizations like the National Black Justice Coalition provided national support, exposure, and acumen in places where it felt like university leaders were immovable or resistant. Collaborations with national organizations were helpful to me as an activist and a professional. During my early years of teaching and organizing at HBCUs, Sharon Lettman-Hicks was a mentor who often helped me navigate career paths and strategically improve policies and climates for Black LGBTQ+ students. The role of the National Black Justice Coalition in my life largely prepared me to serve HBCUs at large.

After leaving NCCU, I joined the National Black Justice Coalition to serve as the program manager of its HBCU LGBTQ-Equality Initiative. I helped develop this initiative, whose mission was to make HBCUs whole and healthy for their LGBTQ populations. Its work has included collecting data, building coalitions, advocating for public policy change, and providing LGBTQ-inclusive cultural competency trainings. The initiative was inspired by the Audre Lorde Black Lesbian Feminist Project (2006–2011) at Spelman College, which the Arcus Foundation funded. We implemented two advocacy efforts through the PrEPing Our Futures Tour at seven HBCUs by facilitating LGBTQ-inclusive cultural competency training and/or Black LGBTQ health and wellness workshops for over 700 students, 300 administrators, and 30 senior-level administrators. Because of this work, more HBCUs have LGBTQ+ resource centers, programs, and policies to ensure that LGBTQ+ students are institutionally supported and protected. My time and work with the National Black Justice Coalition and my involvement with the Human Rights Campaign's HBCU Initiative provided opportunities to work and organize on Capitol Hill and introduced me to grassroots organizing in Washington, DC, where I still live and organize today.

FOUNDING OF THE CENTER FOR DIVERSITY, INCLUSION AND MULTICULTURAL AFFAIRS AT THE UNIVERSITY OF THE DISTRICT OF COLUMBIA

> Everyday something has tried to kill me and has failed.
> —Clifton, 1993, p. 25

I preface this section of my chapter by sharing that my time at the University of the District of Columbia has been some of the most challenging and gratifying in all of my career so far. I eventually found my way back to an HBCU. I also began the next phase of my career on a college campus. The University of the District of Columbia, which Myrtilla Miner founded as a school for "colored girls" in 1851, has been through several shifts over its history; it became a teacher's college that later expanded into an institution of higher education. Today it provides undergraduate, graduate, and juris doctorate degrees in addition to vocational training and professional certifications.

The University of the District of Columbia has long pursued the ideals of social justice and public service. It is a place where historically marginalized people have had access to resources and support that have shifted the trajectory of Black and Brown people across the globe. Because of that history, it was easy to say yes to a position there in multicultural affairs. As an experienced student affairs professional, strategist, and community organizer, I came in ready to work and have made impacts that honor the goals of the institution. However, nothing could have prepared me for the actual work. Probably many other colleagues who share similar ideologies would say the same thing, yet we somehow persevere and honor our commitments. In my case, I choose to change HBCU settings to make them liberatory environments.

The Center for Diversity, Inclusion and Multicultural Affairs at the University of the District of Columbia, which was founded in 2018, is dedicated to promoting social justice through the development of co-curricular programs and educational activities that enhance the personal development, success, and collegiate experience of historically marginalized students. It is committed to fostering an equitable and inclusive campus culture that values the personal, intellectual, and academic growth of all students while prioritizing the experiences of international, undocumented, LGBTQ+, and first-generation students at the University of the District of Columbia. The formation of the center and the development of its mission was rooted in the historical legacy of student organizing movements, the evolution of the concept of intersectionality, and my own commitment to the liberation of oppressed people. As the late bell hooks said, "the personal is political."

For the first few months after I arrived on campus, I spent most of my time talking with students and recent alumni and reading documents in the university archives. During this investigation period, I learned of a significant piece of history, the Kiamsha movement. This was an almost unknown history at the university. In 1990, over 150 students engaged in an eleven-day occupation of the student affairs building in an effort to pressure university officials to meet their demands for student-centered solutions to campus issues. In my oral history research, I learned that the specific incident that sparked the demonstration (in addition to the students' long-standing concerns) was the refusal of the Board of Trustees to meet with student leaders about its decision to spend $80,000 to acquire artist Judy Chicago's controversial art installation *The Dinner Party*.

This artwork was a product of second-wave feminism that is still criticized for ignoring the intersections of race, gender, and class and for erasing the experiences of Black and Brown women and gender-expansive people. What I found most interesting is that some of those issues are still plaguing today's student body. Students are still asking for more student representation on the Board of Trustees and on grievance committees, streamlined admissions processing, and adequate student housing. The bill the students developed with these demands is a part of a long legacy of student organizing on HBCU campuses. When trustees agreed to forty of the students' forty-five demands after eleven days of protests, student organizers ended their demonstration (Harriston, 1990). Learning about the Kiamsha movement inspired many of my students to organize and reactivate student organizations, such as The Alliance Group (T.A.G.), the LGBTQ+ undergraduate student organization, and to create organizations such as Migration Matters, the only student-led advocacy organization that centers the needs and experiences of migrant students at an HBCU. I would also argue that this also prepared students participate in the 2020 Black Lives Matter protests in the midst of the height of the COVID-19 pandemic in Washington, DC, where Black communities organized and protested across generations in record numbers, even during a pandemic.

Another example of the above-mentioned interventions in scholarly praxis on the campus of the University of the District of Columbia is T.A.G., which was originally founded in 2005 to serve as a support for LGBTQ+ students. In 2018, alumnus Taylor Bryant reactivated the organization with a new mission of fostering an LGBTQ+-inclusive climate and educating the campus community through intergroup dialogue, awareness events, community engagement, and national and local partnerships. Since this group was activated (which happened at the same time the Center for Diversity, Inclusion and Multicultural Affairs was founded), its members have led campaigns against homophobia and transphobia, convinced senior-level administrators to develop all-gender restrooms, and hosted the first ballroom culture event in partnership with the leaders of the House of Garcon and the House of Balenciaga. Not only have its members been diligent about pursuing their goals, but most of the group's student leaders have graduated to work in the fields of education, advocacy, and social justice.

The Center for Diversity, Inclusion and Multicultural Affairs strives to provide the programmatic efforts, experiential learning opportunities, and resources students need to transform their thinking and enhance their knowledge and competency in a variety of cultural contexts. Leading it has been one of the greatest honors of my life. It is a testament to what is possible when we center those at the margins. Yet there is still so much work to do and oftentimes feels like I am doing this work alone. But a good organizer never organizes alone, and I have been able to collaborate with amazing colleagues and student leaders for mutual encouragement as we fight against the ivory tower, anti-blackness, sexism, homophobia and transphobia, and the culture of respectability. At the end of 2021, I worked alongside social justice ambassador and T.A.G president Shabre West to develop the first-ever LGBTQ+ Advisory Council at the university and launch the inaugural Kiburi Pride LGBTQ+ Scholarship in honor of Black gay poet Essex Hemphill, a university alumnus.

Even in times of turmoil, resilience and liberation have been at the center for Black queer and trans* communities. In the words of the late Audre Lorde (1984a), "There is no such thing as a single-issue struggle because we do not live single-issue lives" (p. 130). With this as a north star, I hope that each administrator reading this chapter will be inspired to move beyond your biases, knowledge sets, and/or religious beliefs and honor our institutions by doing everything in your power to center marginalized students and create safe, resourced spaces where they can thrive.

CONCLUSIONS AND RECOMMENDATIONS

While there has been tremendous progress at HBCUs as they have moved toward better engagement with their queer and trans* stakeholders, there is still much that can be accomplished. Funding is key. HBCU communities should work to secure funding and resources to provide adequate and safe spaces on their campuses for their marginalized students who embody many intersecting identities. Adequate budgets that support LGBTQ+/non-binary programming, mentorship, and research are vital and would benefit the entire campus culture. These categories of initiatives are usually last on funding priority lists or are not even considered. Institutionalized funding for LGBTQ+ resources should also be allocated to secure several positions that lead social justice, diversity, equity and inclusion work on campus. One position is not enough to sustain this work. In addition, having counseling professionals who are truly in tune with the lived experiences and issues that affect queer and trans* HBCU students is paramount to the well-being of these students (Mobley & Hall, 2020).

I also believe that financial reserves dedicated solely to emergency aid and scholarships specifically geared toward LGBTQ+ students are absolutely necessary. Because of the ways systemic systems of oppression violently attack and erase these students, they need and deserve to be supported so they can thrive in times of both success and crisis. HBCU communities outwardly brag about the diversity of their campuses but they have not actively heralded this type of work. A colleague once said that diversity work without funding is fraud, and I could not agree more. HBCUs need to hire and expand their counseling services departments. If COVID-19 has shown us anything, it is that in a world of suffering and tragedy, mental health care must be prioritized and accessible for those that need it most.

Representation also matters. HBCUs need to hire *and* protect their LGBTQ+ identified faculty and staff. Oftentimes employees who identify with a historically marginalized community or hold political values outside the conservative and/or liberal norm feel unsafe on HBCU campuses. Students can see this. What they see does not motivate them to work and be engaged on their campuses, and it further solidifies their oppression.

HBCUs should also establish and sustain curriculums based on women's studies, gender studies, ethnic studies, and Black studies that offer majors or minors in interdisciplinary studies. Having this option at an HBCU introduces and challenges campus-wide notions surrounding sexual orientation, gender identity, and gender expression for students who may or may not identify as LGBTQ+ or nonbinary. These initiatives would introduce scholarship and pedagogy that forces HBCU campuses to interrogate Blackness through the lenses of race, gender, and class. Also, there needs to be an investment in grassroots

LGTQ+ organizations on HBCU campuses. Have these entities come to your campus and train, present to, and mentor your students. Have these groups help your campuses expand their ways of knowing.

HBCU stakeholders also need to know and be informed about how their queer and trans*students, faculty, and staff have influenced their hallowed grounds. Investing in archivists to document the work and presence of historical and contemporary queer and trans* stakeholders would undoubtedly change our institutions. Time and time again, queer and trans*HBCU students have learned that there are very few accessible records that can help them learn about the history of LGBTQ+ and gender-nonconforming people on their campuses. This signals erasure and is quite divisive.

Finally, treat your students well. All your students. They deserve kindness, support, and respect. These simple acts will change the dynamic on your campus. This should be a must. Our queer and trans* students are often the ones who live on the margins of oppressive systems. Center them first, always.

REFERENCES

Bethune Cookman University. (2022). *Dr. Bethune's last will & testament.* https://www.cookman.edu/history/last-will-testament.html

Clifton, L. (1993). Won't you come celebrate with me. In L. Clifton (Ed.), *Book of light* (p. 25). Copper Canyon Press.

Ford, O., III. (2015). From navigation to negotiation: An examination of the lived experiences of Black gay male alumni of historically Black colleges and universities. *Journal of Homosexuality, 62*(3), 353–373.

Harper, S. R., & Gasman, M. (2008). Consequences of conservatism: Black male students and the politics of historically Black colleges and universities. *The Journal of Negro Education, 77*(4), 336–351.

Harriston, K. (1990, October 10). UDC students rally at district building. *The Washington Post.* https://www.washingtonpost.com/archive/local/1990/10/10/udc-students-rally-at-district-building/cd2446bb-f00d-44b1-aa92-adc7fa5bd24c/

Hirt, J. B., Amelink, C. T., McFeeters, B. B., & Strayhorn, T. L. (2008). A system of othermothering: Student affairs administrators' perceptions of relationships with students at historically Black colleges. *NASPA Journal, 45*(2), 210–236.

Hirt, J. B., Strayhorn, T. L., Amelink, C. T., & Bennett, B. R. (2006). The nature of student affairs work at historically Black colleges and universities. *Journal of College Student Development, 47*(6), 661–676.

Human Rights Campaign. (2022). *HBCU Program.* https://www.hrc.org/campaigns/hbcu-program

Kirby, V. D. (2011). The Black closet: The need for LGBT resource and research centers on historically Black campuses. *LGBTQ Policy Journal, 1,* 93–100.

Lewis, M. W., & Ericksen, K. S. (2016). Improving the climate for LGBTQ students at an historically Black university. *Journal of LGBT Youth, 13*(3), 249–269.

Lorde, A. (1984a). Learning from the 60s. In A. Lorde (Ed.), *Sister outsider: Essays and speeches* (pp. 126–137). Crossing Press.

Lorde, A. (1984b). The transformation of silence into language and action. In A. Lorde (Ed.), *Sister outsider: Essays and speeches* (pp. 28–32). Crossing Press.

McNally, T. (2014). *The study of best practices and resources needed to create inclusion and safe Learning environments for LGBTQ students at HBCUs* [Unpublished master's thesis]. Bethune Cookman-University.

Mobley S. D., Jr., & Hall, L. (2020). (Re) defining queer and trans* student retention and "success" at historically black colleges and universities. *Journal of College Student Retention: Research, Theory & Practice, 21*(4), 497–519.

Mobley, S. D., Jr., & Johnson, J. M. (2019). "No pumps allowed": The "problem" with gender expression and the Morehouse College "Appropriate Attire Policy." *Journal of Homosexuality, 66*(7), 867–895.

———. (2015). The role of HBCUs in addressing the unique needs of LGBT students. In R. Palmer, R. Shorette, and M. Gasman (Eds.), *Exploring diversity at historically Black colleges and universities: Implications for policy and practice* (pp. 79–90). Jossey-Bass.

Mobley, S. D., Jr., Johnson, R. W., Sewell, J. P., Johnson, J. M., & Neely, A. J. (2021). "We are not victims": Unmasking Black queer and trans* student activism at HBCUs. *About Campus, 26*(3), 24–28.

Mobley, S. D., Jr., McNally, T., & Moore, G. (2019). Revealing the potential for HBCUs to be liberatory environments for queer students. In E. M. Zamani-Gallaher, D. D. Choudhuri, & J. L. Taylor (Eds.), *Rethinking LGBTQIA students and collegiate contexts: Identity, policies, and campus climate* (pp. 99–119). Routledge.

Patton, L. D., Blockett, R. A., & McGowan, B. L. (2020). Complexities and contradictions: Black Lesbian, gay, bisexual, and queer students' lived realities across three Urban HBCU contexts. *Urban Education*. Advance online publication. https://doi.org/10.1177/0042085920959128

Reason, P. (1999). Integrating action and reflection through co-operative inquiry. *Management Learning, 30*(2), 207–225.

Suicide Prevention Resource Center. (2011). *Bethune Cookman University grantee*. https://www.sprc.org/grantees/bethune-cookman-university-2

PART 2 ACKNOWLEDGING THE URGENT AND NECESSARY

Organizational Accounts of Cultural Transformation at HBCUs

4 · INCLUSION FLOWS FROM THE TOP

The Role of Boards in Building Inclusive Campuses at HBCUs

FELECIA COMMODORE AND ASHLEY GRAY

Historically Black colleges and universities (HBCUs) are indispensable points of access to higher education for many Black communities. One aspect of the HBCU experience is their affirming and empowering approach to educating those who have been marginalized because of their racial identities. These nurturing environments and their missions focused on the uplift of primarily Black students could lead to the belief that these campus constituencies are monolithic. However, neither HBCUs nor their stakeholders are monolithic. HBCU communities are diverse and have successfully navigated coexisting in their difference on their respective campuses. Within these majority-Black communities are people with various backgrounds, genders, sexual orientations, and sexual identities. As HBCUs look toward the future and the sustainability of their institutions, it is imperative that the needs, concerns, and issues of these diverse groups are not only addressed but also woven into the fabric of their institutional cultures.

Queer and trans* communities have been a part of HBCU communities since their inception, though they are often overlooked and under-researched. Although this institutional sector is lauded for its inclusive environments, much still needs to be understood about the measures of inclusivity for HBCU queer and trans* stakeholders. Most of the studies that have focused on queer and trans* HBCU experiences have focused on student experiences and campus climates (Coleman, 2016; Kirby, 2011; Lenning, 2017; Mobley & Hall, 2020; Mobley & Johnson, 2019; Patton & Simmons, 2008). What is not often present in this discourse is the role of leadership in cultivating HBCU campuses that are truly inclusive and empowering for members of queer and trans* communities. This chapter will explore how HBCU leadership, specifically university presidents and boards of trustees, can approach fashioning queer- and trans*-inclusive campuses through strategic leadership and elements of organizational change. This chapter presents a brief history of HBCUs and campus climate issues at HBCUs and offers a foundational understanding of the role of university boards of trustees and the unique context of HBCU boards and discusses the role that these boards can play in ensuring that a campus approaches queer inclusivity strategically. The chapter ends with recommendations for practice and research.

HBCUS AND QUEER CAMPUS CLIMATES

HBCUs were founded during the Reconstruction era of U.S. history primarily for the purpose of educating newly freed slaves (Anderson, 1988). Various philosophies informed the founding of these institutions, including providing Black communities with labor and industrial skill sets so their members could work and "contribute" to society, a mission of "civilizing" this newly freed populace, and the belief that education would work as a tool of empowerment, uplift, and emancipation (Anderson, 1988). These varying philosophies contributed to the foundation of and pedagogical approaches at early HBCUs. While these perspectives and practices have evolved over time, some elements still remain and continue to influence the cultures of these institutions.

Much like the philosophies undergirding the founding of HBCUs, the identities of HBCU students have evolved. One area where this evolution is evident is the current racial demographics of HBCU students. Additionally, diverse groups on these campuses in areas other than race have grown. The increasing diversity of HBCU students has pushed HBCUs to increase conversations and strategic planning regarding the complexity of their students' needs. This demand for critical conversations about how to engage diverse HBCU students requires many perspectives within these discourses. It is imperative that multiple stakeholders be involved, especially those in institutional leadership. Thus, a more nuanced understanding of how to support HBCU students with intersecting identities is crucial. This chapter will focus on those who identify as both Black and queer.

Although recent efforts have been made to create campus climates that are welcoming and supportive of queer students, challenges still exist in the quest of HBCU campuses to achieve sustained levels of inclusivity (Lewis & Ericksen, 2016; Mobley & Hall, 2020). One of the barriers that several HBCUs must navigate in their attempts to develop more queer-inclusive campuses is the culture of conservatism that is present on many campuses (Commodore, 2019; Harper & Gasman, 2008).[1]

The Culture of Conservativism

While HBCUs are arguably some of the most prolific and long-standing institutions in American society that promote the understanding and affirmation of Black identities, an acknowledgement of their founding is necessary. Many were established by white benefactors who had their own sociopolitical agendas. These white founders not only educated newly freed slaves but also instilled the values of white morality that have manifested in respectability politics and the conservatism that often counteracts empowerment for queer and trans* students and their intersectional identities (Decker, 2014). The aim in naming these origins is not to place judgment but to provide an understanding of the historical context that laid the foundation for existing conservative campus environments at HBCUs (Mobley et al., 2021b).

In considering the aforementioned, it is vital to note that respectability politics were a mechanism to aid in the protection of Black communities (Higginbotham, 1993; White, 2001). As Commodore (2019) notes, "Engaging in the politics of respectability, at times, served as a reasonable intervention for Black people attempting to shield themselves from the effects of living in a racist, anti-Black society.... Exhibiting 'respectable' behaviors and engaging in other markers of respectability served as a tool among many to be used to ensure survival" (p. 443). These "survival" mechanisms derive from Black Christian church cultures (Higginbotham, 1993; White, 2001). In some cases, the Christian denominational affiliations of HBCUs affect their campuses.

These religious affiliations have often resulted in traditionalist norms that have negatively shaped the experiences of sexual minorities. Queer and trans* HBCU students have sometimes been rendered invisible within these postsecondary contexts. Mobley and Hall (2020) note that "the complexities of their sexuality, gender identity, and gender expression(s) often present as an affront to Black 'respectability politics' and disrupt widely accepted notions of conservatism and 'decency' within Black communities" (p. 503). The manifestation of conservatism on HBCU campuses raises several questions. Who do these prescriptive set of norms implicitly and explicitly exclude and are they beneficial to the future of HBCUs?

The Closet Created by Conservatism

Experiencing marginalization due to heteronormative culture is a common experience of queer and trans* HBCU students (Mobley & Johnson, 2019; Patton, 2011; Strayhorn & Scott, 2012). As Mobley and Johnson (2015) observe, "Rather than encouraging students to walk in their own truth and embrace their authentic selves, many HBCUs compel students who identify as gay or lesbian to suppress these identities while on campus" (p. 79). The suppression of these identities causes queer and trans* HBCU students to become outsiders within their own institutions. But being out can also present challenges.

Students who openly acknowledge their queer and/or trans* identities can face social consequences in their peer relationships and in other areas of their campus experiences (Mobley & Johnson, 2019; Patton & Simmons, 2008; Strayhorn & Scott, 2012).

For queer and trans* students seeking college campuses as places for free expression of their diverse identities, being on a campus that explicitly or implicitly communicates that doing so may result in ostracization and marginalization could negatively impact both their development and their engagement and success. HBCUs, much like other institutional sectors in higher education, are examining best practices for supporting their queer students. In 2012, Bowie State University opened the Gender and Sexual Diversities Resource Center, making it the first HBCU with a dedicated center for queer-identified individuals (Mobley & Johnson, 2015). Currently, there are eight queer and trans* resource centers at HBCUs—Bowie State University (Maryland; est. 2012), North Carolina Central University (est. 2014), Fayetteville State University (North Carolina; est. 2015), University of the District of Columbia (est. 2018), Prairie View A&M University (Texas; est. 2019), and North Carolina A&T State University (est. 2020), Texas Southern University (Texas; est. 2020, and Howard University (Washington, DC; est. 2022).

Spelman College began sponsoring national conferences on HBCU and queer identities in 2011 (Gasman et al., 2013). Morehouse College launched its first course focused on Black queer content in 2013 through its Sociology Department (Lee, 2013). The creation of queer resource and research centers at HBCUs is not merely about following a higher education trend; it is about protecting the students who have chosen to attend those institutions (Kirby, 2011). As is the case with many movements, many of the initiatives regarding queer communities at HBCUs were born out of student demands, challenges, and activism. In 2019, 32 percent of HBCUs had recognized LGBTQ student organizations (Mobley & Johnson, 2019), a significant increase from the 21 percent in existence on HBCU campuses in 2013 (Gasman et al., 2013). One groundbreaking example is the MOSAIC student group formed in 2016 at Hampton University. MOSAIC (Motivating Open-Minded Social Acceptance and Inspiring Change) is a designated safe space for queer Hampton University students and allies. This organization is significant because for over twenty years, previous generations of Hampton's queer students had attempted to establish a recognized LGBTQ student group but were denied this distinction.

Although there have been increased advancements toward inclusion, HBCUs still have much work to do to fully support their queer and trans* students (Mobley & Johnson, 2015). Queer and trans* HBCU students have often carried the burden of pushing their campuses toward more inclusive climates, practices, and policies, and this burden should not be theirs to bear (Mobley et al., 2021b).

Those at the highest level of institutional leadership will prove key in achieving queer- and trans*-inclusive HBCU campuses.

THE ROLE OF THE HBCU BOARD

Boards of trustees are key institutional leaders. They have a fiduciary duty to the university and they participate in the institution's short-term and long-term planning. In addition to these major responsibilities, boards of trustees also work with college presidents to construct and support the implementation of policies and practices that aid in the life, brand, culture, and climate of campuses. Although trustee boards play an important role in an institution's leadership and life, they are often an afterthought when discussions regarding campus practices arise, if they are thought of at all. While campus actors such as faculty, student affairs personnel, and facilities workers interact more with students than board members do, governing boards make decisions that impact students and their experiences.

Recent events in higher education have directed increased attention to boards. Abrupt firings of presidents, administrative scandals, fiscal mismanagement, and controversial practices and policies across institutional types have raised the question of the role of the board in preventing and addressing such situations. For example, when students at University of Missouri-Columbia began to question and speak out against campus climate issues for Black students, attention shifted toward university leadership. As in most cases, much focus was directed at the institution's president.

This incident also raised questions about what role a board has in making sure that institutional leaders such as presidents and upper-level administrators are engaging in practices that create campus climates that are conducive to the learning and engagement of diverse groups. Even more targeted questions arose. They included: What is the role of the student trustee on university governing boards? What is the state of and role of diversity on governing boards? How are governing boards held accountable? Some consider it a stretch to draw a connection between governing boards and student experiences and outcomes. However, we offer the perspective that it is the decisions and strategic planning of boards that guide an institution and its leadership team, from student and faculty recruitment goals to establishing campus initiatives and centers. Furthermore, how a board approaches decision-making and strategic planning processes and which voices and viewpoints are included in these processes can affect which decisions are made and which strategic plans are constructed. If an institution strives to be one that services all of the campus's diverse communities well and also strives to create a campus climate conducive to all students feeling a sense of belonging, it must discuss the role of the board of trustees.

Context Matters

Members of governing boards have a unique set of responsibilities to institutions that involve setting their mission, making strategic plans, and setting institutional goals (AGB, 2011). The research on boards of trustees within higher education is scant. Much of it focuses mostly on the history and structure of such boards (Kezar & Eckel, 2004; Kezar, 2006; McLendon, 2003; Minor, 2006; Schwartz, 1998; Tierney, 2004). Many of these studies, analyses, and commentaries either focus on institutional sectors (e.g., public or private) or center predominately white institutions. Boards of trustees and governance within the HBCU context are represented in only a few works (Commodore, 2018; Ezzel & Schexnider, 2010; Minor, 2004, 2005, 2008). This underrepresentation and understudy of HBCUs within higher education governance scholarship is problematic. The argument could be made that this underrepresentation is proportionate to the proportion of higher education institutions that HBCUs represent, about 3 percent. However, considering that HBCUs still enroll 9 percent of all Black students enrolled in postsecondary education and confer approximately 16 percent of the bachelor's degrees earned by Black students, more should be understood regarding how HBCUs are led and governed (U.S. Department of Education, National Center for Education Statistics, 2019).

Whether the members of a board of trustees are self-selected, appointed, or elected, they play a major role in shaping the mission and values of an institution. However, the decisions an institution's board makes and implements can aid in the creation, dismantling, or solidifying of institutional culture. HBCUs have a unique and complex terrain to navigate in the area of culture. HBCU leaders not only have the task of navigating institutional and organizational culture, they also must navigate the racial culture embedded in the nature of their founding and missions. HBCUs find that their institutional culture overlaps with racial culture (Commodore, 2018). This ultimately impacts everything from board composition to decisions made and the process through which those decisions are examined. Although Black culture and politics can and often do play a role in decision-making processes at HBCUs, how these various politics manifest can vary from campus to campus.

Because HBCUs have been noted for embodying conservative campus cultures (Njoku et al., 2017), navigating and shifting these conservative cultures, specifically in the area of queer and trans* concerns, is not a task that occurs simply by changing student demographics, proclaiming catchy slogans, or creating onetime programs. A cultural shift must occur. However, creating organizational and cultural change is hard (Kezar, 2011; Schein, 2010; Tierney, 2008). Culture has many levels, and changing a culture can be a long and tedious process for any organization (Schein, 2010). In higher education institutions, internal and external factors can impact when and how cultural shifts are approached and achieved (Kezar, 2011; Tierney, 2008). Factors such as strategic planning, mission setting, and executive leadership hires play important roles in the processes of setting or changing culture. For this reason, boards of trustees are important entities in the process of shaping and changing institutional cultures and climates.

Relationship to Policy and Practice

Although healthy boards of trustees do not handle day-to-day institutional operations, they make high-level decisions that ultimately impact policies and practices enacted daily. Short-term and long-term strategic plans, which are heavily driven by and approved by boards of trustees, set university goals and strategies for reaching those goals. An institution's mission, vision, and values are also elements of institutional identity that boards of trustees approve. These elements communicate internally and externally the characteristics an institution finds important and salient to its identity. These elements inform the policies and practices in departments and offices across campuses. Lastly, boards of trustees play a major role in establishing and approving an institution's budget. Which initiatives and offices receive funding and how much funding they receive signals what institutional leadership deems important, but this also has very practical implications for how and if initiatives, programs, and services are implemented across a campus. For these reasons, more attention must be paid to boards of trustees at HBCUs, thus increasing conversation regarding the role they can play in the cultivation of campuses that are queer inclusive. As more focus is placed on the decisions and decision-making processes of boards, more focus must be placed on the importance of board composition. It is important to understand how the representatives making the decisions impact campuses.

The Role of Board Composition in Decision-Making

Board composition is an area of higher education that is not often discussed (Commodore, 2018; Rall et al., 2018). However, due to increased media headlines, more attention has been paid to the actions of boards of trustees as well as to who holds board seats. People come to serve on boards in various ways. In public institutions, board members are either appointed by gubernatorial administrations appointed by the state senate or they are elected. The boards of private institutions are often self-selecting. Although public HBCUs have less control over their board composition, forward-thinking presidents can develop strong relationships with governors and state legislatures to create room for dialogue regarding the characteristics of board members most needed by the institution. Private HBCUs have much more input and control over who sits on their boards. For this reason, private HBCU leaders interested in cultivating queer-inclusive campuses should work with their board leadership and nominating committees to curate boards that consist of members who buy in to this vision. It would be naïve to believe that a president can build a board consisting completely of members who agree with everything set forth by the administration, nor would this be considered healthy. In fact, the literature informs us that this approach could lead to ineffective leadership through the development of groupthink, a dysfunctional decision-making process and culture whereby a tightly knit group begins to value the group and membership in the group above anything else (Janis, 1973). Groupthink results in members aiming for quick decisions and minimizing or altogether eliminating conflict (Janis, 1973). Dissenters are silenced and suppressed and outside influences are nullified. Boards operating in groupthink are susceptible to making decisions that too swift or are ill-informed due to a false belief in their own strength (Janis, 1973; Legon et al., 2013). In order to prevent groupthink from occurring, it behooves private HBCUs to curate diverse boards.

Board diversity has also been discussed only minimally (Rall et al., 2018). In instances when the topic is broached, the discussion mostly focuses on topics related to race and gender (Pusser et al., 2006). In the case of HBCU boards, the topic of board diversity is both important and more nuanced in nature. It is to be expected that the majority of most HBCU boards will be Black. This is important when taking into consideration how Black people have been and continue to be systemically excluded from the power structures and decision-making arenas of higher education. In the founding of many HBCUs, with the exception of institutions such as Wilberforce University, which was founded by Black persons such as Mary McLeod Bethune or groups such as the African Methodist Episcopal Church, Black leaders were not given the ability as presidents or board members to have a significant say in the existence or future of their institutions. However, as Black leaders became more educated and attained more access to social and economic capital, Black communities began to be more assertive about self-determination in the area of higher education leadership. This self-determination included having control and decision-making power by taking hold of presidencies and board seats at HBCUs, the institutions that were primarily educating Black communities.

Although membership on HBCU boards of trustees may have increased Black people's access to seats of power, that does not mean that HBCU boards do not face challenges in achieving diverse board composition. Opportunities still exist for HBCU boards of trustees to ensure a diverse representation of Black members with intersecting identities. The membership of HBCU boards still consists primarily of men, older individuals, and alumni of their respective institutions (AGB, 2013). This is not unique to HBCU boards of trustees; most boards across the U.S. higher education landscape are made up of older White males (AGB, 2013). In private HBCUs, specifically church-affiliated HBCUs, it is not uncommon to find boards with a disproportionate number of clergypersons or members who have official capacities in the churches affiliated with the institution. Some may argue that this type of composition should be supported because it ensures that board members are tied to the institution's mission and values. However, this logic does not necessarily hold. In a case study of three private church-affiliated HBCUs, Commodore (2018) found that members of the institutional board that was most diverse in composition had more confidence in their decision-making process than members on boards that were less diverse. This diversity was not limited to race, as discussions of diversity so often are. Rather, it included gender, religious and denominational affiliation, HBCU and non-HBCU alumni, and clergy and non-clergy.

The presence of various perspectives and experiences helps institutional leaders have a prismatic and dynamic approach to institutional policymaking and practices. Boards that focus specifically on issues surrounding queer and trans* support on HBCU campuses are essential for ensuring that certain campus populations are supported through institutional policies and budgetary resources. Having board members who identify as members of queer and trans* communities and who take the issues and concerns of these constituents seriously heightens the chances that these populations will be better engaged and supported. In other words, more diverse boards provide an opportunity for more nuanced thoughts and voices to be included in HBCU strategic planning processes. Structural diversity alone cannot be the goal; diversity of perspectives and values is also important.

Values

Although most board members are aware that they are to engage in their work objectively, it is rare that this occurs; their values often inform their work (Commodore, 2018). Often discussions regarding the selection and appointment of board members centers on the financial and social capital of the prospective member and focus very little on their values (Commodore, 2018). Institutional boards could benefit from a more holistic approach to board member selection processes (Minor, 2008). HBCUs committed to creating campuses that affirm and include queer and trans* students must be diligent about selecting or appointing board members who hold values that align with this institutional value. In addition, board processes, by-laws, and standard operating procedures should establish a structure for board dynamics and practices that give diverse voices the ability to engage in meaningful participation in board work.

It is equally important for institutional leaders to be aware of board members whose value systems do not align with such values. This is not to suggest that this warrants board member removal. However, by taking inventory of the value systems of board members, leaders can identify areas where board members may need more training or education. This also can help institutional leaders assess what challenges may arise in the crafting of and implementation of policies and programming. Attention must be paid to the role values play in the composition, work, and dynamics of the board of trustees.

External Relationships

The importance of board members' characteristics such as social capital and networks are also important in understanding the role of board composition in building queer supportive campuses. Board members can be key players in university development and advancement (AGB, 2010; Legon et al., 2013). This can occur through personal giving but also through how members leverage their external relationships and networks. Campuses should seek board members who have established external relationships with communities, organizations, and donors who are interested in partnering with and supporting HBCUs. Likewise, HBCUs should strive to attain board members who have relationships that can produce an investment in tangible supports and services for their queer and trans* communities. As campuses move toward being more queer-friendly, HBCU leadership should be aware of the external relationships board members have with organizations and donors who are anti-queer. Although these relationships do not directly indicate that board members share these values or views, it is important for leaders to be aware of them. In the age of social media and call-out culture, institutions that proclaim to be queer-affirming that have ties with companies and organizations that are anti-queer could find themselves having public relations challenges. More philosophically, institutional leaders must decide whether these relationships are aiding the institution in fulfilling its mission and vision. This could be a difficult deliberation given that many HBCUs are underresourced within a strained funding environment. But it is a necessary task.

Having board members with values and external relationships that align well with an institution's visions and strategic plan can play a vital role in an institution's progress. For example, Spelman College has become known as a top producer of Black women in STEM graduate study and professions. Spelman's board has a strong presence of representatives of STEM corporations and organizations. Xavier University of Louisiana is known for being one of the top feeders of Black students into medical and health sciences careers. Xavier's board members include several people affiliated with the medical and healthcare industries present. Intentional and strategic board membership can translate into fruitful development relationships. It can also translate into procuring the necessary resources for an institution to position itself as queer-affirming and inclusive.

RECOMMENDATIONS

HBCUs have always been open to students from marginalized and disenfranchised communities. HBCUs produce celebrated leaders and great minds who make an invaluable impact in the world and in their respective communities. Queer and trans* students have always been an integral part of HBCU communities. The current imperative for HBCU leaders is to be intentional about meeting the needs of and creating campus climates conducive to the engagement and development of this student population. When recommendations are provided for practice and research regarding supporting queer and trans* HBCU students, the focus tends to be on student affairs programming and initiatives. Although these elements of university supports are extremely important for creating supportive campuses, it is equally as important to provide recommendations for institutional leaders. The recommendations provided in this chapter are designed to help HBCU leaders consider how they can play a vital and active role in creating and reinforcing an institutional infrastructure that supports creating campuses where their queer and trans* students can thrive.

Recommendations for Practice

A board of trustees is often a group of individuals that has a significant impact on how an institution shapes itself. They are often able to do this while remaining somewhat invisible and unnoticed. HBCUs that take seriously the task of building queer and trans* supportive campuses need to also curate boards with members who are affirming in their professional, personal, and philanthropic lives. This means being intentional in securing trustees whose values align with a campus vision that embraces and empowers queer and trans* HBCU students. It is understood that for public HBCUs, board composition is mostly out of the control of institutional actors due to gubernatorial appointment processes. However, institutional leaders and stakeholders in public HBCUs should find ways to communicate to those who influence board appointments the desired values and skill sets of potential board members who are viewed as pertinent to institutional success. (It is noted that this task may be more challenging in heavily conservative states.) Having HBCU presidents, board members, and political allies who are informed and savvy can be extremely beneficial. The intentional building of a board based on a mix of financial capital, social capital, and vision-aligning values can be instrumental in helping HBCUs bring their vision to fruition.

Board members report that they commonly feel as though they are not sure exactly what their role entails (AGB, 2011). Further complicating this situation is that boards of trustees are becoming increasingly populated with members whose backgrounds are outside higher education. Board members are increasingly hailing from business and industry (AGB, 2011, 2013; Pusser et al., 2006). For HBCUs who want to be strategic about integrating queer and trans* support in their institutional vision, it will be helpful to take the time to educate their board members regarding the issues and high-impact practices that affect these students. These discussions and trainings should make sure to highlight the concerns and practices that are sensitive to the intersectionality of Black queer and trans* HBCU stakeholders. Black women, men, gender-nonconforming, and trans* folx have unique experiences, needs, and journeys to navigate. As institutional leaders engage in strategic planning and budget allocation, having a working knowledge of these populations will create an informed and efficient decision-making process. The dissemination of this knowledge could occur as periodic workshops and sessions at board retreats and should be included in all onboarding trainings for new board members. It would be beneficial to bring in national thought leaders and experts to shape these trainings, and opportunities also exist to partner and engage with campus student affairs and counseling leaders. Board members may question why these issues are of concern to them as this work appears to fall purely under student affairs. To ensure buy-in, presidents, board chairs, and facilitators should explicitly connect being cognizant of queer issues when making institutional decisions and engaging in strategic planning with performance outcomes (e.g., retention rates, graduation rates) and their fiduciary duty. Boards that are well versed in issues that impact student experiences and ultimately student outcomes are positioned well to make decisions that will contribute to the long-term health and sustainable future of their HBCUs.

Developing board membership and fostering external relationships for the purpose of supporting queer campus initiatives is advantageous for HBCUs. Partnering with the Human Rights Campaign and other advocacy groups will create opportunities for increased outreach and resources for the institution. Additionally, HBCU alumni affairs and development offices should work to connect with their queer and trans* alumni. Fund-raising is viewed as the most important factor for the long-term sustainability of HBCUs (Bowman & Gasman, 2012). Howard University has established the Lavender Fund (highlighted in chapter 9), which provides scholarship and programming for students in queer and trans* communities and their allies. Howard University is the first HBCU to establish an initiative of this type to support queer and trans* students with campus initiatives that are intended to promote a culture of inclusion through scholarship, research, and service (Hall, 2018). Building strong relationships with this network and offering this alumni group opportunities to be involved with and support the institution and students can aid in building the infrastructure needed to support current and prospective queer and trans* student populations. This strategy can also benefit queer and trans* faculty and staff.

As important as it is to build and fortify HBCU boards, external relationships, and alumni networks in the quest to foster supportive campuses, it is equally as important to take inventory of the challenges related to the needs and experiences of queer and trans* students. HBCU leaders should take care to identify and address institutional barriers for these students. Taking inventory of what elements of the campus climate may be creating non-welcoming environments and devising strategies to address these elements allows leaders to lay the foundation for needed institutional cultural change. It also helps leaders become aware of climate issues that might not be easily detected on their respective campuses. Likewise, the cultures of departments and programs must also be examined for barriers and challenges. These subcultures sometimes operate under the radar of upper-level leaders. For both boards and presidents, being unaware of these subcultures can, in the long run, create challenges and scandals. Having a working understanding of departmental and program-level cultures without interfering with their day-to-day operations gives HBCU leaders the opportunity to address problematic cultures before they cause irreparable damage; in some cases, damage that is a legal liability. This is important as the institution attempts to create an inclusive, affirming climate for queer and trans* HBCU communities.

These are recommendations that directly impact leadership practices. However, institutional practices can often be enhanced and further developed with the support of insightful and relevant research. Scholars who work to support HBCUs in efforts to create queer-supportive campuses can do so by focusing on some aspects of institutional leadership, organizational behavior, and organizational culture at these institutions. As HBCUs are often researched and reported through a deficit laden lens (Williams et al., 2018), HBCU scholars should take the time to identify HBCU campuses that are successfully supporting their queer populations. Although research in this area often focuses on programmatic aspects and experiences, it would be beneficial for HBCU leaders to learn about how these programs and practices are developed and implemented from an organizational leadership standpoint. Being able to access information about what a successful program is, what it does, and how it was designed and proposed would prove valuable. Knowing what organizational theory concepts have been put into play would help leaders find ways to replicate programs or elements of programs at their campuses. Research that answers questions such as how resources were identified and allocated, how campus and constituency buy-in was navigated and achieved, and what was needed from the institution and institutional leaders to successfully implement the program would both highlight HBCUs doing this work as exemplars and provide information regarding the organizational elements of program development.

Another area where scholars can partner with HBCUs is to learn more about if and how HBCUs have been able to integrate queer and trans* needs and concerns into their institutional strategic plans. Learning the specific areas of HBCU strategic plans, including the roles of their presidents, boards of trustees, and strategic planning committees, is important for understanding how these institutions reach their goals and achieve their desired outcomes. Specifically, understanding how board subcommittees focused their attention on the needs of the queer population would prove beneficial. Knowing how a subcommittee handled discussions about budget allocations for strategic initiatives could prove invaluable to leaders on other campuses. Knowing more about which strategies were effective during negotiations could provide a working blueprint for other HBCUs. Answering questions such as how these strategies have been put into practice, how are they currently being implemented, and how these processes have been actualized at fiscally strained institutions is research that can inform practice and help institutions equip their campuses to be places where queer students and other queer community members thrive.

CONCLUSION

For almost two centuries HBCUs have served as beacons of light, learning, and opportunity for Black students. These institutions have served these same purposes for many other groups of disenfranchised and marginalized persons. When reflecting on this rich history and current reality it can be easy to overlook that within the larger population of Black HBCU students there are students who live at the intersections of multiple identities. It is common for the unique needs, issues, and concerns of Black students who also identify as gender and sexual minorities to be overlooked and lost within the larger Black student narrative. This distinct cultural diversity that lies within the Black student populations who attend HBCUs enriches the campus experience. In a quest to continue to be places of nurturing, inclusion, and empowerment for Black students, more attention must be given to the ways that campus practices, programming, and climate might not be addressing students' intersectional experiences. More intentionality must occur to ensure that campus climates do not explicitly or implicitly communicate that queer students are not supported or welcomed at HBCUs. Although addressing ways to be more supportive and inclusive of queer HBCU students may be seen as the responsibility of student affairs, institutional leadership also plays a role.

HBCU presidents and HBCU boards of trustees must join in the concerted effort to ensure that their institutions are making organizational and cultural shifts and changes to ensure that their queer and trans* students are supported. This means that the voices of those students should be present at various stages of institutional decision-making processes. Boards should consist of members who are committed to and aligned with this institutional vision. Furthermore, it should be clearly communicated to board members that the inclusion of queer and trans* community members is a part of the institutional vision and that they should be working to ensure that that vision comes to fruition via the institution's strategic plan. Developing strong external and alumni relations with queer communities can also prove beneficial for HBCU leaders working toward creating more inclusive campuses and establishing queer initiatives on campus. HBCU presidents and boards of trustees have the hard task of making sure that institutions are fulfilling their missions while at the same time working to achieve the outcomes needed to maintain funding and the support of donors. Although these are challenging tasks, HBCU presidents and boards who recognize the need to support queer communities can do much to ensure that those students are thriving. It has been said that within organizations, culture flows from the top. HBCU leaders who take seriously the inclusion of queer members of their communities must start down the road that leads to a culture of inclusion within their own boardrooms. In doing so, these leaders and boards will continue the HBCU legacy of education, enlightenment, and empowerment.

NOTE

1. Conservatism is any political philosophy that favors tradition (in the sense of various religious, cultural, or nationally defined beliefs and customs) in the face of external forces for change and is critical of proposals for radical social change. Some conservatives seek to preserve the status quo or to reform society slowly and others seek to return to the values of an earlier time.

REFERENCES

Anderson, J. D. (1988). *The education of Blacks in the South, 1860–1935*. University of North Carolina Press.

AGB (Association of Governing Boards of Universities and Colleges). (2010). *Public colleges and universities financial conditions survey*. Washington, D.C.

———. (2011). *2011 AGB survey of higher education governance*. AGB Press. http://agb.org/sites/agb.org/files/report_2011_governance_ survey.pdf

———. (2013). *Building public governing board capacity: Suggestions and recommendations to governors and state legislatures for improving the selection and composition of public college and university board members* (State Policy Brief, Ingram Center for Public Trusteeship and Governance). Association of Governing Boards.

Bowman, N., III, & Gasman, M. (2012). *A guide to fundraising at Historically Black Colleges and Universities: An all campus approach*. Routledge.

Coleman, K. (2016). The difference safe spaces make: The obstacles and rewards of fostering support for the LGBT community at HBCUs. *SAGE Open, 6*(2). https://doi.org/10.1177/2158244016647423

Commodore, F. (2018). The tie that binds: Trusteeship, values, and the decision-making process at AME-affiliated HBCUs. *The Journal of Higher Education, 89*(4), 397–421.

———. (2019). Losing herself to save herself: Perspectives on conservatism and concepts of self for Black women aspiring to the HBCU presidency. *Hypatia, 34*(3), 441–463.

Decker, T. N. (2014). A place at the table: Etiquette and invalidation in the quest for cultural capital at Spelman College. In M. Gasman & F. Commodore (Eds.), *Opportunities and challenges at historically Black colleges and universities* (pp. 235–252). Palgrave Macmillan.

Ezzell, J. L., & Schexnider, A. J. (2010). Leadership, governance, and sustainability of Black colleges and universities. *Trusteeship, 18*(3), 25–28.

Gasman, M., Nguyen, T., Samayoa, A., Commodore, F., Abiola, U., Carter, Y., & Carter, C. (2013). *The changing face of historically Black colleges and universities*. Penn Center for Minority Serving Institutions. https: https://repository.upenn.edu/gse_pubs/335/?utm_source =repository.upenn.edu%2Fgse_pubs%2F335&utm_ medium=PDF&utm_campaign =PDFCoverPages.

Harper, S. & Gasman, M. (2008). Consequences of conservatism: Black male undergraduates and the politics of historically Black colleges and universities. *Journal of Negro Education, 77*(4), 336–251.

Higginbotham, E. B. (1993). *Righteous discontent: The women's movement in the Black Baptist church, 1880–1920*. Harvard University Press.

Janis, I. L. (1973). Groupthink and group dynamics: A social psychological analysis of defective policy decisions. *Policy Studies Journal, 2*(1), 19–25.

Kezar, A. J. (2006). Rethinking public higher education governing boards performance: Results of a national study of governing boards in the United States. *The Journal of Higher Education, 77*(6), 968–1008.

———. (2011). *Understanding and facilitating organizational change in the 21st century: Recent research and conceptualizations.* Jossey-Bass. https://files.eric.ed.gov/fulltext/ED457711.pdf.

Kezar, A. J., & Eckel, P. D. (2004). Meeting today's governance challenges: A synthesis of the literature and examination of a future agenda for scholarship. *The Journal of Higher Education, 75*(4), 371–399.

Kirby, V. D. (2011). The Black closet: The need for queer resource and research centers on historically Black campuses. *LGBT Policy Journal 1*(2010–2011), 93–99.

Lee, M. (2013, January, 4). Morehouse offers LGBTQ course: A student's perspective. *HuffPost.* https://www.huffpost.com/entry/black-lgbt-community_b_2409635

Legon, R., Lombardi, J. V., & Rhoades, G. (2013). Leading the university: The roles of trustees, presidents, and faculty. *Change: The Magazine of Higher Learning, 45*(1), 24–32. https://doi.org/10.1080/00091383.2013.749144

Lenning, E. (2017). Unapologetically queer in unapologetically Black spaces: Creating an inclusive HBCU campus. *Humboldt Journal of Social Relations, 39,* 283–293.

Lewis, M. W., & Ericksen, K. S. (2016). Improving the climate for LGBTQ students at an historically Black university. *Journal of LGBT Youth, 13*(3), 249–269.

McLendon, M. K. (2003). Setting the governmental agenda for state decentralization of higher education. *The Journal of Higher Education, 74*(5), 479–515. https://doi.org/10.1080/00221546.2003.11778887

Minor, J. T. (2004). Decision making in historically Black colleges and universities: Defining the governance context. *Journal of Negro Education, (73)*1, 40–52. https://doi.org/10.2307/3211258

———. (2005). Faculty governance at historically Black colleges and universities. *Academe, 91*(3), 34–37.

———. (2006). A case of complex governance: A structural analysis of university decision-making. *Journal of the Professoriate, 1*(2), 22–37.

———. (2008). Groundwork for studying governance at historically Black colleges and universities. In M. Gasman, B. Baez, & C. S. Viernes Turner (Eds.), *Understanding minority-serving institutions* (pp. 169–182). State University of New York Press

Mobley, S. D., Jr., & Hall, L. (2020). (Re)Defining queer and trans* student retention and success at historically Black colleges and universities. *Journal of College Student Retention: Research, Theory & Practice, 21*(4), 497–519.

Mobley, S. D., Jr., & Johnson, J. M. (2015). The role of HBCUs in addressing the unique needs of LGBT students. In R. Palmer, R. Shorette, & M. Gasman (Eds.), *Exploring diversity at historically Black colleges and universities: Implications for policy and practice* (pp. 79–90). Jossey-Bass.

———. (2019). "No pumps allowed": The "problem" with gender expression and the Morehouse College "Appropriate Attire Policy." *Journal of Homosexuality, 66*(7), 867–895. https://doi.org/10.1080/00918369.2018.1486063

Mobley, S. D., Jr., Johnson, R. W., Sewell, J. P., Johnson, J. M., & Neely, A. J. (2021). "We are not victims": Unmasking Black queer and trans* student activism at HBCUs. *About Campus, 26*(3), 24–28.

Mobley, S. D., Jr., Solomon, S. L., II, Johnson, A. C. & Reynolds, P. (2021). "Troubling the waters": Unpacking and (re)imagining the historical and contemporary complexity of historically Black college and university cultural politics. In B. C. Williams, F. Tuitt, & D. Squire (Eds.), *Campus rebellions and plantation politics: Power, privilege, and the emancipatory struggle in higher education* (pp. 77–97). SUNY Press.

Njoku, N., Butler, M., & Beatty, C. C. (2017). Reimagining the historically Black college and university (HBCU) environment: Exposing race secrets and the binding chains of respectability and othermothering. *International Journal of Qualitative Studies in Education, 30*(8), 783–799.

Patton, L. D., & Simmons, S. (2008). Exploring complexities of multiple identities of lesbians in a Black college environment. *Negro Educational Review, 59*(3–4), 197–215.

Pusser, B., Slaughter, S., & Thomas, S. (2006). Playing the board game: An empirical analysis of university trustee and corporate board interlocks. *The Journal of Higher Education, 77*(5), 747–775. https://doi.org/10.1080/00221546.2006.11778943

Rall, R. M., Morgan, D. L., & Commodore, F. (2018). Invisible injustice: Higher education boards and issues of diversity, equity, and inclusivity. In R. Jeffries (Ed.), *Diversity, equity, and inclusivity in contemporary higher education* (261–277). IGI Global.

Schein, E. H. (2010). *Organizational culture and leadership* (4th ed.). John Wiley & Sons.

Schwartz, M. (1998). *A national survey of board performance assessment policies and practices* (AGB Occasional Paper No. 35). Association of Governing Boards of Universities and Colleges.

Strayhorn, T. L., & Scott, J. A. (2012). Coming out of the dark: Black gay men's experiences at historically Black colleges and universities in R. T. Palmer & J. L. Wood (Eds.), *Black men in college: Implications for HBCUs and beyond* (pp. 26–40). Routledge.

Tierney, W. G. (2004). Improving academic governance: Utilizing a cultural framework to improve organizational performance. In W. G. Tierney (Ed.), *Competing conceptions of academic governance: Negotiating the perfect storm,* (pp. 202–215). Johns Hopkins University Press.

———. (2008). *The impact of culture on organizational decision-making: Theory and practice in higher education*. Stylus Publishing.

White, E. Frances. (2001). Africa on my mind: Gender, counter discourse, and African American nationalism. In D. M. Juschka (Ed.), *Feminism in the Study of Religion: A Reader* (pp. 474–497). Bloomsbury Academic.

Williams, K. L., Burt, B. A., Clay, K. L., & Bridges, B. K. (2018). Stories untold: Counternarratives to anti-Blackness and deficit-oriented discourse concerning HBCUs. *American Educational Research Journal, 56*(2), 556–599. https://doi.org/10.3102/0002831218802776

U.S. Department of Education, National Center for Education Statistics. (2019). *Historically Black colleges and universities.* https://nces.ed.gov/fastfacts/display.asp?id=667

5 · BLAZING THE TRAIL

Creating an LGBTQIA-Inclusive Campus

CHEVELLE MOSS-SAVAGE, LETIZIA GAMBRELL-BOONE, AND MAKOLA M. ABDULLAH

Historically Black colleges and universities have always served many purposes. These institutions were created to serve Black communities that were denied the opportunity to pursue higher education due to racism and discrimination (Anderson, 1988; Brazzell, 1992). HBCUs have consistently functioned as purveyors of social change and racial uplift. They are among the few spaces in the United States where Blackness is appreciated and sustained (Mobley, 2017; Patton, 2016). In this respect, HBCUs remain a safe haven of sorts for Black communities. This is the case at Virginia State University (VSU). In a survey VSU conducted of nearly 25 percent of its students, one of the top reasons students gave for choosing VSU was feeling a sense of belonging (Gambrell-Boone, 2018).

HBCU research conveys that HBCU students experience intentional peer support and positive interactions with faculty and staff that ultimately have a positive impact on their sense of belonging (Brown & Davis, 2001; Strayhorn, 2014). Additionally, HBCUs have long provided social acceptance and environments that affirm commonality and community among many minoritized groups (Mobley, 2017). This chapter analyzes how lesbian, gay, bisexual, transgender, queer or questioning, intersex, and asexual or allied (LGBTQIA) HBCU communities can be best engaged and seen at these institutions in the same manner and why this must be done. This scholarship highlights how an HBCU president and their administration can effectuate this type of change on an HBCU campus. If HBCUs are to remain a staple of academic and community comforts as well as a contender among postsecondary options, then LGBTQIA communities and their families must benefit from the same welcoming essence that has been the foundation of the HBCU student experience since the inception of these schools.

A HISTORY OF INCLUSION AT HBCUS

In 1837, Cheyney University of Pennsylvania was the first HBCU to be established. Its primary goal was ensuring that people of African descent had access to education at an institution of higher learning. The creation of HBCUs was a necessary response to segregation during that era. It would take over a century for numerous segregation laws to be overturned to "allow" Black communities to be educated at historically white institutions within P-20 sectors. HBCUs have always been a resource that levels the playing field for Black students by allowing them to get an education without the threat of conscious and unconscious bias and discrimination based on race (Goings, 2016; Morton, 2020; Williams et al., 2021, 2022). However, the same courtesy has not completely been afforded to those who identify with LGBTQIA communities.

The mission of HBCUs has always been larger than merely rewarding diligence with degrees. Their core missions have included social justice and civil rights and they have long served as testaments of the right of all to pursue higher learning (Douglas, 2012). These ideals are continually reinforced in many diverse Black communities. However, open and affirming recognition for queer and trans* stakeholders has developed at a snail's pace at a majority of HBCUs. Many HBCUs have failed to create institutional supports that ensure queer-friendly campus environments before, during, and after graduation (Mobley & Hall, 2020).

Inclusion is the action of including a group or the state of being embraced within a group or structure. When paired with diversity, the concept promotes organizational togetherness and individual strength that manifests in a fulfilling environment. Inclusion puts the concept and practice of diversity into action by creating an environment of involvement, respect, and connection, one in which the richness of ideas, backgrounds, and perspectives is harnessed to create business value. HBCUs need both diversity and inclusion to be successful (Jewell, 2002; Killough et al., 2019). An effective educational organization is reflected in its students' social and academic health. It might also be determined by how a university's administration embraces and then enacts change in the campus options students have and in the curriculum. HBCUs must take the initiative to formally embrace their LGBTQIA communities in a way that translates into policy and systemic change. When they do so, students gain the confidence to thrive while they are students and after they graduate.

Sharing social and living quarters with like-minded individuals often creates an ease that makes success more attainable on a college campus. Administrations, faculty members, and staff members who are sensitive to the social imbalances LGBTQIA youths experience must challenge and confront such experiences within the traditionally conservative cultures of HBCUs.

WHY IS LGBTQIA INCLUSION IMPORTANT AT HBCUS?

HBCUs have long been sustained with staunch support from alumni who believe in their institutions because of the positive experiences they had while attending. However, there is a sector that has not had all of the positive benefits of the HCBU experience—queer and trans* HBCU alumni. Thus, establishing safe spaces for LGBTQIA communities is a model of modernization that is necessary if HBCUs are to remain competitive and appealing among other institutions of higher learning. Although several HBCUs have created safe spaces where queer students can convene, celebrate, and have representation in their academic and social spheres, there is more work to be done. HBCUs must be advocates for and support all Black identities—especially those that are on the margins (e.g., of social class, sexuality, gender, gender identity, religion) (Mobley, 2017).

Unfortunately, pervasive hetero-cisnormative norms and standards in the broader social context attempt to silence and erase Black queer communities (Blockett, 2017). The same hostile rejection of Black queer communities is present at our nation's HBCUs (Means & Jaeger, 2013; Patton et al., 2020). Queer and trans* HBCU students often have to reconcile pressures associated with being accepted as their authentic selves and rejection due to their sexuality and/or gender performance (Mobley & Johnson, 2005, 2019). Several HBCUs have made tremendous improvements in how they engage and support their queer and trans* stakeholders. This is encouraging because college is a critical time when many queer students begin to further explore their sexuality but often find very little support during that process (Poynter & Washington, 2005).

A key element of the success that Black students at HBCUs achieve is a sense of belonging they experience from the supportive and nurturing environments those institutions provide (Strayhorn, 2014). But for whom do HBCUs provide that all-important resource? Mobley and Hall (2020) note that "HBCU communities have been openly criticized for their tendency to engender socially conservative ideals" (p. 498). This conservatism is usually accompanied by cultural standards that attempt to regulate and/or quell how queer and trans* HBCU stakeholders navigate and show up on HBCU campuses (Coleman, 2016). The challenges queer and trans* HBCU communities face are often due to the conservative religious affiliations inherent within many HBCU contexts (Mobley & Johnson, 2015). HBCU cultures are deeply influenced by their roots in Christian denominations that adhere to religious doctrine that condemns queer and trans* populations. Consequently, the inviting "come as you are" type of atmosphere linked specifically to the Black church culture that often manifests at HBCUs often does not include queer stakeholders. The aforementioned factors manifest as homophobia and transphobia on HBCU campuses. When HBCUs do not holistically engage their queer and trans* populations, their environments render these individuals invisible (Kirby, 2011).

VIRGINIA STATE UNIVERSITY'S ROAD TO ADDRESSING LGBTQIA INCLUSION

VSU's road to inclusion began in 2013 and continues to the present day. The director of the University Counseling Center, who was committed to fostering a welcoming environment for all students, hired an outreach coordinator for the counseling center. The counseling center had a dual focus on providing therapy services to students and creating programs geared toward eradicating stigmas associated with mental health, physical disabilities, spiritual/ethical belief systems, and LGBTQIA identities. To gauge the university's performance regarding LGBTQIA inclusion, the outreach coordinator compiled a campus climate report based on in-person interviews and surveys of past programming. That work revealed that no culturally competent LGBTQIA-specific training had been offered within the previous five years. The qualitative data also showed three primary areas that needed to be included in such trainings: (1) basic LGBTQIA terminology, (2) moving VSU from tolerance to acceptance, and (3) educating the campus community about the impact of verbal and nonverbal communication.

To address the specific needs of the university, VSU conducted a university best practice tour, created an educational model, and implemented various tools to assist in educating the VSU community at large about the importance of LGBTQIA inclusion. During the outreach coordinator's tenure, a thriving LGBTQIA+ student advocacy group was born (Rainbow Soul), a Safe Zone Ally program was established that boasted thirty-five allies in its inaugural year, and Diversity Speaks—a LGBTQIA-specific therapy support group—was created and facilitated by a licensed therapist. The LGBTQIA Advisory Council was established under the aegis of the Provost/Vice President of Academic Affairs and specific programs such as Pride Week, the Pride Ball, Open Mic Night, National Day of Silence, and National Coming Out Day were instituted. However, although educational tools were made available throughout the campus, very few departments took advantage of those resources. Although VSU is a public, non-faith-based institution, themes of religiosity are present on campus that can prevent colleagues from supporting students/faculty/staff who have different identities than their own.

In 2015, a noticeable shift occurred within the student body. Rainbow Soul started gaining social capital and began forming partnerships with other student-run organizations. Members of the organization were selected to attend a summer LGBTQIA leadership academy called Camp Pride. During the weeklong program, students attended workshops that empowered them to affect social change on their college campuses. After a visit to a neighboring predominantly white institution to attend a Lavender Graduation ceremony, student leaders advocated for a Lavender Ceremony to be hosted at VSU. On April 30, 2015, Virginia State University became the first HBCU within the Commonwealth of Virginia to host a Lavender Ceremony. The ceremony celebrates the academic accomplishments of students who identify as members or allies of LGBTQIA communities. Although the ceremony was a momentous occasion, complete administrative buy-in on the need for university-wide affirming activities was lacking, and that disposition was not limited to the administration. There was also limited campus buy-in from VSU's queer communities. In order to transform the campus into a true place of inclusion, support from senior leaders was paramount. In 2016, students requested a meeting with Dr. Makola Abdullah, the newly appointed president of Virginia State University. The president provided an open forum for students to share their concerns. VSU students shared accounts of blatant discrimination and of not feeling safe due to their sexual orientation or gender identity/expression. During the forum, the president said, "Our mission is to foster a campus where all Trojans are granted the pursuit of a quality education in a safe learning environment." Inclusivity is the way that is accomplished.

HOW TO MAKE HBCU INCLUSION INCLUSIVE

In 2017 and 2018, the Human Rights Campaign Historically Black College and Universities Program hosted forums with HBCU leaders that focused on LGBTQIA inclusion. Among the topics discussed were HIV prevention, corporate diversity, and supporting families. The summits also included parents of queer and trans* youths. These types of conversations with HBCU decision makers who are committed to enacting change and then evaluating the results of these discussions are a major way to effectuate change for LGBTQIA stakeholders on HBCU campuses. An organization's journey to becoming inclusive begins with a critical but simple inquiry: What actions is my organization taking to foster an inclusive work culture where uniqueness of beliefs, backgrounds, talents, capabilities, and ways of living are welcomed and leveraged for learning and for informing better business decisions (Rall et al., 2018)?

Because many HBCUs have been slow to enact policies and practices that can best support their queer students, progress at several of these institutions has been due to the efforts and labor of activists (Mobley et al., 2021). HBCUs that have made strides toward building an infrastructure that supports the needs of queer and trans* student have found that dedicated employees and external supports can make a considerable difference (McMurtrie, 2013). This work should be the responsibility of all HBCU campus stakeholders and go beyond those whose sole responsibility is "diversity" work. Queer and trans* HBCU inclusion should be the labor of the entire campus. Creating a climate of change involves action that can begin with a core leadership group and a plan of action. However, that group must make a dedicated effort to grow its numbers and it must make certain to place the needs of queer and trans* populations at the forefront of its work.

A key to institutionalizing LGBTQIA services is having senior-level administrators who recognize and are invested in the need to support the development of queer spaces on HBCU campuses. What is often a challenge is that the perception of having a "small" LGBTQIA population often causes administrators to be dismissive or less inclined to invest in much-needed resources that include Safe Zone trainings, LGBTQIA-centered events, and LGBTQIA resource centers. HBCUs have done a tremendous job of centering and affirming Black racial identities. However, sexual minoritized identities are often ignored within these contexts and HBCU administrators often refuse requests for services that support the healthy exploration and development of students' gender and sexual orientations (Lenning, 2017).

A key starting point for inclusivity at HBCUs is recognizing the need for LGBTQIA programmatic and policy campus interventions. These critical resources can be implemented by carefully selecting faculty, staff, and students to spearhead this progress. These planning groups must also be aware that LGBTQIA communities are diverse and must consider their myriad identities (e.g., based on race, gender, social class, age) so that holistic measures are enacted. For LGBTQIA initiatives to be successful on HBCU campuses, race must be considered. As Garvey et al. (2019) note, Black queer and trans* students contend with racism and other forms of intolerance from their white queer and trans* counterparts. Thus, it is imperative that Black queer and trans* HBCU students receive resources where their Black, queer, and trans* identities are given equal consideration. When this does not occur, some queer and trans* HBCU students may seem completely uninterested in fighting for space and recognition. Thus, there must be faculty and staff who are willing to do the work of nuancing conversations regarding the intersectionality of Black queer and trans* identities (Lenning, 2017; Mobley et al., 2021).

VIRGINIA STATE UNIVERSITY UNIVERSITY'S "RAINBOW BLUEPRINT"

VSU has taken proactive steps to make its campus inclusive. Before Dr. Makola M. Abdullah took the helm as president in 2016, institutionally backed programming that acknowledged and affirmed the LGBTQIA community did not exist. However, with the rise of activism and of policy efforts geared toward validating the needs of LGBTQIA communities in the broader societal context, change became a pressing need for VSU's student body. Several steps were taken to bring about considerable progress for VSU's LGBTQIA communities.

First, an LGBTQIA+ diversity and inclusion consultant was hired at the behest of VSU's administration after President Abdullah made the determination that that demographic was not properly represented or advocated for on campus.

TABLE 5.1 Goals of and Action Steps Taken by the Virginia State University Advisory Board for LGBTQIA+ Inclusion

Goals	Action Steps
Educate faculty, students, and staff by way of Safe Zone trainings, departmental trainings, and student programing	• Nine diversity and inclusion trainings/programs conducted for the academic community in academic year 2017–2018 (students, faculty, administrators) • Four-tiered training program that provides levels of training based on participants' previous education level and interest in becoming LGBTQIA+ students, faculty, and staff
Provide resources for departments campus-wide on sexual identity, gender identity, gender expression, and strategies for inclusion of all students, faculty, and staff	• Review forms for campus departments to ensure language is inclusive for any gender identity, gender expression, and sexual orientation • Offer opportunities for department-specific trainings, targeting certain areas such as student housing, campus police, student accounts, etc.
Advocate for LGBTQIA students with campus entities	• Update VSU website to reflect previously adapted diversity statement, which includes inclusivity for gender identity, gender expression, and sexual orientation • Work to incorporate resources and activities for LGBTQIA+ students in VSU student social media
Work toward increasing perceived feelings of safety for Trojans in the LGBTQIA+ community	• Identify and publish a directory identifying gender inclusive spaces and allies with Safe Zone training • Survey LGBTQIA+ students on feelings of safety

The consultant was tasked with assessing the current state of the university and assisting the campus in becoming more culturally competent about LGBTQIA issues. Additionally, Dr. Abdullah created the President's Advisory Board for LGBTIQA+ Inclusion. Open invitations to sit on the board were given to members of the president's cabinet, vice presidents, associate vice presidents, deans, department chairs, and directors of programs. The president provided a detailed proposal on LGBTQIA+ inclusion that became the origin of the university's diversity and inclusion initiatives. An LGBTQIA+ Advisory Board Working Group was then formed to spearhead VSU's queer and trans* endeavors.

Members of the advisory board volunteered their time and resources. The initial working group agenda covered board structure, board mission/vision, an LGBTQ Inclusion Analysis that was generated by VSU's rating on the Campus Climate

Index for LGBT Inclusion, and the advisory board's goals for a specific academic year. Once goals were set, the working group began incorporating action steps to move the initiative forward through a mission/vision plan. Action steps were then evaluated with a strategic follow-up plan that highlighted next steps and goals.

The President's Advisory Board for LGBTQIA+ Inclusion has advanced the mission of VSU by working collaboratively with all academic, auxiliary, and administrative departments in support of VSU's LGBTQIA+ community. The advisory board oversees the establishment of education, resources, and advocacy to shape and maintain a campus community that provides a safe, inclusive, and respectful environment for Trojans of all sexual orientations, gender identities, and gender expression. This advisory board has been dedicated to several goals:

1. Acquiring a full-time employee dedicated to addressing the needs of students, faculty and staff who are members of the queer community and seek to pursue systemic change for the campus culture.
2. Creating a gender studies track as a major or minor option for students. It also recommends an LGBTQIA+ 101 course that would provide basic information about and correct terminology for queer and trans* communities and culturally appropriate responses to members of those communities.
3. Implementing required training for all faculty, staff, and students on queer and trans* issues.
4. Having at least one member of each department on campus be identified as a Safe Zone–trained ally.

There have been noticeable changes to our campus culture as we seek to fully embrace and protect our LGBTQIA students. VSU administers the Beginning College Survey of Student Engagement to all first-year students in order to understand student perceptions and expectations. It also administers a survey so it can learn of students' genuine interests. Parents are also welcome to reside on campus during the university's freshman orientation.

Also, upon acceptance at VSU, each first-year student is assigned a peer mentor for the summer before they begin classes and during the official Welcome Week. Peer mentors receive training about fundamental LGBTQIA issues and topics. Considerable efforts have been put into place during recruitment and matriculation to ensure that VSU is creating a welcoming and safe place for queer and trans* students. As a result of some of these efforts, there have been noticeable shifts, particularly within the study body. And while we acknowledge these strides, the need for continuous quality improvement exists.

LOOKING TO THE FUTURE

Moving forward, it will be critical for HBCUs to ensure that they are equipped to fully accommodate their queer stakeholders academically and socially. Given the uneven legal protections for queer and trans* students in the broader societal context, it is incumbent on postsecondary institutions to create and maintain policies and practices that ensure full inclusion and prohibit discrimination (Renn, 2017). VSU has been intentional in fostering this type of change. For example, our university website now has updated language in our diversity statement that relays the university's commitment to our LGBTQIA communities. We also prominently feature our interventions in the social media presence of various departments and entities, including but not limited to the Office of the President, the vice-president of student success and engagement, and the Residence Life and Housing Offices. VSU has also developed campus maps that indicate Safe Zone areas and gender-inclusive spaces (i.e., gender-neutral restrooms). In fact, VSU is the first HBCU in the state of Virginia to have gender-inclusive bathrooms on campus. Stalwart support from senior-level administrators who take a genuine interest in the concerns of their LGBTQIA campus stakeholders and make concerted steps toward change will be vital for HBCUs. This level of buy-in will ensure that HBCU campus communities will thrive in a manner that reinforces their missions that are steeped in an ethos of racial uplift and societal change.

We understand that not every HBCU has the resources to establish a queer and trans* resource center. VSU does not have one—yet. However, responsibility for the work that must be done to serve queer and trans* HBCU stakeholders should not be placed solely on the shoulders of their diversity and inclusion or student affairs divisions. The entire campus must take up the mantle of doing the work that purposefully underscores queer and trans* interests on HBCU campuses.

Three core issues among the many important concerns higher education leaders need to be aware of regarding queer students are identity development, campus climate, and state and national social and policy contexts (Mobley & Hall, 2020; Renn, 2017). This work does not have to be viewed as overwhelming or impossible to implement. Measures that can be put into place across various sectors of HBCU campuses to better engage their queer and trans* students include but are not limited to

1. clearly labeling Safe Zone areas that identify HBCU personnel who are available and can be attentive to these students' needs;
2. creating administrative advisory panels that meet routinely to discuss and implement best practices for queer and trans* HBCU stakeholders;
3. holding ongoing faculty, administrator, and staff trainings across campus with content tailored toward the needs of queer and trans* students. Most importantly, these trainings must include all campus sectors (athletics, student health, campus police, enrollment management, etc.);
4. working toward actively engaging prospective queer and trans* students and their families during the recruitment and admissions processes to communi-

cate how their campus can best serve their needs and address any potential concerns prior to enrollment and through the orientation processes. This particular intervention can aid in making sure that first-year students are holistically welcomed to their HBCU.

Above all, care must be taken with any of these initiatives to ensure that the time and resources invested will develop into an HBCU context that is conducive to student success. It is the aim of VSU, and it should be the aim of all HBCUs, to create environments that are receptive to the entire community.

REFERENCES

Anderson, J. D. (1988). *The education of Blacks in the South, 1860–1935*. University of North Carolina Press.

Blockett, R. A. (2017). "I think it's very much placed on us": Black queer men laboring to forge community at a predominantly white and (hetero) cisnormative research institution. *International Journal of Qualitative Studies in Education, 30*(8), 800–816.

Brazzell, J. C. (1992). Bricks without straw: Missionary-sponsored Black higher education in the post-emancipation era. *The Journal of Higher Education, 63*(1), 26–49.

Brown, M. C., & Davis, J. E. (2001). The historically Black college as social contract, social capital, and social equalizer. *Peabody Journal of Education, 76*(1), 31–49.

Coleman, K. (2016). The difference safe spaces make: The obstacles and rewards of fostering support for the LGBT community at HBCUs. *SAGE Open, 6*(2), 1–12. doi:10.1177/2158244016647423

Douglas, T. M. O. (2012). HBCUs as sites of resistance: The malignity of materialism, western masculinity, and spiritual malefaction. *The Urban Review, 44*, 378–400.

Gambrell-Boone, L. (2018). *Division of student success and engagement report to the board of visitors, November 15–16, 2018*. Virginia State University.

Garvey, J. C., Mobley, S. D., Jr., Summerville, K. S., & Moore, G. T. (2019). Queer and trans*students of color: Navigating identity disclosure and college contexts. *The Journal of Higher Education, 90*(1), 150–178.

Goings, R. B. (2016). Investigating the experiences of two high-achieving black male HBCU graduates: An exploratory study. *Negro Educational Review, 67*(1–4), 54–75.

Jewell, J. O. (2002). To set an example: The tradition of diversity at historically Black colleges and universities. *Urban Education, 37*(1), 7–21.

Killough, A., Killough, E., Burnett, J., & Bailey, G. (2019). The contemporary role of the HBCU in diversity, equity and inclusion in the absence of ongoing historical relevance. In C. Davis, A. Hilton, & D. Outten (Eds.), *Underserved populations at historically Black colleges and universities: The pathway to diversity, equity and inclusion* (pp. 41–68). Emerald Publishing Limited.

Kirby, V. D. (2011). The Black closet: The need for LGBT resource and research centers on historically Black campuses. *LGBTQ Policy Journal, 1*, 93–99.

Lenning, E. (2017). Unapologetically queer in unapologetically Black spaces: Creating an inclusive HBCU campus. *Humboldt Journal of Social Relations, 39*, 283–293. https://www.jstor.org/stable/90007885

McMurtie, B. (2013, October 28). Spurred by activists, HBCUs expand their services for gay students. *The Chronicle of Higher Education*. https://www.chronicle.com/article/Spurred-by-Activists-HBCUs/142559

Means, D. R., & Jaeger, A. J. (2013). Black in the rainbow: "Quaring" the Black gay male student experience at historically Black universities. *Journal of African American Males in Education, 4*(2), 124–140.

Mobley, S. D., Jr. (2017). Seeking sanctuary: (Re)Claiming the power of historically Black colleges and universities as places of Black refuge. *International Journal of Qualitative Studies in Education, 30*(10), 1036–1041.

Mobley, S. D., Jr., & Hall, L. (2020). (Re)Defining queer and trans* student retention and success at historically Black colleges and universities. *Journal of College Student Retention: Research, Theory & Practice, 21*(4), 497–519.

Mobley, S. D., Jr., & Johnson, J. M. (2015). The role of HBCUs in addressing the unique needs of LGBT students. In R. Palmer, R. Shorette, and M. Gasman (Eds.), *Exploring Diversity at Historically Black Colleges and Universities: Implications for Policy and Practice.* (pp. 79–90). San Francisco, CA: Jossey-Bass.

———. (2019). "No pumps allowed": The "problem" with gender expression and the Morehouse College "Appropriate Attire Policy." *Journal of Homosexuality, 66*(7), 867–895. https://doi.org/10.1080/00918369.2018.1486063

Mobley, S. D., Jr., Johnson, R. W., Sewell, J. P., Johnson, J. M., & Neely, A. J. (2021). "We are not victims": Unmasking Black queer and trans* student activism at HBCUs. *About Campus, 26*(3), 24–28.

Morton, T. R. (2020). A phenomenological and ecological perspective on the influence of undergraduate research experiences on Black women's persistence in STEM at an HBCU. *Journal of Diversity in Higher Education, 14*(4), 530–543.

Patton, L. D. (2016). Disrupting postsecondary prose: Toward a critical race theory of higher education. *Urban Education, 51*(3), 315–342.

Patton, L. D., Blockett, R. A., & McGowan, B. L. (2020). Complexities and contradictions: Black lesbian, gay, bisexual, and queer students' lived realities across three urban HBCU contexts. *Urban Education, 58*(6). https://doi.org/10.1177/0042085920959128

Poynter, K. J., & Washington, J. (2005). Multiple identities: Creating community on campus for LGBT students. *New Directions for Student Services, 111*(Fall), 41–47

Rall, R. M., Morgan, D. L., & Commodore, F. (2019). Invisible injustice: Higher education boards and issues of diversity, equity, and inclusivity. In R. Jeffries (Ed.), *Diversity, Equity, and Inclusivity in Contemporary Higher Education* (pp. 261–277). IGI Global. https://doi.org/10.4018/978-1-5225-5724-1.ch016

Renn, K. (2017, April 10). LGBTQ students on campus: Issues and opportunities for higher education leaders. *Higher Education Today.* https://www.higheredtoday.org/2017/04/10/lgbtq-students-higher-education/

Strayhorn, T. L. (2014). Making a way to success: Self-authorship and academic achievement of first-year African American students at historically Black colleges. *Journal of College Student Development, 55*(2), 151–167.

Williams, K. L., Mobley, Jr. S. D., Campbell, E., & Jowers, R. (2022). Meeting at the margins: Culturally relevant and sustaining practices at HBCUs for underserved populations. *Higher Education, 84*(5), 1067–1087.

Williams, K. L., Russell, A., & Summerville, K. (2021). Centering Blackness: An examination of culturally-affirming pedagogy and practices enacted by HBCU administrators and faculty members. *Innovative Higher Education, 46*(6), 733–757.

6 · WHEN HBCUs SPEAK OUT

Navigating HBCU Culture and Queer Student Expectations as Student Affairs Professionals

DARRYL B. HOLLOMAN, DARYL LOWE, BONNIE TAYLOR, AND LESLIE HALL

> Lots of people believed that because I was trans, I didn't belong at Spelman but there was nowhere else I would rather be.
>
> —Keo Chaad O'Neal, 2018

The quote above expresses the feelings of Spelman alumnus Keo Chaad O'Neal, who made history in 2018 as the first openly trans* man to graduate from Spelman College, a historically Black college for women, located in Atlanta, Georgia (Amatulli, 2018). During the 2018–2019 academic year, Spelman College revised its admission policy to allow the retention and graduation of students regardless of their gender assignment at birth. Dr. Mary Schmidt Campbell wrote at the time the revised admission policy was announced that retaining women students, including students who consistently live and self-identify as women, regardless of their gender assignment at birth, continues the college's fervent belief in the power of the Spelman sisterhood (Campbell, 2017). Like other historically Black colleges and universities (HBCUs), Spelman College fosters environments in which Black students can be unapologetic about being Black and celebrate Black culture among peers who share similar identities.

The student experience on HBCU campuses is a highly coveted one that is difficult to quantify but continues to serve as a significant driving force for Black students' choice of college. Unfortunately, queer students often arrive on HBCU campuses with a sense of trepidation, a flood of misperceptions, and the expectation that their identities will be marginalized. Because we know that queer students may arrive in HBCU contexts feeling as if they will not belong, it is imperative for student affairs professionals to demonstrate astuteness in their interactions with queer students as they arrive on campus. Programmatic initiatives such as first-year seminar courses should be structured in ways that explore topics of gender identity and sexual orientation. HBCU administrators should ensure that policies, procedures, and guidelines such as student handbooks include information related to queer students. Publications, particularly those emanating from student affairs, should reflect the experiences of queer students on campus. It is also important for HBCU administrators, faculty, and staff to be aware that not only students but parents and family members of prospective students will also have expectations that HBCUs should be prepared to engage and support queer students throughout their college years (Mobley & Hall, 2020).

Although supporting the matriculation and retention of queer students is a campus-wide effort, divisions of student affairs at HBCUs play pivotal roles in ensuring that queer students find welcoming spaces on their campuses. Although the role and scope of HBCU student affairs offices vary, student affairs educators can serve as social change agents in developing policies, programs, and instructional opportunities that inform HBCU stakeholders about the needs, expectations, and perceptions of queer students (Broadhurst et al., 2018). Student affairs practitioners should take care to develop programing and initiatives throughout the year that are specifically developed to support a sense of belonging for queer student and that can attract a broad spectrum of participants from the larger student body. Such resources will ensure that an array of HBCU campus stakeholders can learn from and with queer communities on campus.

Senior-level student affairs administrators should be knowledgeable about current trends related to the experiences of contemporary college students and be equipped to lobby on behalf of queer students at the president's cabinet, among the board of trustees, alumnae affairs, and various stakeholders on and off campus. Divisions of student affairs should be equipped to create campus-wide programs and physical spaces where queer students feel included and welcomed. Although educational and safety programs are also extremely important in ensuring that queer students feel comfortable on campus, student affairs professional should also take care to ensure that enjoyable activities are scheduled so these students also feel that their campus has embraced them. The work that student affairs professionals do to serve as social change agents for queer students on HBCU campuses can help provide these students with a sense of agency as they navigate the social, political, and cultural aspects of their campus (Mobley & Johnson, 2015).

Creating affirming and inclusive environments for queer HBCU students requires education to raise the awareness of the various stakeholders at HBCUs on issues that queer communities face. It is critical that vice presidents of student affairs at HBCUs lead in promoting this awareness. The vice-president of student affairs must not only be aware of international and national trends related to the concerns of queer communities but, must also have a pulse on what is occurring at regional, state, and campus levels. The vice-president of student affairs has a powerful vantage point from which to inform entities that include the president's cabinet, board of trustees, state and city leaders, alumni, and donors. The vice-president of student affairs also has many opportunities to advance funding initiatives that support queer culture on their campus.

Higher education research has revealed that many HBCUs maintain rigid or conservative environments that may be unconsciously embedded in their founding (see Commodore, 2019; Harper & Gasman, 2008; Mobley & Johnson, 2019; Njoku et al., 2017). For example, many HBCUs were founded by religious entities and still maintain close religious affiliations. Although some HBCUs may no longer promote those religious ties, some dated policies or mottos may linger within their cultures. It would be important for HBCU presidents to review their mission and vision to ensure that they are inclusive and fit within a modern framework. The discipline that HBCUs instill in students is often mistaken for rigidity and inflexibility, but some of the greatest leaders and thinkers have emerged from HBCU culture. HBCUs have long stood at the forefront of civil rights advances worldwide, and just as these institutions have advanced racial and civil rights, they also have the full capacity to foster equity in support of their queer students.

Following the horrific murder of Matthew Shepard in the fall of 1998, colleges and universities across the country began to recognize the importance of creating safe and welcoming spaces for queer students and their allies. While this murder was not the first violent atrocity committed against queer individuals, it was the first time that national outrage was felt about the violent loss of life due to a person's sexual orientation. The 1990s were a decade when the conversations about the continued maltreatment and harassment of queer students as they were in the process of self-discovery, as all students are, exhibited the need for policies to protect these individuals.

Postsecondary institutions began to acknowledge the importance of creating safe spaces for queer students that are easily identifiable for students seeking allies on their campuses. Further, to support queer students being open and affirmed on college campuses, legal battles, educational programs, and physical infrastructures arose in response to the loss of Matthew Shepard. While much of the attention surrounding these initiatives centered on white queer student communities, Black queer students were also raising their voices about the need for protection and greater education for the community at large about their concerns.

This chapter uses a theory-to-practice paradigm to provide context for HBCUs that seek to establish procedures and practices that support the matriculation and success of queer students. Using the work of such scholars as Shaun Harper, Steve D. Mobley Jr., Nadrea Njoku, and Lori Patton-Davis as a framework, we will offer recommendations for implementing policies, providing educational opportunities, hiring personnel, and creating the broad resources needed at HBCUs to establish and maintain welcoming environments for queer communities.

OVERVIEW OF QUEER EXPERIENCES AT HBCUS

HBCUs serve as open and inclusive learning environments for Black students, who often seek refuge at these institutions in the face of global systems of systemic oppression (Fries-Britt & Turner, 2002; Goings, 2016; Mobley, 2017). Systemic oppression, however, is quite complex for Black students whose intersecting social, cultural, and political identities are not nurtured on their college or university campus (Crenshaw, 1989, 1995). Patton and Simmons (2008) noted the complexities of intersecting identities and challenges that Black lesbian students encountered at HBCUs as they explored their racial, sexual, and gender identities. This can be true for Black queer students who navigate HBCU campus cultures in search of an environment to support their success (Mobley & Hall, 2020). Like their peers, queer students come to HBCU campuses seeking a place where their racial identities are celebrated and are attracted to the traditions at those institutions (Squire & Mobley, 2015).

However, queer HBCU students do not always find that their identities are openly celebrated within their campus cultures. They may find that events at their HBCU are heteronormative and patriarchal. For example, queer students may attend new student orientation and not find a program that is designed especially for them. It is likely that an HBCU will have diversity programs that speak to a variety of cultures, but such programs may sometimes reinforce the isolation of queer students because they fail to acknowledge their queer identities. HBCUs should pay close attention to their events and activities to ensure that emphasis is placed on queer cultures and identities so that these students are aware of their institution's commitment to embracing the full spectrum of Blackness present on their campus.

Hetero-cis normative cultures present at HBCUs further marginalize students who do not conform to these identities. Mobley and Johnson (2015) directly challenge HBCUs to create policies that help eliminate these cultural biases. They state that HBCUs should, "reexamine their traditions and policies that impose strict rules that often inhibit individual expression and must also begin to recognize how institutional practices [such as] dress codes, lack of student health services geared toward gay and lesbian students, and same-sex housing policies often silence and "other" members of LGBT communities" (p. 82). An examination of heteronormative and exclusionary policies and practices at HBCUs would provide an opportunity to create welcoming environments in which Black queer students feel a sense of belonging and affirmation. Because the retention and success of students who identify with queer communities contributes to the well-being of the student community at large, HBCUs should provide queer-informed education for individuals across campus, including faculty, staff, administrators, alumni, and trustees (Mobley & Hall, 2020; Patton, 2016).

Njoku et al. (2017) refer to "othermothering" in their research on the parental oversights HBCU campus communities provide. They note that, "HBCUs replace the parents and church as guardians of their student bodies" (p. 784). In addition to the tradition of conservative and respectable environments at HBCUs (Njoku et al., 2017), these institutions often restrict the definitions of masculinity, which further represses women due to the inherent sexism in the frameworks of operation in these institutions. HBCUs should remember that their students are adults who have the freedom to make decisions, and although students may need support, it is not the responsibility of the institutions to direct those decisions as if the institutions were the students parent.

Historically, HBCUs have been slow to develop policies, procedures, and programs that embrace Black queer student identities and those who embrace other forms of sexual or gender expressions. However, HBCUs are facing increasing pressure from queer students and their allies to address polarizing incidents of bias on their campuses so that measures are developed to support queer and trans* HBCU communities. Incidents such as vandalism on doors of residence halls, expressing homophobic slurs, verbal harassment, physical and sexual assault, lack of administrative support, and denial of request for non-gender-identified restrooms at many HBCU institutions have been noted nationwide (Baldacci, 2018; Mobley et al., 2021).

However, several HBCUs have worked to create supportive environments for their queer communities. Examples of these efforts include the work of Black feminist and founder of Spelman College's Women's Research and Resource Center, Dr. Beverly Guy-Sheftall, whose work as an early pioneer of gender and queer equity in HBCU settings, prompted a national conference on HBCU and LGBT issues at Spelman College in 2011. Dr. Guy-Sheftall also co-edited Traps: African American Men on Gender and Sexuality (Byrd & Guy-Sheftall, 2001), which centered the intersections of race, gender, and the sexuality of Black men. She also fashioned a handbook for HBCUs that centered Black queer topics titled Facilitating Campus Climates of Pluralism, Inclusivity and Progressive Change at HBCUs (Guy-Sheftall & Alexander, 2006). Under the leadership of Dr. Guy-Sheftall, the Women's Research and Resource Center at Spelman College has been an innovator in promoting queer-inclusive culture on HBCU campuses. In addition, Spelman College's Division of Student Affairs has created a professional staff position for an LGBTQIA+ liaison. This student affairs professional works exclusively to develop and create campus-wide programming for queer students.

Additional sexuality and gender work on HBCU campuses includes the first Lesbian, Gay, Bisexual, Transgender, Queer, Intersex, and Allies Resource

Center, which opened on the Bowie State University campus in 2012. Also, an academic course that centers on Black Queer history was launched at Morehouse College in 2013. North Carolina Central University has implemented affirming policies, practices, and programs that embrace queer students on its campus. It was the second HBCU to open a resource center for queer students (Mobley & Hall, 2020).

Understanding their historic role in promoting civil rights efforts, HBCUs in theory, if not always visible in practice are working to cultivate efforts to support the success of queer students on their campuses (Simon, 2017; Williams, 2018). Steve D. Mobley Jr., a graduate of Howard University and a queer HBCU researcher, has noted that, "HBCUs now stand at a crucial horizon. The way they address, respond to, and begin to provide support for their LGBT populations will speak volumes not only to higher education, but also to Black communities and the larger society as a whole" (quoted in Gasman, 2013, p.9). When student affairs professionals at HBCUs including deans of students, Title IX coordinators, student conduct officers, and vice presidents for student affairs swiftly address incidents of transphobia and homophobia on campus through policy and procedural efforts, they are also helping to eliminate misperceptions that HBCUs are not responsive to the needs and concerns of Black queer and trans* students on their campuses.

While it is the responsibility of all members of HBCU contexts to act, senior student affairs administrators can serve as catalysts for cultural change in response to the concerns of queer students. This can be achieved by supporting recognized student organizations created by queer communities, celebrating the achievements of queer students through events such as lavender ceremonies, spearheading policy changes regarding equity in facilities, developing residence hall policies, and supporting the use of student name change processes. Each of these activities can aid in the support of queer students who have chosen to attend HBCUs. In addition, an increase in education and cultural awareness presented in partnership with HBCU diversity and inclusion offices and student organizations could help further eliminate the sense that HBCU cultures are bastions of conservatism that are unwilling to embrace the needs of queer students.

HBCU student affairs professionals should serve as leaders in erasing the bias and phobias that arise in their campus communities. Their efforts not only lift the specific campus where they work but also helps to reduce homophobias and transphobias that may exist in Black and African American cultures at large (Hurtado et al., 1999; Williams, 2018). Hurtado et al. (1999) suggest that "Campuses are complex social systems defined by the relationships maintained between people, bureaucratic procedures, structural arrangements, institutional goals and values, traditions, and the larger sociohistorical environments where they are located" (p. 80). Creating more inclusive spaces on HBCU campuses requires that campus leaders, especially those in student affairs, acknowledge queer students as campus community members rather than "others" who are different and who are unable to connect to the HBCU student experience due to their gender or sexual identity (LePeau, 2015; Mobley & Johnson, 2015).

Black Queer Student Isolation

Unfortunately, there is scant literature that specifically addresses the experiences of queer students at HBCUs, but the scholarship that does exist offers researchers pathways for exploring in greater depth the experiences of queer community members as they navigate HBCU cultures. Mobley and Johnson (2019) advocate for reaffirming and nonjudgmental stances within HBCUs through the creation of safe spaces for Black queer students. They also noted tensions between Black queer communities and HBCU communities. Queer and trans* HBCU students have fought for positive peer relationships and encouraging social and academic communities on their respective campuses. However, the more conservative nature of some HBCU communities can make Black queer students feel as though their unique needs are being ignored or overlooked, which leads to a sense of feeling "othered" on a HBCU campus (Mobley & Johnson, 2015).

Unfortunately, HBCUs have been widely perceived as unwelcoming environments for queer and trans* students. HBCUs have been behind in terms of providing resources and support initiatives that affirm queer student cultures on their campuses. Lenning (2017) has noted that "although studies of the experiences of [queer] students on HBCU campuses are limited and often based on extremely small sample sizes, they do reveal that [queer] students do not necessarily view administrators and faculty as supportive" (p. 4). This is in part due to the challenges these students face in their attempts to find spaces that are affirming of their sexual and gender identities.

QUEER HBCU COLLEGIANS

Queer students arrive on HBCU campuses with their own perceptions or misperceptions related to HBCU cultures and often have feelings of exclusion, self-doubt, and neglect. This may be reinforced when they encounter harassment, disregard for policies designed to ensure fair treatment, or non-responsiveness to bias incidents that provide challenges for them as they navigate potentially unwelcoming environments. Perceptions of HBCU culture as homophobic, transphobic, or lacking in education regarding queer students' need for protection often serve as the first impression queer students form. In addition, queer students may have been told by their families or members of their supportive networks that they will not be accepted in the HBCU community due to their sexual or gender identities, given the perceptions that HBCUs are unsupportive of queer communities. Any unwelcoming spaces at HBCUs can reinforce for queer students their preconceived notions that they are not wanted at their institution.

Unwelcoming HBCU spaces that Black queer students encounter can cause them to retreat from the HBCU experience that many students come to campus expecting. Queer students at HBCUs who fear retribution, isolation, retaliation, or oppressive environments because of their queer identities may seek more inclusive spaces by withdrawing from HBCUs and then seeking refuge at predominately white institutions, or suppressing their identities until graduation (Mobley & Johnson, 2015; Patton & Simmons, 2008). For many queer students, this crucial period in student development is the time when they choose to disclose their sexual or gender identity to others. If this "coming out" is met with hostility, dismissiveness, or fear, the psychological and emotional impact of that harm prevents the continued growth and development of these students (Mobley & Johnson, 2015; Njoku et al., 2017; Patton, 2011).

RECOMMENDATIONS FOR BEST PRACTICES AT HBCUS

Intense work to support queer students can begin with assessing campus climates, setting strategic goals, and allocating resources for programmatic initiatives. Assessing the HBCU campus climate will help determine the various levels of tolerance, acceptance, and inclusion of queer students. Campus climates analyses are important because of the higher rates of harassment of queer students on college campuses compared to the harassment of their heterosexual peers experience (Young & McKibban, 2014). Once a baseline assessment of the climate of a HBCU campus had been made, a plan to address areas of opportunity and challenge can be incorporated into a strategic plan to address the specific issues on the campus. During the development phases of the strategic plan both students and external stakeholders must have a voice at the table.

Divisions of student affairs or college-wide strategic goal setting initiatives can provide an idea of the needs or concerns of queer students. Within the strategic plan there must be an evaluation of the current services provided to queer communities as well as an assessment of the institutional resources needed to raise the awareness of the general community about queer culture on the campus specifically and within the larger community generally. The strategic plan should include an inventory of current financial resources, physical spaces for LGBTQ resource centers, distribution of educational resources, personnel dedicated to supporting queer students, and clear direction about how to support the implementation of a plan.

A review of current resources will determine the most significant funding sources available to support programs and activities that promote queer cultures on campus. If funding sources are limited, the president's cabinet should find ways to generate funding through the offices of institutional advancement or the office of alumni affairs. Vice-presidents for student affairs should seek ways to reallocate funds from their budgets to ensure that Black queer students feel a sense of belonging on the campus. Support for queer students on an HBCU campus have long-term term effects for the institution in terms of ensuring student success and building a strong alumni base and contributing to a vibrant campus climate.

College services such as those offered through the counseling center, Title IX offices, faculty engagement, and student programming units reflect an HBCU's commitment to be responsive to the stress and isolation queer students may experience. If such services are not provided, it could lead to queer students departing higher-education contexts (Young & McKibban, 2014). Additional measures such as housing, anti-discrimination efforts, campus and community education, and health care are significant advances in the creation of an inclusive environment for queer students attending HBCUs (Williams, 2018).

RECOMMENDATIONS FOR POLICY ANALYSIS, EDUCATION AWARENESS, AND FISCAL RESOURCES

HBCU stakeholders should consider four target areas in their efforts to support the needs and concerns of queer students: policy, education, personnel, and fiscal resources. These key areas will also help eliminate the perceptions that HBCUs are unwelcoming and uninviting spaces for queer and trans* students. Although actions related to these target areas can begin in student affairs, these recommendations must be replicated throughout the college or university it they are to expand to campus-wide initiatives that transform campus cultures. A commitment to enhancing campus-wide resources for queer student communities works to elevate the entire student body by providing a voice to other groups that may feel marginalized (Gasman, 2007; Mobley & Johnson 2015).

HBCU stakeholders must "intentionally structure conversations and provide forums where individuals from diverse communities can learn from their differences to build mutually respectful interactions" (Mobley & Johnson, 2015, p. 8). The creation of spaces for queer students on HBCU campuses will foster a culture of inclusivity and promote tolerance and acceptance (Mobley& Hall, 2020; Williams, 2018; Young, 2014). Whether through safe zones, promotion of student-run queer organizations that foster student leadership skills, or a physical center that is fully supported by the campus, HBCUs can foster an open environment in which all students are free to express themselves in a safe and reassuring environment. To accomplish this goal, HBCUs should focus on the following issues:

Policy Analysis

HBCUs will need an ongoing review of their institutional policies to ensure that those policies reflect queer voices. Over the past twenty years, a few HBCUs have had highly public and visible bias incidents involving members of their queer student populations. An institutional policy analysis ensures that HBCUs are compliant with federal laws in support of queer communities, which are constantly evolving. Efforts to delay a review of institutional policies could make HBCUs appear unresponsive to the needs and concerns of queer student communities on campus.

This policy review should begin with an analysis of the HBCU's admission policies and procedures. This analysis starts the process of raising awareness across the campus that the institution is committed to developing welcoming spaces for queer students. Additional policy reviews should involve areas that are typically located in student affairs areas. Four critical student affairs areas need review: the health clinic, the student disability or access office, the office of housing and residence life, and the counseling center. These four areas are the functional areas where queer students have the most direct impact regarding their campus experiences.

It is important to analyze the policies for these four areas because these are the places queer students will turn to for direct services. For example, queer trans students will seek the health clinic or student access center for support in their gender transition. The office of housing and residence life could be the first place where students feel a sense of being excluded or face cultural biases. The counseling center can be a place of refuge where queer students can confidentially process information regarding their feelings and thoughts about themselves and their connections to campus.

However, policy analysis cannot be done exclusively within the division of student affairs. Policy development will also need to be fostered within the president's cabinet and the Board of Trustees to ensure systematic implementation on a broad scale. Although the alumni affairs office at many HBCUs does not serve as a key player in the daily operations of the institution, alumni groups can be important stakeholders in introducing, vetting, and promoting policy analyses that some graduates of the institution may view as controversial.

Education and Awareness

It is important for HBCUs to develop campus-wide education and awareness campaigns to enlighten their campuses about queer culture, queer terminology, and the expectations of queer student communities and their allies (Broadhurst et al., 2018). This education will help destigmatize queerness and highlight the historical contributions of Black queer members such as those of Bayard Rustin, the orchestrator of the March on Washington. Focusing on a comprehensive education and awareness campaign will assist queer students who may arrive on campus needing to learn more about queer culture and iconic queer figures. Providing education about correct queer terminology will heighten awareness of how members on campus can actively engage queer students without relying on queer students themselves to provide that education. That campus-wide education and awareness will reduce the incidences of faculty, staff, and students using offensive language or doing actions that further marginalize queer students. Education and awareness campaigns will also elevate queer voices within the HBCU campus culture.

Student affairs can take a lead in this education through such things as campus programming units and Title IX offices. The office responsible for campus programs and activities may be one of the areas in student affairs that has a robust budget that is exclusively dedicated to creating a welcoming and inclusive environments for HBCU students. These offices can take the lead in developing programs and activities that queer students can observe and participate in. One of the areas where queer students can find immediate affirmation is through new student orientation activities that affirm their identities. Title IX offices can help HBCUs ensure that their campuses comply with ever-changing federal regulations that involve sexual assaults and harassment. However, these efforts cannot be exclusively located in student affairs units. It is also important that faculty and academic affairs unit at HBCUs create academic courses that focus on gender affirmation and gender education and partner with student affairs units on programming initiatives. Oftentimes academic departments that focus on gender work may be small or underfunded and partnering with student affairs could provide the funding they need to support such efforts.

HBCU vice presidents for student affairs should take the lead in reaching out to department chairs and college deans to develop these partnerships. The alumni engagement office is another important resource that can help HBCU campuses support queer students. Alumni offices can help promote the gender identity and queer initiatives of graduates who are active members of larger Black communities. In addition, alumni engagement units should plan events around Founder's Day, or HBCU reunions, and other such events. Partnerships between alumni engagement offices and student affairs units can be forged to help develop an inclusive environment for queer students and queer alumni. Student government associations at HBCUs could also be strong allies in the work of addressing the needs and concerns of queer students. Student government associations should be viewed as a vital part of the governance structure at HBCUs and student affairs professionals should seek to partner with the representatives of these associations to ensure that they are adequately advocating for queer students.

Fiscal Resources

Human and financial capital is important to the sustainability of any initiative within HBCUs (Gasman, 2013). These colleges often rely heavily on tuition dollars, federal funding, funding campaigns, and institutional gifts to support and sustain staffing, academic, campus programming, and infrastructure. As is the case at other colleges and universities, these sectors of HBCUs constantly compete for fiscal resources, and many chief financial officers at these institutions strike a delicate balance in order to support the various initiatives fostered on the campus (Gasman, 2013). In some cases, competing budgetary demands at HBCUs could fuel misperceptions among queer students lack of understanding of how their college or university is funded or how those funds are disseminated could cause students in general and queer students in particular to feel that their concerns are not being addressed in a timely fashion. Student affairs units can have a direct impact on eliminating these misperceptions by closely reviewing their budgeted allocations to assess ways to support queer students.

Campus programming efforts should ensure that queer student representation is included, is visible, and integrated into mainstream programmatic efforts. Budgetary support of queer students at HBCUs should not be seen as the exclusive responsibility of student affairs because the impact of queer initiatives benefits the entire campus. Faculty should seek to propose courses or course modifications to ensure that queer culture is highlighted during curriculum development. Faculty and staff can seek to become queer allies by designating their offices or departments as safe space zones, partnering with other units to fund queer programming, and attending safe zone trainings in order to become educated about queer terminology.

Although the creation of cultural centers is costly, HBCUs should seek rooms or suites as startup initiatives that can be converted into sexuality and gender equity resource centers in a cost effective way. Counseling centers and health clinics should invest in literature and resources that reflect queer culture. A review of staff could reveal that existing personnel can be re-classified or individuals can be identified who can develop targeted and intentional programs and services for queer students.

FINAL THOUGHTS

Historically Black colleges and universities are not alone in facing perceptions that they do not support or address the needs of Black queer students. Many predominately white institutions that are religiously affiliated, and focused on minorities also face challenges in terms of how best to support queer students on their campuses. Because of their strong connections to civil rights movements throughout the twentieth and twenty-first centuries, HBCUs have a special obligation to foster environments in which Black queer students can grow and thrive. Often faced with unsurmountable challenges as they navigate the complex microaggressions surrounding their gender, race, sexual orientation, and gender identities, queer students should view their HBCU experience as one that is affirming. In some cases, these students may not have the luxury of "coming out" in their homes or churches. Being out is a performative privilege that Black HBCU students have not been afforded (Garvey et a., 2019). Thus, HBCUs could be a refuge for them as they explore their identity and their queerness evolves within the larger society.

REFERENCES

Amatulli, J. (2018, May 15). Meet the first openly trans man to graduate from Spelman College. *Huffington Post.* Retrieved January 31, 2021, from https://www.huffpost.com/entry/meet-the-first-openly-trans-man-to-graduate-from-spelman-college_n_5afae6c1e4b09a94524c336e

Baldacci, M. (2018, May 2). Spelman College investigating hateful notes sent to LGBTQ students. *CNN Health.* https://www.cnn.com/2018/05/01/health/spelman-hateful-notes-lgbtq-students-trnd/index.html

Broadhurst, C., Martin, G., Hofshire, M., & Takewell, W. (2018). "Bumpin' up against people and their beliefs": Narratives of student affairs administrators creating change for LGBTQ students in the South. *Journal of Diversity in Higher Education, 11*(4), 385–401.

Byrd, R. P., & Guy-Sheftall, B. (Eds.). (2001). *Traps: African American men on gender and sexuality.* Indiana University Press.

Campbell, M. S. (2017, September 5). President's letter to the community: Spelman admissions and enrollment policy update. Spelman College. https://www.spelman.edu/about-us/president's office revised/letters to the community/letter/3017/09/05/spelman admissions and enrollment policy update

Commodore, F. (2019). Losing herself to save herself: Perspectives on conservatism and concepts of self for Black women aspiring to the HBCU presidency. *Hypatia, 34*(3), 1–23. doi:10.1111/hypa.12480

Crenshaw, K. (1989). Demarginalizing the intersection of race and sex: A black feminist critique of antidiscrimination doctrine, feminist theory, and antiracist politics. *The University of Chicago Legal Forum, 1989,* 139–168.

———. (1995). Mapping the margins: Intersectionality, identity politics, and violence against women of color. In K. Crenshaw, N. Gotanda, G. Peller, & K. Thomas (Eds.), *Critical race theory" The key writings that formed the movement* (pp. 357–383). The New Press.

Fries-Britt, S., & Turner, B. (2002). Uneven stories: Successful Black collegians at a Black and a white campus. *The Review of Higher Education, 25*(3), 315–330.

Garvey, J. C., Mobley, S. D., Jr., Summerville, K. S., & Moore, G. T. (2019). Queer and trans* students of color: Navigating identity disclosure and college contexts. *The Journal of Higher Education, 90*(1), 150–178.

Gasman, M. (2007) Swept under the rug? A historiography of gender and Black colleges. *American Educational Research Journal, 44*(4), 760–805. doi:10.3102/0002831207308639

———. (2013). *The changing face of historically Black colleges and universities.* Penn Center for Minority Serving Institutions. https://repository.upenn.edu/gse_pubs/335

Goings, R. B. (2016). Investigating the experiences of two high-achieving Black male HBCU graduates: An exploratory study. *Negro Educational Review, 67*(1–4), 54–75.

Guy-Sheftall, B., & Alexander, J. (2006). *Facilitating campus climates of pluralism, inclusivity and progressive change at HBCUs.* Spelman College Women's Resource Center.

Harper, S. R., & Gasman, M. (2008). Consequences of conservatism: Black male undergraduates and the politics of historically Black colleges and universities. *Journal of Negro Education, 77*(4), 336–351.

Hurtado, S., Milem, J. F., Clayton-Pedersen, A. R., & Allen, W. R. (1999). *Enhancing diverse learning environments: Improving the campus climate for racial/ethnic diversity in higher education* (ASHE-ERIC Higher Education Reports Series No. 26-8). Jossey Bass

Lenning, Emily. 2017. Unapologetically queer in unapologetically Black spaces: Creating an inclusive HBCU campus." *Humboldt Journal of Social Relations, 1*(39): 283–293.

LePeau, L. (2015). A grounded theory of academic affairs and student affairs partnerships for diversity and inclusion aims. *The Review of Higher Education, 39*(1), 97–122. https://doi.org/10.1353/rhe.2015.0044

Mobley, S. D., Jr. (2017). Seeking sanctuary: (Re)Claiming the power of historically Black colleges and universities as places of Black refuge. *International Journal of Qualitative Studies in Education, 30*(10), 1036–1041.

Mobley, S. D., Jr., & Hall, L. (2020). (Re)Defining queer and trans* student retention and "success" at historically Black colleges and universities. *Journal of College Student Retention: Research Theory & Practice, 21*(4), 497–519. https://doi.org/10.1177/1521025119895512

Mobley, S. D., Jr., & Johnson, J. M. (2015). The role of HBCUs in addressing the unique needs of LGBT students. In R. Palmer, R. Shorette, and M. Gasman (Eds.), *Exploring diversity at historically Black colleges and universities: Implications for policy and practice.* (pp. 79–90). Jossey-Bass. doi.org/10.1002/he.20133

———. (2019). "No pumps allowed": The "problem" with gender expression and the Morehouse College "Appropriate Attire Policy." *Journal of Homosexuality, 66*(7), 867–895.

Mobley, S. D., Jr., Johnson, R. W., Sewell, J. P., Johnson, J. M., & Neely, A. J. (2021). "We are not victims": Unmasking Black queer and trans* student activism at HBCUs. *About Campus, 26*(3), 24–28.

Njoku, N., Butler, M., & Beatty, C. C. (2017). Reimagining the historically Black college and university (HBCU) environment: Exposing race secrets and the binding chains of respectability and othermothering. *International Journal of Qualitative Studies in Education, 30*(8), 783–799. https://doi.org/10.1080/09518398.2017.1350297

Patton, L. D. (2011). Perspectives on identity, disclosure and the campus environment among African American gay and bisexual men at one historically Black college. *Journal of College Student Development, 52*(1), 77–100.

———. (2016). Disrupting postsecondary prose: Toward a critical race theory of higher education. *Urban Education, 51*(3), 315–342

Patton, L. D., & Simmons, S. L. (2008). Exploring complexities of multiple identities of lesbians in a black college environment. *Negro Education Review, 59*(3), 197–215, 237.

Simon, M. (2017, September 11). Spelman College becomes second women's only HBCU to admit transgender students. Retrieved January 17, 2021, from https://www.nbcnews.com/news/nbcblk/spelman-college-becomes-second-women-s-only-hbcu-admit-transgender-n799536

Squire, D., & Mobley, S. D., Jr. (2015). Negotiating race and sexual orientation in the college choice process of Black gay males. *The Urban Review, 47*(3), 466–491.

Williams, S. (2018, June 21). It's time for HBCUs to address homophobia and transphobia on their campuses. *THE Nation.* www.thenation.com. https://www.thenation.com/article/archive/time-hbcus-address-homophobia-transphobia-campuses/

Wymer, K. (2016, June 3). It's time to speak up for your gay and transgender students. *The Chronicle of Higher Education.* https://www.chronicle.com/article/It-s-Time-to-Speak-Up-for/236710

Young, S. L., & McKibban, A. R. (2013). Creating safe places: A collaborative autoethnography on LGBT social activism. *Sexuality & Culture, 18*(2), 361–384. https://doi.org/10.1007/s12119-013-9202-5

7 · UNDERSTANDING THE ENGAGEMENT AND POLITICS OF QUARE HBCU STUDENT LEADERS

TOBIAS RAPHAEL MORGAN

When the label queer was introduced in the United States in 1914, it was a term of opprobrium that was used to identify homosexuals. This usage continued for most of the twentieth century until activists reclaimed it during the gay rights movement and the AIDS epidemic of 1980s and 1990s (Perlman, 2019). Political in nature, the concept of queer embraces and opposes adverse systems and circumstances. Today, LGBTQ people around the globe use the concept of queer as a political statement to foster unity across the LGBTQ spectrum. As T. R. Morgan (2020) notes, queer theory unites the personal with the political. A key component of queer theory is its insistence that intersecting identities specific to race, class, gender (Marfield, 2012), and sexuality are undeniably associated.

However, "queer" has also been associated with whiteness and privilege in the LGBTQ community. The pervasive racism and white supremacy in LGBTQ communities often relegate Black queer and trans* communities to the margins (Blockett, 2017; Garvey et al., 2019). Thus, as an act of resistance many Black queer and trans* individuals have chosen not to use the term "queer" to describe themselves. In this chapter, the term "quare" will be used in place of "queer."

Quare theory, which E. Patrick Johnson (2001) introduced, provides a space for exploring the intersections of oppression related to race, gender, sexuality, and class for Black LGBTQ individuals. Quare theory creates room to recognize queer and trans* HBCU cultures. A participant in a study Obie Ford (2015) conducted among gay Black alumni of HBCUs noted, "Going to an HBCU, being Black had a lot of pride associated with it, especially being a Black man. There were things you shouldn't say or do. You shouldn't have any feminine characteristics. I have been gay all my life. It was evident. I'm not the most masculine man in the world, but I'm also not the most effeminate. The pressure to be masculine was challenging" (p. 59). In essence, quare theory makes clear how important it is to understand that Blackness and LGBTQ identities are not separate and should not be treated as such.

Today a generation of quare student leaders is visible on HBCU campuses, in their communities, and on social media. For example, Keadrick Peters, the coordinator of multicultural programs and services at Bowie State University, told Vanessa Roberson (2021) that students who had been marginalized in high school and hadn't been able to choose who to take to the prom were the ones who started the Gay-Straight Alliance and the LGBTQIA resource center at Bowie State. They also started planning a prom at their university.

HBCU Out Loud Day, an initiative that the Human Rights Campaign began in 2019, has become a popular trend among LGBTQ students at HBCUs. The purpose of this national partnership is to celebrate HBCU quare and trans* communities while also bringing awareness of LGBTQ equity and inclusion opportunities, programming, and pride events on HBCU campuses (Human Rights Campaign, 2021).

Quare and trans* HBCU students are also challenging social norms and campus policies and are partnering with national LGBTQ organizations to call out administrators who attempt to other them (Mobley et al., 2021). For example, in 2015, after decades of rejection from their administration, Hampton University's LGBTQ students fought for and gained clearance to form a university-recognized student organization for LGBTQ students called MOSAIC. In 2019, Morehouse students initiated the hashtag #MorehouseCannotEraseMe on social media in response to a transgender admissions policy that they deemed restrictive and transphobic toward current and future students. The students at these two HBCUs forced their administrations to listen and resisted the conformity that was being forced upon them.

Many Black quare and trans* student activists can be found in leadership roles in student government or the student senate or in the royal court as campus kings or queens. But many other quare and trans* students at HBCUs do not feel comfortable about being out and are hiding in plain sight. Research indicates that quare students at HBCUs struggle with their involvement on campus due to their gender identity and/or expression. These students are at risk of experiencing isolation, a lack of resources, and a lack of professional leadership from administrators (Lewis & Ericksen, 2016).

This chapter describes how quare student leaders navigate and negotiate their roles at HBCUs. What follows is a conversation about the experiences of quare student leaders based on my personal points of view in the past and present. The literature on the experiences of quare student leaders at HBCUs is scant

(T. R. Morgan, 2020; Kilmartin, 2007). Previous studies that focused on Black LGBTQ students have drawn upon models and theories constructed from research on white students (Washington & Wall, 2010). Scholarship that examines Black LGBTQ student experiences at HBCUs warrants attention that is specific to lesbian and trans* students. This chapter presents my personal experiences as a Black quare HBCU student leader and now a Black quare student affairs professional as a resource for future dialogue.

The chapter will also offer recommendations to student affairs professionals from a critical lens that views HBCUs as political institutions that promote conservative values (Patton et al., 2020). I offer this chapter as a resource for shedding light on the importance of valuing all students and creating welcoming spaces, actions that will further advance the missions of HBCUs by ensuring that all of their students are able to thrive in co-curricular environments.

HBCUS AND CONSERVATIVISM

The campus cultures of HBCUs have been shaped by their religious affiliations (Commodore, 2018). As the landscape of higher education evolved, the Second Morrill Act of 1890 gave rise to Black land-grant institutions. This legislation provided grants of land to states for the purpose of establishing postsecondary institutions and expanded post-secondary opportunities for Black communities. In essence, this government intervention further mobilized HBCUs by broadening access to college for Black students and increasing diversity and program offerings on college campuses that served Black students. Brown and Freeman (2004) note that the origins of HBCUs fall into three key categories: schools founded by missionaries, schools founded by Black religious denominations, and schools founded by white industrialists and abolitionists.

The American Missionary Association founded several HBCUs, including Fisk University, Dillard University, Tougaloo College, and Talladega College (Spry, 2010). Missionary organizations affiliated with northern white denominations worked alongside the Freedmen's Bureau to aid in the education of Blacks (Decker, 2014). Even though white missionaries assisted in founding HBCUs, these groups and individuals had their own agendas and viewed Black people through a judgmental lens that led them to enact Christian values on these campuses (Anderson, 1988b; Mobley et al., 2021). Black churches, Black missionary societies, and former slaves founded Edward Waters College, Morris Brown College, and Wilberforce University (Anderson, 1988b). In addition, at the end of the nineteenth century, white northern industrialists provided funding for HBCUs as private Black colleges began to experience a decline in funding (Peeps, 1981). This funding was attached to Christian values and a hidden agenda that sought to influence Black education (Anderson, 1988a). Allen & Jewell (2002) contend that early white supporters of HBCUs "sought to divest Blacks of their 'peculiar' cultural past and to teach them the ways of middle-class white Americans" (Allen & Jewell, 2002, p. 246). While white philanthropists and former abolitionists provided funding for HBCUs in an effort to educate Black populations in the South, "this benevolence toward the former slaves was not without its disturbing side" (Decker, 2014, p. 235). White philanthropists who invested in HBCUs used education to control Black communities in efforts to ensure that they would remain subordinate in the postbellum social order (Anderson, 1988a; Decker, 2014; Mobley et al., 2021). These roots led to a culture of conservatism that still exists in contemporary HBCU contexts.

Students on today's HBCU campuses represent many religious affiliations, cultures, and ethnicities. Unfortunately, as Green-Hayes (2017) notes, "like many other Black cultural institutions, such as the Black church, Historically Black Colleges and Universities (HBCUs) have traditionally been depicted as 'behind the mainstream' with regards to gender and sexuality" (p. 2). As political awareness continues to rise around queer and trans* issues, a noticeable shift is occurring in postsecondary contexts and at HBCUs in particular. HBCUs must develop a strategy to support the shift toward acceptance of LGBTQ communities and develop key outcomes that promote supportive environments (T. R. Morgan, 2020).

QUARE STUDENT LEADERSHIP

Student leaders at HBCUs set the tone for pride, culture, policies, and the campus climate. Serving as a member of a student government association, the royal court, or the student senate or as officers of a club or organization impacts the campus fosters student development and inspires future generations to sustain HBCU experiences. However, quare HBCU students often find it difficult to navigate their experiences in student leadership because they are not fully included in their campus communities and because they lack resources and institutional leaders who support them (Lewis & Erickson, 2016; Mobley et al., 2021; Patton et al., 2020). Elsewhere (T. R. Morgan, 2020), I have noted that quare HBCU student leaders may have issues with coming out on their campuses because in the context of heteronormative campus cultures, that act may be viewed as rebellion.

The lack of support for quare student leaders sends a clear message about an institution's feelings toward its quare students and their experiences. For example, quare students who assume responsibilities as a campus king or queen may face challenges from both their peers and administrators whose views force them to live a closeted life, thus denying their sexual identity during a critical stage of development. As Byrd (2020) notes, "The lack of tolerance for fluid gender expression on the HBCU campus leaves students in a position where they have to hide their queerness for fear of insult or other discrimination." (p. 111). Additionally, trans* or non-binary students may be denied opportunities to participate in the royal court pageant because administrators reject their gender identity. HBCUs located in the Deep South have subscribed to specific mores and standards regarding how HBCU student leaders should (re)present their institution. For example, Alabama State University and Southern University and A&M College have never bestowed the title of "Mister" upon a student, nor have they designated class kings. Alabama State University and Southern University and A&M College have refrained from conferring the title of "mister" or appointing students as class king on the royal court. This reluctance can be linked to the conservative stance often associated with HBCUs and with university administrators avoiding discussions surrounding gender expression and identity. This stance is intriguing, because in recent years several HBCU kings have identified as quare.

Invisible Quares as HBCU Student Leaders

Black quare and trans* individuals have been forced to hide in plain sight and often feel compelled to force themselves to perform socially acceptable roles so as not to disturb stereotypical notions of Blackness or queer identity (Boykin, 2005; Mobley et al., 2020). I was the "invisible" quare student leader at my HBCU. My experiences and my advisors motivated me to work in student affairs. My experience as a student leader throughout my high school years provided a foundation of service, advocacy, and development. Student leadership was a familiar frame of thought and student engagement opportunities were a critical factor as I chose which college I would attend. What was unfamiliar was my attraction to my own gender in the new environment of college and having that identity be viewed as problematic in a conservative binary system. The alarming question that echoed in my mind was, How do I present my authentic self and participate in student government, the royal court, or serve in a leadership role in student clubs and organizations without being othered?

I vividly remember leaving Rendall Hall (the freshman male residence hall) one day, heading to the cafeteria to meet a few friends for dinner. As I walked through a group of male upper-class students, words that sounded like gunshots echoed throughout the quad: "this gay-ass n——." Even though I sensed I might have been the subject of their conversation, I remained unsure if the comments were aimed at me. Still, the negative thought was triggering. I walked as fast as I could to escape their ignorance. This was a time when I honestly did not understand my own sexual identity. I felt forced to pass as heterosexual and present myself in a way that society deemed "manly." The campus climate was not a welcoming space for quare individuals. Although quare students were present at my HBCU, we were seldom discussed or acknowledged. At the time, the institution did not support a LGBTQ student organization, and I do not believe I would have even considered becoming a member because of my fear of being ostracized. In addition, the student leadership opportunities on the campus did not reflect diversity and inclusion. Consequently, many quare students found community primarily on the margins of my campus.

During the first few weeks of school, my peers voted me Mister Freshman. This was a prestigious ambassador title awarded to a male-identified first-year student. I did not know much about HBCU campus kings and queens at the time, but I was soon educated about how the position of an HBCU king was viewed as less masculine. "Playing dress-up" and participating in coronation or a pageant were viewed as feminine activities. I endured the pressure of having to change who I was to fit in to a new environment that was very different from high school. In an effort to become more socially accepted across the campus, I unconsciously adapted to imposter syndrome to survive. Clance and Imes (1978) introduced the concept of imposter syndrome in the late 1970s, defining it as a practice of regularly doubting one's abilities even through the evidence shows competence. High levels of rejection and oppression, a culture of heterosexism, and a lack of inclusion were the factors that contributed to my experiencing imposter syndrome.

Quare student leaders oftentimes negotiate gender expression and campus involvement in efforts to acquire acceptance, belonging, and status. This is especially true for students seeking top leadership positions such as student government association president or vice-president or student trustee or a position on the royal court. Postsecondary contexts impact how quare students develop throughout their college years, when they are strongly impacted by heterosexism and institutional homophobia. My negotiation ended during my senior year with the arrival of a new young male student affairs professional at my HBCU. I saw a reflection of myself in him. He served as a tangible reminder that regardless of my gender identity, the spaces I inhabit hold significance for me and, more importantly, merit my presence as a student at this institution. Although a more accepting environment for student leaders who identify as quare exists today, things are far from ideal. Traditional mores continue to influence HBCU cultures and mid-level and senior HBCU administrators continue to silence and police quare students (M. Morgan, 2020). Students of all sexual and gender identities are evolving faster than our institutions are. Thus, now more than ever, HBCU student affairs professionals must work to meet the needs of this population.

Playing the Game

One in six students at an HBCU who identify as queer are victims of harassment, leading some to believe it's imperative to hide their identities for safety rather than risk being targeted and potentially facing backlash for their sexual preferences (Pinder, 2011). This forces quare student leaders to be selective about disclosing their sexual identity, which increases their invisibility (Garvey et al., 2019). During my junior year, as a newly initiated fraternity man, I encountered harassment from my fraternity advisor. I expressed my desire to become the

National Pan-Hellenic Council president and to run for mister of the university. I anticipated an encouraging response but was met with sarcastic homophobia. As he continued talking down to me, I felt as if I was not even in the room anymore. But I did hear him say, "The university isn't ready for no soft boys to be the face. Now, you made line because of your potential. So let's take things slow."

This was my first encounter with an administrator who questioned my masculinity and my sexuality. Heterosexism and homophobia were both on display, and they made me feel invisible. This meeting influenced my actions throughout the remainder of my junior year. I was not truly able to express my sexual identity. I experienced what Squire and Mobley (2015) described: "Students who have oppressed intersecting identities endure educational environments that are, at the very least, doubly marginalizing in educational contexts" (p. 467). My experiences disprove the notion that HBCUs support the co-curricular achievements of marginalized students.

I learned from that experience with my fraternity advisor to play the game. I also realized in that moment that HBCUs have a way of reinforcing the politics of respectability in their cultures (Byrd, 2020). My campus environment was reminiscent of the military's policy of "don't ask, don't tell" (T. R. Morgan, 2020, p. 90). Evelyn Brooks Higginbotham (1993) introduced the concept of the "politics of respectability" as a method that African Americans have used to avoid societal norms, behaviors, and attitudes that white people considered inferior, instead adopting behaviors and attitudes that they believed will earn respect (Njoku et al., 2017; Patton, 2014). Harris (2003) suggests that "by linking worthiness . . . to sexual propriety, behavioral decorum, and neatness, respectability served as a gatekeeping function, establishing a behavioral 'entrance fee' to the right to respect and the right to full citizenship" (p. 213). Fully immersed in my role as a student leader on campus, I ignored my sexual identity to present what administrators believed was acceptable behavior in the hope of expanding my network.

I did not question my performance or my decisions one time, although at times it felt uncomfortable. I had goals in mind and my sexuality, or what I perceived it to be at the time, put me at risk. I was blind to the idea that I could truly be my authentic self on a Black campus that continuously affirmed the culture of heteronormativity. Ultimately, I served on the royal court, president of the Ziana Fashion Club, pledged a fraternity, became a member of the student government association, participated on the track and field team, and became a resident assistant in the freshman men's hall. Respectability politics played a major role in my day-to-day performance as a student leader who was not acknowledging his quare identity. In retrospect, these decisions presented a way for me to gain social capital, leadership opportunities, and, most important, leadership development. However, the burden of living up to a societal standard of masculinity that my peers, faculty, and administrators subscribed to was so strong that I failed to resist restrictive policies and toxic behaviors and viewpoints. I and my peers on campus who identified as quare and who had a desire for service and student leadership pushed ourselves to obtain leadership positions, but at what cost? In hindsight, I can see that we bought in to the politics of respectability, but our sacrifices also provided a foundation for the liberation and visibility of quare students who were to come after us.

Visible HBCU Student Leaders

Today's generation of college students is the most diverse in terms of race, gender, sexuality, socioeconomic status, and cultural background to date, and quare students are becoming more visible at HBCUs (Byrd, 2020). Quare HBCU student leaders are now in more positions as visible voices on campus, and they have made advancements for the LGBTQ community through student activism (Mobley et al., 2021). As they navigate political systems such as unwritten gender roles, misgendering of students, binary systems, failure to use appropriate pronouns, and restrictive masculinity, quare student leaders continue to combat outdated policies, heterosexism, harassment, and being othered. Although the advancements that exist today for quare HBCU student leaders represent significant strides toward equity and equality, quare HBCU student leaders continue to receive metaphorical slaps on the wrist for not conforming to tradition and conservative standards. I am reminded of a quare student leader at Florida A&M University who once told to me that "as senate president I was told by administration to dress slightly different from my normal dress and not to wear tight clothes, oh and to act a 'certain' way." As a student affairs professional, I still hear colleagues say, "as long as the queen is not trans" or "the [woman identified] Student Government Association president can't wear a suit or dress like a man." These experiences remind me of how I gave my power away to administrators as a quare HBCU student leader. Diminishing my existence allowed administrators to silence me while the cycle of oppression continued (Rankin & Garvey, 2015).

Today, quare HBCU student leaders are still openly challenging heterosexism, toxic campus environments, and biased policies when they face discrimination during their leadership roles. M. Morgan (2020) conducted a qualitative study that examined the experiences and perceptions of six HBCU administrators (who represent five public institutions and one private institution) about LGBTQ student services decisions. The administrators who participated in the study acknowledged that on their campuses, a culture of tolerance for LGBTQ students was assumed. Their statements support Mobley and Johnson's (2019) observation that LGBTQ students at HBCUs may feel invisible in the campus community. M. Morgan's study shed light on societal assumptions and the existence of opinions and behaviors that are not mutually agreed upon related to factors that impact the climate of a campus as HBCU administrators understand them. Morgan did this study to determine if HBCU campus cultures created safe environments for quare students to show up as their true authentic selves.

A senior-level HBCU administrator may accept a meeting request from student leaders who identify as quare to document that they have listened to student concerns but not work to create a campus environment that would support this population of students. Tolerance is when an administrator simply listens to a student and then turns the page to issues that they perceive to be of high importance once the student leaves their office. Tolerant behaviors toward LGBTQ students are typically performed by senior-level student affairs professionals who have strong religious beliefs that create roadblocks for younger student affairs professionals who want to support quare student leaders. When HBCU administrators present characteristics of tolerance, it can be assumed that they are conforming to standards that support conservative systems. These administrators contribute to a climate where "there is difficulty in acceptance from faculty, staff, and administrators" (M. Morgan, 2020, p. 89). Administrators demonstrate acceptance when they show concern; provide support, guidance, and resolve; and follow up with a student to ensure that their difficulty has been resolved.

The conflicting notions of tolerance and acceptance provide additional context for why student affairs professionals at HBCUs may not be equipped to holistically support quare student leaders as they navigate their multiple identities in the midst of leading. Administrators who consciously avoid engagement with their quare students are a primary reason why engaging these students has progressed slowly. As one participant in M. Morgan's (2020) study noted, "We have got some work to do! It has been a 'hot topic' here on campus as of recent because we have some students wanting to participate in certain activities, and they are going through the process of transitioning. I think it has been difficult for the campus community to embrace" (p. 90). Similar discussions are being held on HBCU campuses around the country. These schools are still navigating how to truly embrace and support quare student leaders without compromising the institution's traditional and conservative views on campus, in the community, and on social media. Masculine-presenting female students who seek leadership roles face oppression. Revised campus dress code policies have shifted into discreet one-on-one discussions implying that regulations on attire are not openly articulated but rather enforced confidentially and selectively, targeting only specific individuals behind closed doors. Despite progress in terms of including quare HBCU student leaders, it appears that binary notions of gender and gender expression prevail.

RECOMMENDATIONS FOR HBCU STUDENT AFFAIRS PROFESSIONALS

It is critical for HBCU student affairs professionals to understand that issues relating to sexuality, gender, and gender identity have many manifestations that require their attention. This knowledge is essential for building relationships with the students they advise, teach, and mentor. The following recommendations are intended to further the discussion about providing supportive environments for quare HBCU student leaders. Several HBCUs have been slow to nurture the success of their LGBTQ students. It would be beneficial for all HBCU administrators and faculty members to engage in learning about queer and trans* communities through a variety of strategies.

It is important for administrators to take advantage of professional development opportunities. Attending conferences and workshops pertaining to quare [queer] and trans* issues provides opportunities to build an understanding of these students and their unique needs. Moreover, these sessions offer information about how to enact inclusive and holistic trans* inclusion policies and access to resources for LGBTQ students. Professional development also allows administrators to reflect on best practices for supporting quare student leaders as they navigate their undergraduate experiences. Administrators in the division of student affairs often spend time with student leaders beyond the scope of university hours. These moments can provide opportunities to discuss expectations, leadership, campus climate, and challenges. Intimate discussions can be liberating for a quare student leader at an HBCU when administrators are properly trained to have these conversations.

Each HBCU should develop an LGBTQ task force to develop initiatives that speak to culture, inclusion, and social responsiveness for students, faculty, and administrators. Such task forces are currently in place at Dillard University, Morgan State University, and Virginia State University (Mobley & Hall, 2020). Giving quare student leaders representation on these task forces will provide an outlet for growth and development for them and will give them the opportunity to model representation and possibility for their peers. A major component of an LGBTQ task force should be including partnerships with local and national LGBTQ organizations so they can assist in developing campus workshops and trainings that focus on current issues for the LGBTQ community.

HBCUs can enhance campus inclusivity by implementing initiatives like hosting forums and seminars tailored to the enrichment of LGBTQ students, as demonstrated by the groundbreaking efforts of institutions such as Tennessee State University and Howard University. In 2020, under my leadership, the Office of Student Activities and Leadership at Tennessee State University held its inaugural Student Leadership Institute virtually sponsored by the Human Rights Campaign HBCU Initiative. This monumental moment at Tennessee State University educated participants with three sixty-second public service commercials that focused on the importance of voting, support for LGBTQ students, and how the inclusion and visibility of LGBTQ students shapes allyship on campus. Howard University hosts an annual LGBTA Renaissance Reception during homecoming that serves as a fund-raiser for the Lavender Fund, an initiative that centers its queer and trans stakeholders (see chapter 9 by Cross & Lu, this volume). A major accomplishment of this initiative, which was established by the first openly gay graduate student trustee in 2015, is that it continues as an example of the institution's commitment to a progressive future and to developing strategies to ensure a safe and inclusive environment for all students.

I conclude these recommendations by reminding readers that quare student leaders serve at a disadvantage with an open heart. Quare students recognize when administrators are "speaking from a position of truth and love rather than a position of momentary satisfaction" (T. R. Morgan, 2020, p. 143). Urging senior-level administrators to embrace quare student identities should be a campus priority. As President Obama (2013) noted in his inaugural address, "Our journey is not complete until our gay brothers and sisters are treated like anyone else under the law ... for if we are truly created equal, then surely the love we commit to one another must be equal as well" (para. 22).

Today it is common for institutions of higher education to emphasize using correct pronouns and to create spaces that affirm gender-nonconforming students. However, administrators at HBCUs have not fully embraced supporting the proper use of gender pronouns or creating safe spaces. This often leaves quare HBCU student leaders wondering how to create a space where all students experience the benefits of the campus culture. The issues surrounding gender and sexuality on HBCU campuses require the immediate attention of senior-level leaders. It is the responsibility of administrators and other campus leaders to dismantle toxic practices that are occurring at HBCUs by providing purpose-driven trainings for faculty, staff, and administrators. Targeted sessions can provide awareness of the importance of inclusion, a meaningful social change, a safer campus environment, and a cohesive system of governance.

CONCLUSION

HBCUs have made significant strides over the last decade to support students who identify as quare. However, slow planning and slow implementation of plans characterizes the vast majority of HBCUs, and most still do not provide communal support for quare students in terms of pedagogy and student affairs. Individuals in institutions continue to "other" lesbian, gay, bisexual, transgender, and questioning students based on societal norms and expectations despite changes to institutionalized guidelines and policies. Even though LGBTQ students are more visible on HBCU campuses, these institutions have not fully satisfied the demand to educate, nurture, and develop these students or equip student affairs professionals with the tools and resources they need to holistically support this population.

More students are coming out and organizing on the campuses of U.S. institutions of higher education (Jones et al., 2014). The Human Rights Campaign's annual Leadership Summit for LGBTQ students at HBCUs, partnerships with the National Black Justice Coalition for diversity and inclusion trainings, and the acknowledgment of World AIDS Day with HIV testing on campus provide evidence that quare student leaders are championing important issues. Since 2018, there have been more examples of visible quare student leadership at HBCUs. A Howard University Student Association vice-president and president has openly identified as trans* and a student senate chair at Howard University has identified as nonbinary. Members of the Royal Court at Morehouse College and Spelman College have openly identified as quare. Further, a recent Student Government Association president at St. Augustine's University has identified as quare. Mister Tennessee State University openly campaigned and won as quare, Johnson C. Smith University made history with the first trans* woman to serve on royal court as Miss Junior (previously serving as Mister Freshman and Mister Sophomore prior to her transition), the first Mister Clinton College openly identified as quare, the Executive SGA President at Shaw University identified as nonbinary, and the list continues.

Through conversations with quare student leaders over the years, I have had the opportunity to build meaningful relationships and even mentor them. I have also observed that HBCUs are cautious about embracing the inevitable reality that gender and sexuality cannot continue to be ignored. M. Morgan (2020) has noted that "cultural and institutional practices can shape an administrator's perspective on handling LGBTQ students" (p. 115). As a practitioner in the field, I understand that quare students continue to face conservative political environments on their campuses in part because of student affairs professionals who agree with ideals represented in the Black church and in the broader society.

Although the historical roots of conservatism provided a pathway for HBCUs to uplift the African American community, quare student leaders at HBCUs today grapple with negotiating their identities related to sexuality, gender, and self-expression despite having a platform for change. HBCUs now stand in a critical moment. How HBCUs choose to address, react to, acknowledge, and offer support to quare students will provide an indication of how willing they are to take next steps toward increasing the visibility of these students. Inviting quare student leaders to participate in the conversation beyond having a seat at the table will truly shift HBCUs toward a better future in which they model how to embrace full Blackness on their campuses (Mobley, 2017).

REFERENCES

Allen, W. R., & Jewell, J. O. (2002). A backward glance forward: Past, present and future perspectives on historically Black colleges and universities. *The Review of Higher Education*, 25(3), 241–261.

Anderson, J. D. (1988a). Northern foundations and the shaping of southern Black rural education, 1902–1935. *History of Education Quarterly*, 18(4), 371–96.

———. (1988b). *The education of Blacks in the South, 1860–1935*. University of North Carolina Press.

Blockett, R. A. (2017). "I think it's very much placed on us": Black queer men laboring to forge community at a predominantly white and (hetero) cisnormative research institution. *International Journal of Qualitative Studies in Education, 30*(8), 800–816.

Boykin, K. (2005). *Beyond the down low: Sex, lies, and denial in Black America*. Carroll & Graf Publishers.

Brown, M. C., & Freeman, K. (2004). *Black colleges: New perspectives on policy and practice*. Praeger.

Byrd, K. (2020). *LGBTQ student experiences on historically Black college and university campuses* [Unpublished doctoral dissertation]. The College of William and Mary. https://scholarworks.wm.edu/etd/1593091486/

Clance, P. R., & Imes, S. (1978). The imposter phenomenon in high achieving women: Dynamics and therapeutic intervention. *Psychotherapy Theory, Research, and Practice, 15*(3), 1–8.

Commodore, F. (2018). The tie that binds: Trusteeship, values, and the decision-making process at AME-affiliated HBCUs. *The Journal of Higher Education, 89*(4), 397–421.

Decker, T. N. (2014). Not in my backyard: Puritan morality versus Puritan mercantilism and its impact on HBCUs. In M. Gasman & F. Commodore (Eds.), *Opportunities and challenges at historically Black colleges and universities* (pp. 235–52). Palgrave Macmillan.

Ford, O., III. (2015). From navigation to negotiation: An examination of the lived experiences of Black gay male alumni of historically Black colleges and universities. *Journal of Homosexuality, 62*(3), 353–373.

Garvey, J. C., Mobley, S. D., Jr., Summerville, K. S., & Moore, G. T. (2019). Queer and trans*students of color: Navigating identity disclosure and college contexts. *The Journal of Higher Education, 90*(1), 150–178.

Green-Hayes, A. (2017, April 11). "Black, Gifted & Whole" nonprofit helps gay students thrive at HBCUs. News One. https://newsone.com/3705170/black-gift-and-whole-nonprofit-helps-gay-hbcu-students-thrive/

Harris, P. J. (2003). Gatekeeping and remaking: The politics of respectability in African American women's history and black feminism. *Journal of Women's History, 15*, 212–220.

Higginbotham, E. B. (1993). *Righteous discontent: The women's movement in the black Baptist church, 1880–1920*. Harvard University Press.

Human Rights Campaign. (2021). *#HBCUOutLoudDay*. https://www.hrc.org/campaigns/hbcu-outloudday

Johnson, E. P. (2001). "Quare" studies, or (almost) everything I know about queer studies I learned from my grandmother. *Text and Performance Quarterly, 21*(1), 1–25. doi:10.1080/10462930128119

Jones, K. N., Brewster, M. E., & Jones, J. A. (2014). The creation and validation of the LGBT ally identity measure. *Psychology of Sexual Orientation and Gender Diversity, 1*(2), 181–195.

Kilmartin, C. T. (2007). *The masculine self* (3rd ed.). MacMillan Publishing Company.

Lewis, M.W., & Ericksen, K.S. (2016). Improving the climate for LGBTQ students at an historically Black university. *Journal of LGBT Youth, 13*(3), 249–269.

Marfield, J. D. (2012). *Performing race, gender, and sexual orientation in context: How undergraduates make meaning of the multiple dimensions of their identity* [Unpublished doctoral dissertation]. University of California, Los Angeles.

Mobley, S. D., Jr. (2017). Seeking sanctuary: (Re)Claiming the power of historically Black colleges and universities as places of Black refuge. *International Journal of Qualitative Studies in Education, 30*(10), 1036–1041.

Mobley, S. D., Jr., & Johnson, J. M. (2019). "No pumps allowed": The "problem" with gender expression and the Morehouse College "Appropriate Attire Policy." *Journal of Homosexuality, 66*(7), 867–895.

Mobley, S. D., Jr., Johnson, R. W., Sewell, J. P., Johnson, J. M., & Neely, A. J. (2021). "We are not victims": Unmasking Black queer and trans* student activism at HBCUs. *About Campus, 26*(3), 24–28.

Mobley, S. D., Jr., Solomon, S. L., II, Johnson, A. C. & Reynolds, P. (2021). "Troubling the waters": Unpacking and (re)imagining the historical and contemporary complexity of historically Black college and university cultural politics. In B. C. Williams, F. Tuitt, & D. Squire (Eds.), *Campus rebellions and plantation politics: Power, privilege, and the emancipatory struggle in higher education.* (pp. 77–97). State University of New York Press.

Mobley, S. D., Jr., Taylor, L., Jr., & Davison, C. H. (2020). (Un)Seen work: The pedagogical experiences of Black queer men in faculty roles. *International Journal of Qualitative Studies in Education, 33*(6), 604–620.

Morgan, M. (2020). *Experiences and perceptions of HBCU administrators about LGBTQ student services decisions* [Unpublished doctoral dissertation]. Capella University. ProQuest Dissertations & Theses Global. Retrieved from https://search.proquest.com/openview/c21896ec4c2a5034761e7efb3d70b04b/1?pq-origsite=gscholar&cbl=18750&diss=y

Morgan, T. R. (2020). *Owt on the yard: An exploration of masculinity among African American members of Black Greek-letter fraternities who identify as gay, bisexual, or same-gender loving at historically Black colleges and universities.* [Doctoral dissertation]. Morgan State University. ProQuest Dissertations & Theses Global.

Njoku, N., Butler, M., & Beatty, C. C. (2017). Reimagining the historically Black college and university (HBCU) environment: Exposing race secrets and the binding chains of respectability and othermothering. *International Journal of Qualitative Studies in Education, 30*(8), 783–799. doi:10.1080/09518398.2017.1350297

Obama, B. H. (2013, January 21). *Inauguration address by President Barack Obama.* The White House. https://obamawhitehouse.archives.gov/the-press-office/2013/01/21/inaugural-address-president-barack-obama

Patton, L. D. (2014). Preserving respectability or blatant disrespect? A critical discourse analysis of the Morehouse appropriate attire policy and implications for intersectional approaches to examining campus policies. *International Journal of Qualitative Studies in Education, 27*(6), 724–746.

Patton, L. D., Blockett, R. A., & McGowan, B. L. (2020). Complexities and Contradictions: Black lesbian, gay, bisexual and queer students' lived realities across three urban HBCU contexts. *Urban Education, 58*(6), 1355–1382. https://doi.org/10.1177/0042085920959128

Peeps, J. M. S. (1981). Northern philanthropy and the emergence of Black higher education—do-gooders, compromisers, or co-conspirators? *Journal of Negro Education, 50*(3), 251–69.

Perlman, M. (2019, January 22). How the word "queer" was adopted by the LGBTQ community. *Columbia Journalism Review.* https://www.cjr.org/language_corner/queer.php

Pinder, A. L. (2011). *Lost in reverie: Gay HBCU alumni look back.* Unpublished commissioned paper, Arcus Foundation Project, Spelman College.

Rankin, S. S., & Garvey, J. C. (2015). Identifying, quantifying, and operationalizing queer-spectrum and trans-spectrum students: Assessment and research in student affairs. *New Directions for Student Services, 2015*(152), 73–84. doi:10.1002/ss.20146

Roberson, V. (2021, June 25). HBCUs partner with the human rights campaign to explore best practices for LGBTQ+ students. *HBCU Buzz.* https://hbcubuzz.com/2021/06/hbcus-partner-with-the-human-rights-campaign-to-explore-best-practices-for-lgbtq-students/

Spry, S. (2010). A whole new world: Nine things academic advisors should know about historically Black colleges and universities (HBCUs). *The Mentor: An Academic Advising Journal, 12.* https://doi.org/10.26209/mj1261411

Squire, D. D., & Mobley, S. D., Jr., (2015). Negotiating race and sexual orientation in the college choice process of Black gay males. *The Urban Review, 47*(3), 466–491.

Washington, J., & Wall, V. A. (2010). African American gay men: Another challenge for the academy. In S. R. Harper & F. Harris (Eds.), *College men and masculinities: Theory, research, and implications for practice* (pp. 136–147). Jossey-Bass/Wiley.

8 · CREATING INCLUSIVE ACADEMIC SPACES FOR QUEER STUDENTS AT HBCUs

KATHRYN C. WYMER, JENNIFER M. WILLIAMS, AND W. RUSSELL ROBINSON

This chapter describes the work that has happened over the past few years at North Carolina Central University (NCCU) to foster academic inclusivity for queer students at the undergraduate level. As this public HBCU has increased its advocacy for queer students, it has also had to grapple with legal challenges, such as North Carolina's passage of HB2 in 2016, a law that mandated single-sex bathrooms. Many at the time called it "the most anti-LGBT law in the United States" (Yang, 2016). Educators in North Carolina were forced to contend publicly with the issue of queer equality as the state gained the national spotlight (Spellings, 2016). Although faculty and staff at NCCU had long been working to advance equality on campus, the events of 2016 served as a catalyst for improving university-wide conversations about queer issues, specifically with increased academic offerings that dealt with LGBTQIA (lesbian, gay, bisexual, transgender, queer/questioning, intersex, and asexual/agender) content. We hope that the lessons learned at NCCU can provide guidance to faculty at other HBCUs about what we can do in the classroom to support all students.

Of first importance as we began our recent initiatives was to assess what we were already doing well so that we knew how to focus our efforts for growth and improvement. NCCU, located in Durham, is a public university in the University of North Carolina system with an enrollment of over 8,000 students in graduate and undergraduate programs. The school's motto is "Truth and Service," and NCCU has been recognized for its high level of community engagement by the Carnegie Foundation for the Advancement of Teaching. In keeping with the institution's goal of equitably serving all students and community members, NCCU has long been a leader among HBCUs in supporting queer students.

This support has grown steadily over the last decades. In 1998, activist Mandy Carter, working with the National Black Lesbian and Gay Leadership Forum, spoke to those who had organized the school's first queer student support group, noting at that time that such support was rare at HBCUs and was offered only at "Spelman College in Atlanta, GA; Howard University in Washington, DC; and the newly formed Brothers and Sisters at NCCU" (NCCU Brothers and Sisters, 1998). Those years of leadership were productive and yielded what organizers in 2000 believed to be "the first workshop on sexual diversity at any historically black campus in the nation" (Cheng, 2000).

Progress did not happen overnight, however. Changes in administrative appointments seeded a new training regimen for student staff that included the first Safe Zone training on NCCU's campus in 2004. In 2009, Polychromes was established, an organization composed of out and allied staff and faculty members. After much planning and development, NCCU's LGBTA Resource Center opened its doors in April 2013. The school became the second HBCU in the nation to establish such a center (HRC Staff, 2013). As of 2024, there are eight LGBTQ Resource Centers at HBCUs (Mobley & Hall, 2020). Programs such as Safe Zone training (Young & McKibban, 2014) and Lavender Graduation ceremonies (Sanlo, 2000) have been offered regularly at NCCU and are well attended. From the fall of 2017 through the spring of 2018, NCCU's Department of Residential Life offered Kaleidoscope, a themed residential community for queer students and allies during a pilot program for residential communities (Barker, 2018). The project was reinstated due to student demand after the pandemic in the 2021–2022 academic year.

Although the focus of this chapter is undergraduate education, it is worth noting that graduate and professional schools at NCCU have also made contributions to the shift in campus culture. The North Carolina Central University School of Law has also been working to include queer representation in the curriculum. For example, in summer 2017, Professor Lydia Lavelle offered LAW 8308, Transgender Rights & Social Justice. Professor Lavelle has also guest lectured on Supreme Court rulings on same-sex marriage to undergraduates at NCCU. Also on faculty at the School of Law is Associate Dean Angela Gilmore, who was one of the plaintiffs in the lawsuit against the state's HB2 law (Holpuch, 2016). The School of Law also provided the location for the 2017 Summer Institute that NCCU's Department of Diversity and Inclusion hosted titled Strategies for Resistance, Resilience, and Hope: Supporting QTPOC (Queer and Trans People of Color) on College Campuses, which drew participants from across the nation and from all areas of NCCU's campus (Consortium of Higher Education LGBT Resource Professionals, 2017). Partnerships with the School of Law are ongoing and will undoubtedly yield even more valuable collaborations in the future. Many of these changes have been sparked by student interest and requests. This is true in the psychology graduate program; students in that program have the option of partnering with and interning with the LGBTA Resource Center on campus. Graduate students conduct research and lead programming initiatives in the center.

Despite what we believe to be real and productive accomplishments, our campus has much room to grow. The gains in campus inclusivity at the undergraduate level prior to 2016 were almost exclusively initiated by the Division of Student Affairs. Up to that point, NCCU initiatives supporting queer students followed what LePeau (2015) has labeled a "complementary pathway" in which the Academic Affairs and Student Affairs were working separately to achieve diversity initiatives, though these two units undoubtedly do work together. For instance, faculty members attend Safe Zone training, and Lavender Graduation on our campus would not exist without students' successful completion of coursework. However, before 2016, there was little direct coordination of effort, with the result that students were clearly finding more support in structures outside classrooms than within them. Noting this need for increased student support, faculty and administrators responded by creating academic spaces to facilitate productive conversations. The subsequent course development required partnerships across campus that were more closely aligned with the model of what Dooley and LePeau (2016) have identified as a "pervasive pathway" in which Student Affairs and Academic Affairs "work from a shared vision" and break down the boundaries between the divisions.

This chapter will discuss the importance of incorporating LGBTQIA content in undergraduate academic coursework and the specific courses that have recently been developed and taught at NCCU. Support from the administration in the form of an Academic Innovation Grant has been crucial for these endeavors. That grant funded faculty and student research on the experiences of queer and trans people of color at HBCUs and a public lecture series on queer issues. As a component of the work, the Academic Innovation Grant explicitly invited principal investigators to engage with units across campus. As a result, we formed partnerships between numerous divisions: the Office of Diversity and Inclusion, the LGBTA Resource Center, the Department of Language and Literature, the Department of Mass Communication, the Program in Women's and Gender Studies, and the James E. Shepard Memorial Library. This chapter presents these projects as models for how HBCU faculty and administrators can actively support queer students in academic spaces.

QUEERING CURRICULA: THREE MODELS FOR SUPPORTING AN INCLUSIVE ENVIRONMENT FOR STUDENTS

Ensuring that queer students feel included on campus requires that faculty members integrate LGBTQIA content and concepts in course content. On the surface, this seems like it should be an obvious statement. However, in practice such integration is the exception rather than the norm at HBCUs (Mobley & Hall, 2020; Mobley & Johnson, 2015). It is important to address some of the reasons for this disconnect between what is often a sincere desire on the part of the faculty to welcome queer students in their classrooms and the actual practice that emerges in the day-to-day management of a course. Doing so can help faculty members recognize places in their courses where they have natural opportunities to increase inclusivity.

Incorporating LGBTQIA content in the curriculum not only improves the campus climate for queer students, such gains also reach students who do not identify as queer. Indeed, part of the value of academic study of queer issues is that it educates the wider community and dispels myths and rumors. Education about queer issues in an academic context also removes the burden from queer students to constantly explain themselves, answer intrusive questions, and otherwise be asked in social settings to educate their peers on the queer experience. Queer studies courses are not just for students who identify as part of that community. Many nonqueer students are also interested in these topics because they perceive value in understanding friends, family, future co-workers, and future clients who identify as part of the queer community. Students' success after college depends on their ability to work with people from all backgrounds, and providing academic venues for understanding others' life experiences helps develop those skills.

For the purposes of this discussion, it is useful to identify three broad categories for integrating LGBTQIA content in the curriculum. The first is a lesson plan model in which an instructor incorporates inclusive class lectures or activities in a course that is otherwise not specifically about queer studies. Evidence for how often this happens is necessarily anecdotal because recorded data on course titles and adopted texts do not capture the entirety of what the content of any given lesson might be. There are certainly some instructors who do a good job of including queer representation. However, it is also clear that there are many missed opportunities in which texts are taught without reference to the author's queer identification (Johnson, 2021; Mobley & Hall, 2020; Mobley & Johnson, 2015). It would be unthinkable to teach Alice Walker's works without mentioning her status as a prominent African American author. Nevertheless, instructors often fail to mention Walker's public acknowledgment of her same-gender-loving relationships. Similarly, teaching the works of James Baldwin in a literature or history class without mentioning his prominence as a gay author omits a key aspect of his personal and public life. Yet very often instructors mention only one aspect of a text or an author without also mentioning the intersection of their queer identity. Including a queer author does not equal representation if that author's identification is never discussed.

Courses beyond the humanities have other blind spots. It is easy to imagine colleagues who, although they are well-intentioned individuals, might claim that queer studies are about social issues that are not suitable for discussion in their courses. In reality, social discourses around queer identities rely heavily on information from all fields of study represented in postsecondary environments. Dispelling myths and giving students the tools to connect their analytical skills in ways that help them understand contemporary discussions is key. Although anecdotal evidence suggests that lesson plans that include discussion of queer issues exist, there has not been a clear study of the full extent to which they are used. One area of outreach that corresponds to this model, though, is the LGBTA Center's Lavender Liaisons program, which allows instructors to invite student representatives to their courses to discuss queer issues and/or NCCU programming opportunities that support queer communities.

The second category for infusing LGBTQIA content in the curriculum is a model that encompasses courses that are specifically dedicated to some aspect of queer studies. Evidence for these courses is better attested in higher education because data on course titles and enrollments is more easily obtained. However, the most recent reporting suggests that such courses are extremely rare at HBCUs. Bowie State University made news in 2016 with a new course offering titled Queer Culture, for instance. That year, HBCU Digest reported that Bowie State was the "latest HBCU to offer an elective course in LGBT culture or theory, following Morehouse College's Black LGBT genealogy class launch in 2013, and the first academic offering at Spelman College in 2006" (Carter, 2016). Notable in that report was the fact that only three schools were easily identified as having such offerings in their undergraduate catalogs. Whereas many predominantly white institutions regularly offer courses and academic majors in queer studies, "currently, there are no HBCUs that offer LGBT studies as an academic major, minor, or certificate program" (Mobley & Johnson, 2015, p. 85). NCCU does not offer such a program, though there has been some progress on this front. In 2016, the university created a new minor in women's and gender studies, and that program has helped further the offering and advertisement of courses that deal with LGBTQIA content.

The third category is a lecture model that offers students academically focused LGBTQIA content outside a course in the form of a public lecture or event. These events offer the most potential for overlap in efforts between Student Affairs and Academic Affairs. On our campus, the LGBTA Center regularly offers events for students, and by collaborating with faculty they can invite speakers whose topics enhance discussion already occurring in courses or academic programs. Similarly, professors who have invited guest speakers to their courses can reach out to Student Affairs in order to publicize the talk to the wider campus community. NCCU had programming with positive queer representation even before more recent initiatives. A notable example is the NCCU Lyceum Series presentation by transgender actress and star of *Orange Is the New Black* Laverne Cox in September 2015 (Campus Echo Staff, 2015). However, this type of programming was not always seamlessly integrated between units at the university. In the case of Laverne Cox, the Lyceum committee organized the presentation, but the LGBTA Center, the student organization Creating Open Lives Organizing for Real Success (COLORS), and faculty teaching queer theory were made aware of the already-planned event only through flyers and other campus-wide advertisement. All constituent groups did come together in the days before the lecture, and it was a very successful event. Current practice has developed from lessons learned so that units consult each other during the planning stages of events to improve discussion, representation, and advertising. Such communication is essential if events are to have the kind of impact that contributes to an inclusive campus climate for queer students.

Ideally, any given campus will have offerings in all three categories: courses that include some discussion of queer studies, courses that are fully devoted to queer studies, and public lectures on queer studies topics. Several colleagues at NCCU have recently included queer topics in specific lesson plans or units of study in the following courses: ENG 3300 Applied Literary Criticism (Queer Theory), HEDU 3300 Human Sexuality (Sexual Identity), and PSY 2100 General Psychology (LGBTQIA Psychology). Other courses undoubtedly touch on relevant topics when they arise. For instance, courses in mass communication regularly discuss current events related to LGBTQIA topics. However, there is certainly more than can be done in courses across university curricula. In the example projects referenced below, we have focused primarily on enhancing our work in the categories of course development and public lectures.

COURSE DEVELOPMENT: INFUSING LGBTQIA CONTENT THROUGH WOMEN'S AND GENDER STUDIES AT NCCU

Overview of Course Development since 2016

Fall 2016 was the first semester that NCCU's women's and gender studies (WGST) minor was available for students, and the push to develop more courses that focused on women and gender allowed for the development, offering, and advertisement of courses that focused on LGBTQIA content. The first such course on record at NCCU was offered in Fall 2016. That course was taught in the Department of Language and Literature as ENG 3040 Special Topics: LGBT Literature. Women's and gender studies courses have also been offered on LGBTQIA topics: WGST 3610 Special Topics: QTPOC Research Experience and ENG 3400 Junior-Senior Seminar: Baldwin and Lorde.

These course offerings show that NCCU has momentum in LGBTQIA-related course development and that students remain eager to learn about these topics. Some of this success has been due to partnership with the WGST program and its push to advertise the courses through flyers and advising. Nevertheless, although each of these queer studies courses has drawn student enrollment, the fact that they are not offered with a consistent course code makes it difficult for students to obtain reliable course information and subsequently enroll. Because there is no official course in NCCU's undergraduate catalog for queer topics, each of these courses has had to run as special topics or seminars in a major or minor program. Offering courses regularly with permanent course catalog designations would allow NCCU to match the gains that have been made at Spelman, Morehouse, and Bowie State. Such course development remains a future priority for our campus.

Beyond course offerings and enrollment numbers as a means of evaluating how effectively we have incorporated queer studies courses in the WGST offerings, we have also asked queer-identified community members for their feedback. Two interesting comments have been made on our campus about these course offerings. The first suggests that simply offering queer content changes the climate, whether or not students, faculty, or staff are directly involved in the course. One queer-identified faculty member mentioned their feeling that having texts in the bookstore and courses in the catalog that represent queer communities has the potential to make queer students, faculty, and staff feel validated and conveys that their presence is welcomed and worthy of academic study. In other words, visibility matters. The second comment about course offerings reflects a different viewpoint about campus climate. At a meeting on campus, queer-identified students offered guidance on how student interest in queer studies courses could be increased. Several students expressed that course titles should not overtly advertise their queer content. Indeed, many students on campus expressed strong concerns that their transcripts would reflect that they had taken a queer studies course. It is a complicated dilemma. Because of this conversation, the 2016 English course "LGBT Literature" was renamed "Baldwin and Lorde" in 2018 in an effort to assess whether the title made the course more or less marketable to students. Advising about and advertising of the course on campus still made clear that the main content would engage with queer studies. Enrollment actually reduced by half following the title change, but that is possibly due to the positioning of the course as a junior-senior seminar rather than an open elective. Clearly, this topic merits further study and sensitivity to the needs of the student population.

The dilemma presented by the combination of students' interest in queer studies and their concerns of being outed or impacted by their transcripts has been demonstrated in other areas of student life. One such example is NCCU's annual Lavender Graduation ceremony. This ceremony, hosted by the LGBTA Resource Center, is held at the end of the academic year. NCCU's ceremony is not only a celebration of the accomplishments of queer-identifying students and their allies, it is also a celebration of their contribution to queer life at NCCU. Graduates' names are called, they are given certificates of recognition, and they are gifted lavender regalia cords. Other students receive special recognition for their volunteerism, support for various efforts related to the center, and other notable activities. The event is heavily photographed by participants and university officials, as is typical of many end-of-year celebrations. The lavender regalia cords are a huge incentive for participation. Often participants who are not able to attend stress the importance of still receiving their cord and certificate. Arrangements are made for the items to be picked up at a later date.

Nevertheless, each year there are some students who choose not to pick up their awards and some who have made it clear that they are not comfortable being recorded or photographed at the event because they cannot control who might see the photos. The students who have opted to leave their awards with staff mentioned a variety of reasons: not being completely out to family, complications with living situations if they were to be out, financial ramifications, fallout with support systems, and other obstacles that prevent them from displaying their awards proudly (J. Albright, personal communication, 2022). In many ways, being associated with the center or any efforts to support the queer community is perceived as potentially costly for individuals in the off-campus environment.

ENG 3040 Special Topics: LGBT Literature

It seems straightforward to identify the passage of North Carolina's HB2 law as a catalyst for curricular developments, and in many ways it was (Wymer, 2016). However, the factors behind the origin of the Fall 2016 undergraduate course in LGBT literature are more complex than that. Over the years, student interest in queer studies topics has grown. Our campus had also noticed a trend in student interest in courses that study all aspects of gender and sexuality. The timing seemed right, and both the director of the women's and gender studies program and the chair of the Department of Language and Literature offered their full support.

As we looked through course catalogs and talked with people who have a long institutional memory, we could not identify any other undergraduate course at NCCU that had ever taken queer studies as its primary topic. Admittedly, many courses have addressed topics in individual lesson plans or units of study, and there have been a number of actively engaged faculty members, Dr. David Jolly foremost among them for his vocal involvement in supporting queer students since 1999. Since this 2016 course was the first to include the term "LGBT" in the title, however, it was not clear what student interest or enrollment might look like. As it happened, enrollment was very strong, with eighteen students signing up. (Similar courses require a minimum of ten and a maximum of twenty-five enrolled students.) As expected, several English majors enrolled because the course designation could fill a major requirement. Nevertheless, half of the students were not English majors and had enrolled due to interest in the topic. No one in the class was asked whether they identified as queer, although some students chose to volunteer that information. What became apparent is that the class was a mix of some openly queer students and many who identified as allies rather than as queer. That diversity underscores that such a course should not be depicted as only for queer students. All students can benefit from learning about queer perspectives, and many heterosexual and cisgender students have a genuine interest in learning to be better allies.

Another key factor in making the course a success was the presence of guest lecturers. These included faculty from NCCU and other institutions who were willing to come speak with students about their areas of expertise as they related to queer studies. Bringing in these guests helped establish connections and buy-in from other faculty members, and students enjoyed the opportunity to learn from them. One of the guest lecturers visited the class specifically within her role as the director of NCCU's first-year writing program to talk about inclusive language and pronoun guidance. With her help, the students engaged in a project with immediate real-world advocacy value: they helped transform the handbook used in our composition courses to better support inclusive approaches to writing about sexual orientation and gender identity (Wymer & Fulford, 2019). Another guest lecturer, English professor Dr. Kristen Carella, gave two lectures on literature, one on queer readings of poetry and another on her work on transgender literature as viewed through the work of Laura Jane Grace (Carella & Wymer, 2019, 2020).

USING THE LECTURE MODEL TO BRIDGE CONNECTIONS BETWEEN ACADEMIC AFFAIRS AND STUDENT AFFAIRS

Lessons learned from the value of guest lecturers in ENG 3040 were the inspiration for the speaker series titled Speaking OUT at NCCU: A Celebration of 20 Years of LGBTQ Activism. In the summer of 2017, Drs. W. Russell Robinson and Kathryn Wymer collaborated to apply for and later received an Academic Innovation Grant to study the experiences of queer and trans people of color (QTPOC) on campus. We developed two components for Spring 2018: a course titled WGST 3610: QTPOC Research Experience and a speaker series. The research that we completed for WGST 3610 reminded us that 1998 marked twenty years of student activism on campus and we wanted to celebrate that. We also had strong pedagogical reasons for creating this lecture series. For our course, we wanted to be able to invite experts so that students could learn from and interview them. We realized that there was much to gain by opening these lectures to the wider campus community. This lecture model invited interested NCCU community members to spend an hour or so engaging with an LGBTQIA topic rather than having to invest the time for a full-semester course. Because we could and did share the invitation with the Durham community, we also had numerous participants from outside NCCU.

We also endeavored to represent a variety of experiences in our lecture series. The first speaker, Patrick Riley, reflected on his experience as an out African American gay man in the entertainment industry. His lecture was the largest event, attended by about 250 people in a filled theatre. For his lecture, we were able to partner with faculty in the Mass Communication Department. We also hosted Ariana Brown, a Black Mexican American poet, who performed her poems and spoke to a crowd of sixty about Blackness in a Mexican American context, spirituality, queerness, womanhood, and healing. Her performance was supported by the Office of Diversity and Inclusion as well as faculty in the Spanish program. The Empowering Equality on HBCU Campuses Campaign supported a screening of the documentary film *The New Black* during Pride Week and a grant for a reception that was attended by local activist Mandy Carter. A panel on gender identity that was inclusive of trans* and nonbinary identities was also held with Marie McGwier, Kristen Carella, Kyla Hartsfield, D'atra Jackson, and Harmony Phoenix.[1] Finally, filmmaker and NCCU alumnus Ashley Roque gave a talk about queer representations in Hollywood to a standing-room-only crowd in the LGBTA Center followed by a screening of one of her short films.

Financial support from the Office of the Provost was integral to this series. All of the events also received high levels of administrative support from staff in the Office of Diversity and Inclusion and the LGBTA Center, most especially Emily Guzman and Jennifer Williams. Without their help in organizing, providing catering, and advertising, the series would not have been the success it was. It therefore represented to us the pervasive pathway ideal of working from a shared vision. For one of the events (screening of *The New Black*), Student Affairs asked for faculty help in writing the grant, and for another (the Ariana Brown poetry performance), they specifically requested the speaker because of student input they had received from the NCCU Águilas Afro-Latino student group.

Just as offering courses with LGBTQIA content raised visibility on campus, so did these speaker events. Two positive impacts stand out. First was the impact in the larger Durham community. Having outside speakers allowed us to advertise to the Durham community and build stronger connections to the LGBTQ Center of Durham and to local activists. The second impact was that the influence of these lectures extended beyond the number of attendees. Several queer-identified students reported that they were really pleased to see flyers and felt momentum on campus. Many of those students, however, did not attend any of the events. Just as some students feel hesitant about walking into an LGBT center or signing up for a queer studies course, they may feel hesitant about attending an event about an LGBTQIA topic. Nevertheless, the presence of such events on campus makes a broader impact. A former student has indicated that these types of events not only raise awareness but also further shift the culture of the campus climate around queerness (Albright, personal communication, 2022). Such events work to create community. Faculty and staff may attend an event out of personal curiosity and in turn have a long-standing question about queer culture and identity addressed.

LGBTQIA HBCU ALUMNI REPRESENTATION MATTERS

All of the events in the series were successful and much more could be said about each one. The final one in the series stands out because it gave space to a queer alumnus to reconnect with NCCU. After completing her BA in English at NCCU, Ashley Roque pursued her master of fine arts in motion pictures and television from the Academy of Art University and began working as a filmmaker in California. Drawing on her knowledge of film and television history, she spoke to the audience about how the media portrays queer characters. She then screened her own short fictional film that focused on a lesbian relationship and spoke about her upcoming project, a documentary about queer support in religious communities.

Attendees learned much from the talk, but organizers also learned from Ashley Roque's engagement with the event. The talk took place in the LGBTA Center, which did not exist during her time at NCCU. Although she remains active in the alumni association, she had not been aware that the center existed. It was a timely reminder that even our active and engaged alumni may not be aware of what we are doing on campus if we do not reach out to them directly.

By the time of this final event, the organizers had also learned much about what works and what does not in terms of scheduling and advertising. Inviting faculty and staff to an event that takes place during business hours results in higher attendance and the chance that they will bring students with them. We had the most success with engaging NCCU's broader community beyond the campus gates with evening and weekend programming. We worked to include a variety of times so that we could reach more people. Additionally, advertising through campus channels (such as emails or flyers) was valuable for reaching faculty and staff. Students and community members responded better to social media, with Instagram reaching a younger demographic and Facebook reaching an older demographic. Social media had a powerful influence, and some community members expressed a strong desire for us to make more social media posts to inform alumni and the Durham community about what we were doing on campus. Indeed, our speaker expressed the same desire to know more about what was occurring at NCCU to support queer students, faculty, and staff, and she helped promote her own event on her social media accounts.

CONCLUDING THOUGHTS: GUIDING PRINCIPLES FOR MAKING INCLUSIVE ACADEMIC HBCU SPACES

The work we have done at our institution to promote queer-inclusive academic spaces has offered an opportunity for reflection on what we have done well and what more we could do in the future. Drawing on the seven principles for good practice in undergraduate education put forth by Chickering and Gamson (1991) as inspiration, here are five guiding principles for creating inclusive academic spaces for queer students at HBCUs:

1. *Be proactive in creating inclusive academic spaces.*

    Too often otherwise well-intentioned individuals fail to take an active role in supporting queer students. Faculty and staff who do not identify as queer may feel that it is not their role and may wait for queer-identified individuals to step forward. Meanwhile, queer-identified individuals may not necessarily feel empowered to start initiatives without clear signals of support from colleagues and administrators. There is no value in waiting for the "right person" to come along and start the work. All HBCU stakeholders must engage in this work. Many students who might identify as queer are not out at HBCUs, and thus it is important for allies to learn as much as they can about how to support queer students and to deliberately and intentionally begin engaging them (Mobley & Hall, 2020). It is equally important to support queer-identified colleagues in visible and substantial ways.

2. *Engage in meaningful conversations with stakeholders in units across campus.*

    At NCCU, we found that forming partnerships with units across campus to be transformative. The LGBTA Center was undoubtedly a valuable source of information and resources. The women's and gender studies program offered much assistance as well. Many HBCU contexts do not have such centers or programs, but that does not need to be an obstacle to this work. We found that partnerships with other units on campus were also essential. In order to administer our courses and lectures, we had to have the support of the provost and the dean of the College of Arts and Sciences and of the constituent departments. We also had to collaborate with stakeholders from facilities management, catering, and even the copy center. Bringing all of these stakeholders on board with our initiatives made a huge difference with the work we were doing on campus.

3. *Engage in meaningful conversations with stakeholders in the community and with alumni.*

   A community member who had been telling a friend about our initiatives at NCCU later mentioned the friend's admiration and surprise: "They're doing what?" Although our HBCU has made a recent push to include queer students, our reputation in the community and among alumni has not yet reflected the campus mindset. Over the past couple of years, it has been inspirational to see queer alumni return to campus and become emotional about the gains made here. Partnerships in the Durham community and with alumni provide the kinds of support that administrators seek to cultivate.

4. *Create space for academic inquiry beyond the classroom setting.*

   As important as it is to examine issues deeply in a multi-week course, one-time lectures in which students, faculty, and staff can learn enough to get them thinking about issues facing queer communities also offer several benefits. When these lectures are widely publicized, their visibility helps cultivate an inclusive environment. The emphasis on academic inquiry in these lectures is important. The Student Affairs Division at NCCU has hosted many queer-positive events that focus on entertainment, socialization, and emotional support. Examples include a homecoming drag show, a yearly queer prom, and monthly discussion groups for queer students. These events have immense value. However, adding campus-wide opportunities for education about queer history, sexual health, media representation, and other topics can help all HBCU students recognize that these are valid areas of engagement and gives all members of the campus the opportunity to understand more about queer identity as it is currently represented in the work of different academic disciplines.

5. *Listen to students as guides for best practices.*

   Offering courses and lectures is a valuable practice only if students show up to learn. Just because your campus has a class on the books, it does not mean students will register for it. Understanding what students want and need is essential. For example, students on our campus often needed to focus on taking courses that fulfilled a requirement toward a major or minor. If a student does have elective hours, they may often choose courses that seem likely to focus on a skill required for the workplace. Intentionally engaging students about the reasons why they should choose certain coursework is essential in developing curricular offerings. Similarly, students get excited about lectures that relate directly to their personal interests. Asking students to help in the planning stages improves buy-in for any class or event.

Extending inclusivity initiatives to support queer students, faculty, and staff upholds North Carolina Central University's commitment to diversity, a deeply held value at every HBCU. Making sure that those initiatives find representation in the classroom is key. Administrators, faculty, staff, and students must work together to ensure that queer community members feel welcomed, validated, and supported.

NOTE

1. Marie McGwier is known for their activism with Gender Is Over!, for which they were featured on the cover of *Time* magazine in 2017. Kristen Carella is a transgender professor of literature. Kyla Hartsfield, D'atra Jackson, and Harmony Phoenix are community activists in North Carolina who advocate on behalf of people who identify as trans* and nonbinary.

REFERENCES

Barker, M. V. (2018, October 24). NCCU's LGBT-friendly housing Kaleidoscope enters its second year. *Campus Echo.* http://campusecho.com/nccus-lgbt-friendly-housing-kaleidoscope-enters-its-second-year/

Campus Echo Staff. (2015, October 5). LGBT activist Laverne Cox speaks to overflow audience about her life. *Campus Echo.* http://campusecho.com/laverne-cox/

Carella, K., & Wymer, K. (2019). "You want me to surrender my identity?" Laura Jane Grace, transition, and selling out. *Punk & Post-Punk, 8*(2). https://doi.org/10.1386/punk.8.2.193_1

———. (2020). "Tonight we're gonna give it 35%": Expressions of transgender identity in the early work of Laura Jane Grace. *The Journal of Gender Studies, 29*(3), 257–268. https://doi.org/10.1080/09589236.2019.1604325

Carter, Sr., J. L. (2016, March 2). *Bowie State to offer queer studies course.* HBCU Digest. https://hbcudigest.com/bowie-state-to-offer-queer-studies-course/

Cheng, V. (2000, October 30). NCCU brings gay issues out of the closet. *The News and Observer,* B5.

Chickering, A. W., & Gamson, Z. F. (1991). Appendix A: Seven principles for good practice in undergraduate education. *New Directions for Teaching and Learning, 1991*(47), 63–69. https://doi-org./10.1002/tl.37219914708

Consortium of Higher Education LGBT Resource Professionals. (2017). 2017 *Summer Institute Program & Logistics.* http://www.lgbtcampus.org/index.php?option=com_content&view=article&id=129:2017-summer-institute-program---logistics&catid=22:consortium-news&Itemid=144

Dooley, J., & LePeau, L. (2016). Striving for an inclusive and nurturing campus: Cultivating the intersections. In B. Barnett & P. Felten (Eds.), *Intersectionality in action: A guide for faculty and campus leaders for creating inclusive classrooms and institutions* (pp. 63–76). Stylus.

Holpuch, A. (2016, March 28). Lawsuit challenges constitutionality of North Carolina LGBT discrimination law. *The Guardian.* https://www.theguardian.com/us-news/2016/mar/28/north-carolina-lgbt-discriminiation-law-lawsuit-constitutionality

HRC Staff. (2013, May 28). *North Carolina Central University opens LGBT student resource center.* https://www.hrc.org/blog/north-carolina-central-university-opens-lgbt-student-resource-center

Johnson, J. T. (2021). The category is . . . transformational inclusion: A conceptual framework for (re) imagining the inclusion of Black queer and trans* students attending HBCUs. In G. B. Crosby, K. A. White, M. A. Chanay, & A. A. Hilton (Eds.), *Reimagining historically Black colleges and universities.* Emerald Publishing Limited.

LePeau, L. (2015). A grounded theory of academic affairs and student affairs partnerships for diversity and inclusion aims. *Review of Higher Education.* 39(1), 97–122.

Mobley, S. D., Jr., & Hall, L. (2020). (Re)Defining queer and trans* student retention and success at historically Black colleges and universities. *Journal of College Student Retention: Research, Theory & Practice,* 21(4), 497–519.

Mobley, S. D., Jr., & Johnson, J. M. (2015). The role of HBCUs in addressing the unique needs of LGBT students. In R. Palmer, R. Shorette, and M. Gasman (Eds.), *Exploring diversity at historically Black colleges and universities: Implications for policy and practice* (pp. 79–90). Jossey-Bass.

NCCU Brothers and Sisters. (1998, November 17). Box 152, Mandy Carter Papers. David M. Rubenstein Rare Book & Manuscript Library, Duke University, Durham, North Carolina.

Sanlo, R. (2000). Lavender graduation: Acknowledging the lives and achievements of lesbian, gay, bisexual, and transgender college students. *Journal of College Student Development,* 41(6), 643.

Spellings, M. (2016, May 9). Letter to Vanita Gupta, Principal Deputy Assistant Attorney General. https://static.politico.com/d5/8a/ff5fad1d4df5b5e561366b9164a3/unc-system-responds-to-department-of-justice-on-hb2.pdf

Williams, S. (2018, June 21). It's time for HBCUs to address homophobia and transphobia on their campuses. *The Nation.* https://www.thenation.com/article/time-hbcus-address-homophobia-transphobia-campuses/

Wymer, K. (2016, June 3). It's time to speak up for your gay and transgender students. *The Chronicle of Higher Education.* https://www.chronicle.com/article/It-s-Time-to-Speak-Up-for/236710

Wymer, K., & Fulford, C. (2019). Students as co-producers of queer pedagogy. *Journal of Effective Teaching in Higher Education,* 2(1), 45–59. https://doi.org/10.36021/jethe.v2i1.29

Yang, J. (2016, March 24). *How N.C. signed a bill dubbed most anti-LGBT law in the U.S.* PBS News Hour. Retrieved September 11, 2017, from www.pbs.org/newshour/bb/how-north-carolina-signed-a-bill-dubbed-the-most-anti-lgbt-law-in-the-u-s/

Young, S. L., & McKibban, A. R. (2014). Creating safe places: a collaborative autoethnography on LGBT social activism. *Sexuality and Culture,* 18(2), 361–384. https://doi.org/10.1007/s12119-013-9202-5

9 · THE LAVENDER FUND, THE FIRST OFFICIALLY RECOGNIZED UNIVERSITY-WIDE LGBT FUNDRAISER IN HBCU HISTORY

How It Came to Be and How It Continues

CHRISTOPHER N. CROSS AND DIANA LU

I am Christopher N. Cross, PhD, Howard University's first openly gay graduate student trustee. As a trustee, I led an LGBTQ+ initiative to foster a campus culture invested in breaking down barriers, false narratives, and phobias. I founded The Lavender Fund, the Homecoming LGBTA Renaissance Reception, and the Howard University International Lesbian Gay Bisexual Transgender Ally Alumni Association. I believe that these outcomes are all reproducible across HBCUs. The Lavender Fund is the first top-down LGBTQ+ initiative at Howard, and it continues to be championed by the current university administration. The fund is embedded in Howard University's core development infrastructure.

In 2015, when the first LGBTA Renaissance Reception was held during Howard University's Homecoming, it raised nearly $8,000 for the Lavender Fund. President Wayne A. I. Frederick and his wife, Mrs. Simone Frederick, matched that amount. Since then, the Renaissance Reception has become an annual event. The Lavender Fund has raised nearly $100,000 and there has been a steady stream of donations from alumni, faculty, and university administrators. The fund has awarded over 30 scholarships for queer students. Many high-profile alumni have worked with the fund beyond donating money, including hosting and cohosting the Renaissance Reception and other events, mentoring students, and promoting the fund through their personal and professional networks. Importantly, this enthusiastic alumni involvement not only benefits Howard's queer and trans* students, staff, and faculty by fostering a campus culture of inclusion, it has also benefited Howard University through increased national visibility and alumni support. This work was motivated by my personal experiences of disenfranchisement as a young person and my experiences of empowerment through more positive role models and communities. It is my hope that more Black gay people may experience the latter, particularly in their formative years.

HISTORICAL BACKGROUND

Historically Black colleges and universities were established over 150 years ago by white philanthropists, the federal government, and various factions of the Black church (Anderson, 1988). These institutions were founded in a white supremacist context in which Black people were perceived as a monolith and were seen as subservient, inferior, and unworthy of education or personal identity (Brazzell, 1992). Despite these challenges, HBCUs have more than met their educational charge of educating and uplifting Black communities—albeit under the pressure of having to constantly defend their historical and contemporary contributions (Mobley, 2017; Patton, 2016). However, as Williams et al. (2019) note, "broader narratives about HBCUs—not unlike the narratives attached to Black Americans in general—too often depict them from a deficit perspective" (p. 558). HBCUs are complex, as are their histories. These institutions have been controversial since they were established. They were "shaped in the womb of a country that has and continues to struggle with how and if it values and invests in the education of Black Americans" (Commodore, 2018, p. 400).

Due to conservatism and religious affiliation, HBCUs have often sought to produce a specific brand of Blackness to fit into a particular socially acceptable archetype (Commodore, 2019; Njoku et al., 2017). This idea is not uncommon or specific to HBCUs, but it is necessary to acknowledge this reality. These contextual layers have contributed to a social hierarchy that is enabled by various HBCU stakeholders that relegate queer and trans* HBCU students to the margins (Mobley & Hall, 2020). Because of such practices, queer or queer-perceived HBCU communities have been deprived of recognition, praise, and protection (Patton et al., 2020).

(RE)SITUATING HOWARD UNIVERSITY

Howard University, founded in 1867, is often called The Mecca of Black Intelligentsia. It is considered to be one of the most well known and most prestigious HBCUs. During its inception, Howard was primarily funded by the Freedman's Bureau and by private endowments (Logan, 1969). Although Howard University has deep roots in the Civil Rights Movement, other HBCUs have led the way in terms of queer and trans* rights. For example, Bowie State University in Maryland was the first HBCU to open a queer and trans* resource center in 2012 (Mobley & Hall, 2020). Howard University's impact on and connection to Black communities and its institutional history likely plays an important role in maintaining a heteronormative status quo on its campus.

Because of Howard's unique founding, it is different from many HBCUs in that it has dual status as a federally chartered but private HBCU. Much of its funding comes from the federal government. Thus, the university is often perceived as an extension of a federal agency (Logan, 1969). In fact, the United States secretary of education has had a seat on the Board of Trustees as patron ex officio. Because of its relationship to the federal government, Howard often has to comply with federal law in a much more visible way than other HBCUs and private universities that do not receive federal funds. On June 26, 2015, less than a month before I received the news that I was elected as a trustee, the Supreme Court ruled in favor of legalizing same-sex marriage across the nation in *Obergefell v. Hodges*. The law was now irrefutably in favor of my proposed initiatives for queer and trans* HBCU stakeholders. In addition to my persistence, I believe this timing was crucial for my success. Howard University's proximity to Capitol Hill and the strong role governmental influence plays on campus greatly helped my initiatives make sense for the university administration, even though some members may have been uncomfortable with my ideas.

THE FOUNDER'S NARRATIVE

Personal growth, particularly growth related to an identity as intimately connected to others as sexuality, cannot be achieved in isolation. Discovering one's sexuality happens in communion with others and requires social training and validation. That is an important lesson I learned from my journey of becoming, and it is why I feel so strongly that HBCUs need to provide that space. I had already accepted myself by the time I got to Howard, but not everyone has a supportive household, network, or environment in their formative years. More broadly, there are precious few spaces in which Black gay people can safely take their journeys.

Academic administrators need to hear stories like mine in order to understand the importance of developing a welcoming campus culture for all. My road to self-acceptance and confidence exemplifies how isolating and difficult it is at times and how fantastic and freeing it is at others. As the youngest of nine children in a religious family in small-town Ohio, I was not able to express myself as a full person because of homophobia and racial prejudice. I also did not feel safe about expressing my feelings to the people I was attracted to. I spent much of my youth trying to "pray the gay away" and hide it from myself and others. I siloed myself in my studies so that I could control the things I was able to control.

I felt more like a full person when I moved to Atlanta before college, where I was surrounded by a Black community. I began the journey of stepping into my LGBT self when I reconnected with a dear childhood friend. He came from a household that centered Blackness in a deliberate way and he was comfortable with himself. His family always had his back, and knowing that gave him more confidence to be who he was. By the time we found each other again in Atlanta, his confidence about expressing his authentic self had grown by leaps and bounds. The gap between where he was and where I was seemed as wide as the Grand Canyon. With him, my appreciation for being gay and all the beauty that comes with that identity grew. I came into a new sense of confidence I never knew existed on the other side of trauma. This friendship was one of the defining relationships that made me say "this is something I need to do for my campus" once I became a trustee at Howard.

My time in college was another transformative experience. I moved to midtown Atlanta and found a new social group of Black gay guys. Finding them enabled me to have the college experience I had always dreamed of. During this period, I crafted a mental narrative that allowed me to say to myself, "I'll just explore this temporarily but I'm not really gay." I went through these mental acrobatics to negotiate the cognitive dissonance between who I was and the dominant narrative I still internalized about the "othered" identity of being gay. Then I had a pivotal relationship that made me face myself. I fell in love with a man so deeply that my internal dams broke. A year later, I told my mother I was gay and she broke down crying. It was one of the toughest conversations I have ever had, but looking back, it gave me strength to have more tough conversations in both my personal and professional lives, including as a graduate student trustee at Howard.

It took a lot of digging and replanting over years for me to be able to be me. You need a safe social space in which to do this work. I did not have this space in my family or on my undergraduate campus, and it was hard to create my own community to get there. I made a promise to myself that I would never again live in a place where I could not be openly gay, Black, and proud. There are precious few places anywhere in the world where I can celebrate being Black and gay and feel comfortable. HBCUs providing that space would make a huge impact.

I wanted my graduate school experience to be authentic, and when I got to Howard, I was very intentional about not stifling myself again and was openly gay on campus from the beginning. I thought that being confident and out was the end of my journey and that I would be in an environment at Howard that was totally welcoming and supportive. However, that was not the case. People gave me a lot of verbal affirmation, but their actions were different. Experiencing all this was a major motivation for creating a scholarship for my community. As previously mentioned, the *Obergefell v. Hodges* Supreme Court decision came down a few weeks before I was named a graduate student trustee. I went to the

White House that night to commemorate it. That same night I got the news that I would be joining the Board of Trustees, and I resolved to do my best to help my communities.

BECOMING A TRUSTEE: THE LAVENDER FUND AND THE RENAISSANCE RECEPTION

From a young age, when I participated in sports I was the second in command but not the captain. I always had this narrative in my head that although I was an engineer and an athlete, I was not supposed to be the person in the center of the room making things happen. This was another internalized barrier: I had been socialized to see myself as a supporting character, the gay sidekick in someone else's story. This narrative did not align with my interests or my skills, and as I came into myself, I accrued leadership experience and honed my interpersonal and communication skills. I gradually began to see myself as a leader and a policymaker when I found the courage to stand first-in-command and run for graduate student trustee.

At Howard, I got involved with student government activities and became friends with the then-president of Howard's Graduate Student Council. I loved her confidence and positive energy. She became one of the few graduate students in Howard's history who was elected to the position of graduate trustee. The graduate trustee is a prestigious role that students from any of the graduate and professional schools can run for. Howard has several schools and colleges: the Graduate School, School of Business, Communications, Divinity, Education, Social Work, College of Engineering and Architecture, College of Nursing and Allied Health Science, College of Medicine, College of Dentistry, College of Pharmacy, and the School of Law. The graduate student trustee has traditionally been a law student, maybe because such students tend to have political ambitions and may want to leverage the benefits of the role. Each school at Howard has its own graduate student council that sends representatives to the university-wide Graduate Student Alliance (GSA), where preliminary voting and politicking occurs. In 2014, I was selected as the representative from the Graduate School's student council to the GSA.

When my friend broke down the barrier for a graduate student to become a graduate trustee, she encouraged me to run for graduate trustee the next term. It was great timing for me because I was seeking new experiences outside of science policy. Through conversations with my childhood friend, I found a think tank called the Potomac Institute for Policy Studies. I applied to be a neuroscience fellow at the Center for Revolutionary Scientific Thought (CReST), and I interned there for nearly a year. This experience opened my eyes to why policy is important.

All of this was in the context of working with stakeholders on Capitol Hill to get legislation across based on new neuroscience technology, which was what I was privy to as a CReST Fellow. Through this experience I met other interns, including one woman who was a postdoc and a Congressional Science Fellow. She suggested I take up her position after she stepped down, and she made that happen with an email. I interviewed with the Congresswoman's chief of staff and senior legislative assistant and they offered me the position. Because of these fellowships, I was working on Capitol Hill before I got my PhD. To be that junior and be in such a prestigious position as Congressional Science Fellow was rare, especially as a Black person, let alone a Black and gay person. The people I worked with, some of whom are still there, still remember me. It was a phenomenal experience. My boss, Congresswoman Frederica Wilson, was on the House Committee for Science, Space, and Technology. I was her committee liaison. That opened my eyes to how policy is made, how legislation is done, and who the key stakeholders are that can make things happen. This experience gave me confidence in my people management skills within the context of policy. I also learned the importance of leadership behind the curtain and leadership in front of it and when to use each type to advance your goals.

That experience showed me the power of top-down initiatives and gave me the confidence to run for trustee at Howard. During my run for graduate trustee, the initialism in my election campaign slogan, Cross Leading by D.E.S.I.G.N., stood for Discover, Endeavor, Share, Institute, Grow, Next (see fig. 9.1).

My platform issues included increasing student comradery, improving administrative support, creating incubator spaces for graduate students, and enlisting better alumni support. I used my student loan refund, about $4,000, to pay for my election campaign. Dr. Terrence Tarver was my friend and brilliant campaign manager. He was instrumental in my winning the election. Even to this day, people tell me they remember my campaign posters. It turned out to be a very competitive election, with 40 percent voter turnout university-wide. On July 17, 2015, I received notice from Howard University's Board of Trustees that I had been vetted and confirmed as the 2015–2016 graduate student trustee.

Now that I was officially in a position to lead, I felt that I could launch a historic effort to address homophobia at what I believed to be the most prestigious HBCU in the country. I had learned from the previous trustee, that we only have one year in the position, so I would need to hit the ground running. With my time limited, I felt I had to get this right, and there were a lot of political games to be played to finesse that. I was now representing the Board of Trustees. I was also the first openly gay man in this role, and I wanted to push for initiatives that would impact Howard's queer and trans* stakeholders. In this environment, I knew I had to *represent*. I was hyperaware of how I needed to dress, speak, and present myself in that boardroom at all times.

I put a lot on my shoulders, and I felt like I had to be perfect. That is how I think a lot of people saw me, as the perfect "power gay." I did not mind that, but it was still a lot of pressure. In my personal life, it was also really hard to be dis-

FIGURE 9.1. Christopher Cross's graduate trustee election campaign poster.

creet about my interactions with people but also still be me. I felt that a lot of things became embargoed and I experienced a lot of imposter syndrome. Truth be told, I was so driven that I could not allow myself to be as terrified as I really was. I discussed it with many friends and colleagues who shared my excitement and fears. Ultimately, I decided "f-ck that, I only have a year to make this happen," and I went all in. In the end, it really was all worth it.

I first asked myself and others what I could realistically accomplish in one year. What vehicle could I use to create lasting change and gain visibility for my Black queer community? What could I do that would generate a perpetual return on investment for my university? Considering my experience of having my PhD funding suddenly disappear, the idea for a fundraiser for queer students began to brew. I decided that creating a scholarship and a fundraising reception were the best ways I could make a lasting contribution, given the time and resources I had.

Many similar projects had been started and had failed, so I was intentional about creating a lasting infrastructure from the inception of the fund. I had a few conference calls with former student trustees. One created a successful summer abroad program. The other was credited as the first openly queer trustee. During her term as an undergraduate trustee, she created *The Lavender Report*, a document that captured the state of queer and trans* life at Howard up to that point. She discussed with me the history of Howard's lesbian, gay, bisexual, and trans* student organization (now known as CASCADE), distinguished LGBT alumni, and other support vehicles that helped improve life for queer students. I named the fund in honor of this landmark report.

At first, I received the normal degree of administrative pushback that comes with any initiative from an ambitious new student trustee trying to institute change without knowing the landscape. In response, I developed a strategic plan based on all that I had learned about politics on Capitol Hill. I learned that the university president and the members of his cabinet are the managers of the university and that their support would be critical. Furthermore, I knew that I would increase my odds of success if I aligned the fundraiser with Howard's mission and traditions.

My strategy implemented a top-down approach with three key pillars: leadership, mission, and tradition. To be completely top down, the initiative needs to be started by the chair of the Board of Trustees, the most powerful member of the board. Typically, the board then directs the president and their cabinet. However, I leveraged my position as a trustee to have meetings with President Frederick and his cabinet to align my mission with theirs and get their help with implementing my initiative.

The other benefit of being a trustee was being on committees, which are much smaller groups where you can network and ask questions more freely. I asked to be on the Research and Science Committee, which has since been disbanded. I had looked into what committees were available and wanted to be on this one because it was aligned with my expertise and I could make valuable contributions to it.

My participation on the committee enabled me to build rapport with the provost and the chair of the board and with specific cabinet members. In particular, I became acquainted with an external affairs cabinet member who also had government experience. Next, I got to know Laura Jack, the director of development at the time. I knew she would be essential to making the Lavender Fund and a fundraising reception a reality. I also knew that I needed buy-in from the Division of University Advancement and the Division of Student Affairs and general support from the Board of Trustees.

Finally, I did a lot of student engagement. I convened the presidential chats that Kelechi had started, in which leaders from the student councils met with the president to discuss general student issues throughout the professional schools. For these meetings, I created special student trustee reports for the president that captured student issues in the different schools. In particular, my work improved constituent communication with the administration during the #TakeBackHU protests. After these events, President Frederick created a university ombuds position to help address issues central to my work.

Although none of these activities directly related to the Lavender Fund and the Renaissance Reception, they helped establish my relationship with the president and initiated intraleadership communication and trust with many different groups on campus. Meeting with the student boards and their presidents and figuring out what their issues were, establishing the trust of the president, and mediating difficult conversations between these entities were key. Fortunately, these endeavors were second nature to me due to my lived experiences. I had already served as a bridge across different groups, and that allowed me to be a representative of the students and gain the leadership's trust as well. During my time on Capitol Hill, resolutions and campaigns can be all fanfare and not mean a thing, *but* they can also be used to start initiatives and conversations with people you need to work with to create change. I knew this and worked feverishly to get my initiative enacted by the president and the Board of Trustees. Without that endorsement, I would not have been able to engage Howard's alumni to create an endowed grant that is embedded in the university's development infrastructure.

Eventually, I met with President Frederick to discuss my idea of creating the Lavender Fund, a scholarship for Howard LGBTA students, and the Renaissance Reception—an annual fundraising event to be held during homecoming to celebrate Howard's queer and trans* students and alumni. I mentioned the long history of abuse, discrimination, and hurt that queer students had endured over the university's 150-year history and how the passage of same-sex marriage rights made us well positioned to be the first HBCU to lead the change in this arena. He was very supportive. President Frederick greenlit my next steps of connecting with a key member of his cabinet, the vice president of development and alumni relations. To determine feasibility and needs for implementation, I had several meetings with the vice president and her staff, which included the director of advancement services, the special assistant to the vice president, the senior director of annual giving, the director of administration, and the director of special events. The input I gained from these people enabled me to generate an official university letter that was published on August 29, 2015.

After the letter was published, the next step was to create a university-endowed account for the contributions to the fund. Creating such an account usually required a minimum deposit of $5,000. However, I asked the president for help. He created a holding account for us until we had raised enough to create the endowed account. After the fund was established, I could start the grassroots fundraising campaign. During this time, I enlisted key alumni and friends to help coordinate the fundraiser and give donations. The most effective method was to mimic a Capitol Hill fundraiser where you offer name recognition to hosts and cohosts of the event with a set donation. For hosts, the donation was $500+ or services provided (e.g. promotion, entertainment, or emceeing) and for cohosts it was $250. I personally paid for all the food and decorations and we raised the baseline money for the fund account.

President Frederick later complimented my use of the Capitol Hill strategy. He really appreciated the process I went through to create the fund: the official announcement letter, the account, the meetings with his cabinet, doing the event, hosting, and then a follow-up meeting with the development office to give the recap reports in person. I also built rapport with the board and the secretary to the board of trustees.

I was able to accomplish all of this by understanding the assignment, so to speak. I knew that I needed to impress the board as a whole, do my research, be present and on time, and be insightful. A times it was difficult because I was still a student and I also had to be a representative for my peers who could also be an advocate. Trustee board members were also really busy and our meetings were only thirty minutes to an hour, so time was limited for building rapport. I had to take advantage of every opportunity. When we had board meetings, I would do the prep work, then follow up with people who had interesting ideas with emails or set up times to talk with them offline. Through my persistent dedication, I was able to engage with top leadership on their levels in a way that few students were able to.

I proceeded with the fundraiser event in the same way that I came out to my mom: unabashedly. I wanted it to be a homecoming event because for me this initiative was about celebration. I have always been intentional about celebrating Black queer and trans folks. This was a personal need that had gone unmet in my romantic relationships, so I wanted to celebrate my community. I reflected on my feelings from late June, when I had stood with my best friends seeing the White House lit up in a rainbow in acknowledgment of the Obergefell decision. I grieved the deep loss of all the celebration I could have had if the culture and the law been different when I was younger. I wanted to make the future better for all who had to love furtively and experience heartbreak alone.

I named the event the LGBTA Renaissance Reception to channel the beauty and excitement of the Harlem Renaissance. This was an era when Black music, art, and poetry were booming and Black people were ascending to high social economic spaces they had never been in before. It is lauded as an amazing period for Black Americans. Many queer and trans* artists, musicians, poets, and other creators were involved in the Harlem Renaissance (Knadler, 2002). The most challenging aspect of my initiative was finding people to work with on the event committee. Many promised a lot but failed to deliver. One person on the committee even held a competing event at the same time. However, I had a very clear vision about what I wanted and how I wanted it done, so I ended up doing a lot of things for the first reception myself. It was a huge learning experience for me, and it was ultimately successful.

In total we raised just under $8,000 with President Frederick and Mrs. Simone Frederick's monetary match. Since the first event in 2015, the Renaissance Reception has continued each year and has become an annual event during Howard's Homecoming festivities. To date, it has raised ~$100,000 and has awarded 33 scholarships to queer students. There has since been a steady stream of donations from alumni, faculty, and university staff administrators.

I cannot emphasize enough how critical President Frederick's support was to the beginning and continuation of the fund. He gave reasonable, clear metrics that we met. He did not initially promise any matching and I did not ask for it either; he just started doing it. He remains very supportive and shows up and is present at these events each year. He has noted that his wife is a major supporter, and both have matched the funds raised every year. This is a lesson in how change needs to happen. The president decides what policies get implemented and how and if students thrive or get sidelined and erased. Policies start at the top, which means that it is important to hire leaders who are progressive and supportive of marginalized communities.

CONTINUING OUTCOMES

In 2017, the Lavender Fund initiative was moved from the Office of Development and Alumni Affairs to the Office of Student Life and Activities. It is operated under the Howard University LGBTQ+ Advisory Council. This council was created to increase the visibility of queer students, staff, and faculty. At the sixth Annual Renaissance Reception in 2020, Howard University president Wayne A. I. Frederick remarked, We are recognizing those who have helped transform Howard into a home. . . . We have to turn the spotlight back on ourselves to see what we can do to make our institution more welcoming and inclusive." As I was ending my term as trustee, I and nine Howard alumni paid dues to formalize the Howard University LGBT Alumni Association, the nation's first LGBT alumni organization at an HBCU. This also has continued to grow and has recently undergone new leadership with increased membership.

To focus and increase alumni donation and engagement with the Lavender Fund initiative, we worked with the Office of Development and Alumni Relations to initiate the Howard University International Lesbian, Gay, Bisexual,

Transgender, Ally, and Alumni Association. The original bylaws for the club were approved in 2017 and were updated in 2022 with an official rename as the Howard University Rainbow Alumni Association (HURAA).

HURAA is not geographically bound and serves as an all-encompassing constituent group. This was done instead of an affinity group or local/satellite alumni club to increase inclusion, engagement, and visibility. This organization was established with the intention of creating a collective connection in which all LGBTQ+ and allied alumni can participate. The National Howard University Alumni Association regulates its organizational structure and is responsible for providing an official email account, account information, social media accounts, membership plans, programming/activities and fundraising. Mandated positions include president, vice president, treasurer, recording secretary, and historian. The term limits were set for two years, excluding the historian, whose term is not limited in order to maintain continuity.

GUIDE FOR ADMINISTRATORS

A top-down approach was implemented to break ground on this particular LGBT HBCU initiative. The following is a suggested stepwise guide informed by Howard's initiative that may be transferable to other HBCUs.

Beginning Steps

- Locate the university's organizational chart and become familiar with the hierarchy and associated positions of influence.
- Identify person(s) in leadership at the highest level of the institution who will support the initiative and dedicate time and resources to launch it.
- Generate a document that describes the aim(s) of the initiative, including its scope and its supporters in leadership positions.
- Leverage both the document and supportive leadership to collaborate with key institutional staff responsible for the Office of Development and Alumni Affairs (or its equivalent).
- Understand how success is being measured (e.g., fundraising and attendance goals).

Engaging HBCU Stakeholders

- Develop a fundraising and engagement strategy to achieve success with input and approval from appropriate university staff. For Howard, the key positions were:
  - Development
  - Alumni Affairs
  - Marketing and Branding

- Advancement Services
  - University Communications
  - University Events and Protocol
- Acquire knowledge of and adhere to the institutional rules regarding
  - Marketing
  - Advertising
  - Creating events
  - Establishing financial accounts
  - Establishing alumni chapters or clubs
- Create a budget for the event
- Create an agenda/program for the event
  - Invite key university administrators and offer them an opportunity to speak at the event. We invited
    - the university president
    - the dean of chapel
    - a representative from the Office of Student Life and Activities
    - members of the Alumni Association
    - LGBT alumni
    - members of local media
- After the event, develop a report to detail metrics and outcomes:
  - Names of VIP guest(s) and individual and organization attendees
  - Donor information
  - Monies raised
  - Amount of monies given (if scholarships)
  - Media presence and photos of the guests and awardees

CONCLUSION

Academic institutions are businesses and they are always open to raising more funds and increasing alumni giving. Typically, any initiative that improves these outcomes will be welcomed. Altruistic initiatives are often launched that require resources such as direct contributions of funds, staff, space, time, and effort. The Lavender Fund was initiated by a queer graduate student in a position of power on the Board of Trustees. It could not have been created without the leverage conferred by the position. The official letter about the fund communicated support from the president and Board of Trustees with a clear stance and direction for an LGBT initiative. Taken together, this enabled action from members of the president's cabinet, including the vice president of development and alumni affairs. Execution of the vision required forethought, extensive collaboration, persistence, and upfront monetary resources.

The success of the Lavender Fund was measured by event attendance, monies raised, and media attention, but what was most important was its impact on university staff, students, and alumni. The LGBT initiative served as a predecessor to the LGBTQ+ Advisory Committee and the Howard University International Lesbian Gay Bisexual Transgender Ally Alumni Association/Howard University Rainbow Alumni Association, which was created as the sole place for all LGBTA alumni to commune and connect with one another through our alma mater. Importantly, the Lavender Fund had support from the administration but no university monies were allocated until the following year. Because it was a new initiative, the administration was not prepared to sponsor or allocate funds without demonstration of proof of principle. After the success of the first year, the administration allocated $3,000 from the budget of the Office of Development and Alumni Affairs to sponsor the LGBT homecoming event.

The Lavender Fund, the homecoming LGBTA Renaissance Reception, and the Howard University Rainbow Alumni Association are reproducible. This chapter advocates for a top-down approach that produces downstream benefits once key leadership and support have been identified. The success at Howard University was contingent on acknowledging the hurt and neglect of the past in order to move toward a more inclusive future. I recommended that institutions wishing to reengage detached queer students and alumni first acknowledge the hurt and neglect of the past, then provide an opportunity to allow vulnerability and visibility, followed by celebration. At Howard University this process has led to a more inviting campus that is continuing the work of recognizing past wrongs and ongoing improvement and reconciliation. I hope administrators will continue to push the envelope and show the next generation of leaders the diversity of love. Love wins.

REFERENCES

Anderson, J. D. (1988). *The education of Blacks in the South*. University of North Carolina Press.

Brazzell, J. C. (1992). Bricks without straw: Missionary-sponsored Black higher education in the post-emancipation era. *The Journal of Higher Education, 63*(1), 26–49. https://doi.org/10.1080/00221546.1992.11778338

Commodore, F. (2018). The tie that binds: Trusteeship, values, and the decision-making process at AME-affiliated HBCUs. *The Journal of Higher Education, 89*(4), 397–421.

———. (2019). Losing herself to save herself: Perspectives on conservatism and concepts of self for Black women aspiring to the HBCU presidency. *Hypatia, 34*(3), 1–23. doi:10.1111/hypa.12480

Knadler, S. P. (2002). Sweetback style: Wallace Thurman and a queer Harlem renaissance. *MFS Modern Fiction Studies, 48*(4), 899–936.

Logan, R. W. (1969). *Howard University: The first hundred years, 1867–1967*. New York University Press.

Mobley, S. D., Jr. (2017). Seeking sanctuary: (Re)Claiming the power of historically Black colleges and universities as places of Black refuge. *International Journal of Qualitative Studies in Education, 30*(10), 1036–1041.

Mobley, S. D., Jr., & Hall, L. (2020). (Re)Defining queer and trans* student retention and success at historically Black colleges and universities. *Journal of College Student Retention: Research, Theory & Practice, 21*(4), 497–519.

Njoku, N., Butler, M., & Beatty, C. C. (2017). Reimagining the historically Black college and university (HBCU) environment: Exposing race secrets and the binding chains of respectability and other mothering. *International Journal of Qualitative Studies in Education, 30*(8), 783–99.

Patton, L. D. (2016). Disrupting postsecondary prose: Toward a critical race theory of higher education. *Urban Education, 51*(3), 315–342.

Patton, L. D., Blockett, R. A., & McGowan, B. L. (2020). Complexities and contradictions: Black lesbian, gay, bisexual, and queer students' lived realities across three urban HBCU contexts. *Urban Education, 8*(6), 1355–1382. https://doi.org/10.1177/0042085920959128

Williams, K. L., Burt, B. A., Clay, K. L., & Bridges, B. K. (2019). Stories untold: Counter-narratives to anti-Blackness and deficit-oriented discourse concerning HBCUs. *American Educational Research Journal, 56*(2), 556–599.

PART 3 DELIBERATE AND INTENTIONAL QUEER AND TRANS* SCHOLARLY HBCU EXPLORATIONS

10 · A MANIFESTO FOR BLACK QUARE LIBERATION AND INCLUSION AT HBCUs

JARREL T. JOHNSON

This is an invitation for all HBCU stakeholders (e.g., senior leadership, faculty, staff, and students), especially cisgender heterosexual stakeholders, to proactively participate in the progression of an inclusive Black liberation that must transpire across all HBCUs. HBCUs have been focused on centering Blackness since their inceptions. They are some of the few spaces in the United States where Blackness is intentionally centered in an institution's organizational practices and policies (Mobley, 2017). This manifesto calls for recognizing and expanding the diversity within Black communities by acknowledging and supporting Blackness at the intersections of queerness and transness. HBCUs are known for leveraging their social justice tenets to enact social change in U.S., international, and Black communities (Mobley, 2017; Patton, 2016). HBCUs can and, I argue, have a mandate to expand their current institutional practices and policies to support the liberation and inclusion of their Black queer and trans* stakeholders.

But what happens when Blackness intersects with queerness and transness at HBCUs? Scholarship that examines the lived experiences of Black queer students at HBCUs has exposed the ways HBCU campus environments often undermine and erase the existence of those students (e.g., Ford, 2015; Mobley & Johnson, 2019; Patton et al., 2020). However, empirical research to investigate the collegiate experiences of Black trans* students attending HBCUs remains absent from the body of scholarship, although media reports have documented how Black trans* students encounter unfriendly campus environments (King, 2020; Williams, 2018). To date, only 8 of the 101 HBCUs in the United States have active queer and trans* student resource centers on their campus (Mobley & Hall, 2020). While such resource centers are not the only way HBCUs can demonstrate their support for queer and trans* students, their absence on most HBCU campuses speaks to the dismal progress of inclusion efforts in support of these students. That is why senior leaders, staff, and faculty at HBCUs must participate in the "quaring" of HBCUs.[1] This manifesto draws from a Black queer theory framework (e.g., quare theory and the queer of color critique) and the literature on Black queer experiences at HBCUs to empower HBCU stakeholders to participate in the work of the transformational inclusion and liberation of Black queer and trans* students. I propose four tenets that can serve as a guide for HBCU stakeholders who seek to become knowledgeable about the lived experiences of Black individuals who identify as queer and/or trans*, understand the connections between theory and practice, and disassemble forces of power and oppression that push queer and trans* students to the margins of HBCUs.

1. Quaring student identities
2. Quaring organizational structures
3. Quaring student policies and practices
4. Quaring for co-conspirators

While this manifesto presents only four tenets, I hope that future engagement in the quaring of HBCUs will extend these tenets and reveal additional foci. I begin by explaining the Black queer theory framework that anchors this document. Next, I explain the tenets in further detail and include some concrete examples of how HBCU administrators could work toward inclusive campus environments for queer and trans* students using the tenets. I conclude with an appeal to HBCUs to accept the challenge and reward of becoming sites of greater and more inclusive Black liberation.

CENTERING BLACKNESS AT THE INTERSECTIONS OF QUEER AND TRANS* IDENTITIES: A BLACK QUEER THEORY FRAMEWORK

To call attention to the identities and lived experiences of Black queer and trans* students at HBCUs, I draw from two Black queer theories—quare theory (Johnson, 2005; Johnson & Henderson, 2005) and the queer of color critique (Brockenbrough, 2013; Ferguson, 2004; Marquez & Brockenbrough, 2013). Quare theory is focused on the intersectional social identities (e.g., race, gender, class, and sexuality) that Black queer and trans* people hold and how their identities shape their lived experiences (Johnson, 2005). It places a strong emphasis on the lived experiences of Black queer and trans* individuals in the southern region of the United States (Johnson, 2005). Quare theory helps make sense of the identities of Black queer and trans* students because a majority of the HBCUs are located in that region. Unlike queer theory, quare theory contests white Western queer and trans* liberation norms such as coming out, rigid conceptualizations of identities, and the notion that an individual's social identities can be detached from one another (Johnson, 2005).[2]

Muñoz's (1999) concept of disidentification is a major precept of quare theory. Disidentification is the expression of resistance to hegemonic forms of identity and the altering of cultural logic and structures in society. These behaviors are often personified by Black queer and trans* individuals (Johnson, 2005; Muñoz, 1999). Disidentification can be used to defy Black cultural norms such as othermothering[3] and Black respectability politics[4] that sometimes harm queer and trans* students and restrict the ways they exist within HBCU settings (Mobley & Johnson, 2019; Njoku et al., 2017; Patton, 2014). Johnson (2021b) notes that disidentification can be used to disrupt and dismantle institutional "policies and practices that undermine and inhibit the existence of queer and trans* students on HBCU campuses" (p. 155). Disidentification is also a tool that administrators at HBCUs can employ to ensure that the responsibility of designing and implementing queer and trans* inclusion efforts is shared across multiple organizational structures (Johnson, 2021b).

The queer of color critique (Brockenbrough, 2013; Ferguson, 2004; Marquez & Brockenbrough, 2013) is the second theory that grounds this manifesto. This theory evolved from a materialist lens and was introduced to initiate a deeper analysis of sexuality in the context of race, poverty, and economic discrimination (Ferguson, 2004). This critique requires an interrogation of the cultural politics entrenched in heterosexist communities of color that frequently marginalize queer and trans* people of color (Marquez & Brockenbrough, 2013). It is informed by an understanding of how the social identities of queer and trans* people of color cross social and historical perspectives. These identities generate nuanced understandings of what it means to be queer of color and the inconsistent relationships among queers of color to systems of power (Marquez and Brockenbrough 2013). Through a queer of color critique lens, scholars confront policies and laws that prescribe advantages based on a singular identity (e.g., race) without attention to the intersectional and interlocking identities of gender, class, and sexuality (Ferguson, 2004). Including the queer of color critique in this manifesto offers an analysis of how HBCUs can resist cultural politics informed by heterosexist ideologies and work to revise policies, programs, and services that benefit only individuals with cisgender and heterosexual identities (Johnson, 2021a, 2021b). The Black queer theory framework serves as a guide for centering the multiple and intersecting identities of queer and trans* collegians at HBCUs. Together, quare theory and the queer of color critique work to hold HBCUs accountable for addressing the unique needs of students whose Blackness exists outside cisgender and heterosexual realities.

Tenet One: Quaring Student Identities

HBCU stakeholders who want to begin the process of ensuring that their campuses are liberatory and inclusive spaces for queer and trans* students must understand, value, and honor the various ways that Black queer and trans* students show up in their institutions. Promoting a culture in which all stakeholders seek this understanding so they can value and honor the complex identities of Black queer and trans* students is a first step HBCUs can take to address the various tensions these students experience on HBCU campuses and understand the assets they bring to their schools. Therefore, I suggest that HBCU stakeholders begin at the place of quaring student identities. This process is about understanding that Black queer and trans* students hold multiple identities (e.g., race, gender identity, gender expression, class, sexuality, religion) that intersect and cannot be disentangled from one another (Johnson, 2005; Means, 2014). Black queer and trans* students experience their Blackness concurrently with their gender identity and gender expression, their sexuality, their class, and their religious identities, to name a few (Ford, 2015; Mobley & Johnson, 2015).

Black queer and trans* students at HBCUs are regularly confronted with the pressure to align either their Black identity or their queer identity with societal and cultural politics (Mobley & Hall, 2020). Black queer men feel forced to choose between their Black identity and their queer identity as early as the process of deciding which college to attend. For some Black queer men, the decision to attend an HBCU was influenced by the need to attend a racially affirming institution rather than a queer-affirming one (Squire & Mobley, 2015). Squire & Mobley (2015) found that some Black queer men chose a predominantly white institution specifically because they felt it would be affirming of their queer identity. However, they tended to select those schools without much consideration of how they would affirm both their racial and sexual identities. Findings from this study suggest that HBCUs must consider how they can design institutional efforts that affirm all the identities of their students. Doing so will allow HBCUs to appeal to a broader range of students.

At times, the coalescing of the multiple identities Black queer students hold creates conflict for them when they encounter ideologies that claim that one cannot be Black, gendered, *and* queer (Barmore, 2019; Ford, 2015; Patton, 2011). Ford's (2015) study of the undergraduate experiences of Black queer men who were alumni of HBCUs illuminated the tensions they encountered as they sought to understand their Black, gender, and queer identities. Participants in Ford's study discussed how they arrived at their HBCUs questioning their ability to be Black and queer, as queerness was considered to be a white man's trait. However, participants recalled being able to use their HBCU experience as a means of resolving their Black, gendered, and queer identities. In fact, one participant credited coursework that featured readings from Black queer authors with his ability to make sense of his multiple identities. Similarly, Barmore's (2019) study found that Black queer women attending HBCUs often felt that they had to emphasize their Black identities over their queer identities to be accepted by administrators, peers, and faculty at their HBCUs. Unfortunately, the Black queer women in this study felt that they had to "shelve" their queer identities and that they needed to find communities off campus to access queer-affirming spaces.

Black queer and trans* individuals sometimes reject white Western norms of coming out. The quaring of student identities requires the realization that Black queer and trans* students exist on a spectrum of visibility. Patton (2011) and Means & Jaeger (2013) found that Black queer men did not feel that it was important to publicly disclose their queer identity while they were attending their HBCUs. Participants in Means & Jaeger's study stressed that it was more important for them to feel "comfortable in their skin" than to declare their sexuality to others publicly. For a variety of reasons (e.g., personal/physical safety, continued access to social networks, and/or financial resources from family), Black queer and trans* students often engage in passing (McCune, 2014) to fit in in the spaces they inhabit.[5] Some Black queer students make the conscious decision to camouflage their queer identity to maintain access to social networks and professional opportunities (Means & Jaeger, 2013; Patton, 2011).

When institutional stakeholders at HBCUs honor the lived experiences of Black queer and trans* students, they can glean many insights that have implications for how they can engage and empower Black queer and trans* students on their campuses. Quare theory is a "theory of the flesh"[6] (Johnson, 2005). I argue that paying attention to the ways that Black queer and trans* students physically show up on HBCU campuses will give institutional stakeholders the information they need to frame their lived experiences as assets to the campus community. It is not enough to just witness how Black queer and trans* students show up on their campus environments; HBCU stakeholders must also challenge ideologies such as Black respectability politics and heterosexism that privilege Blackness and support only heterogendered notions of sexuality and gender. A queer of color critique lens will help HBCU administrators, faculty, and staff understand why they must challenge and reconstruct policies and practices (e.g., the royal court, gendered campus residential policies) that sustain cultural politics that work to reduce and erase the existence of Black queer and trans* students (Ferguson, 2004; Johnson, 2021b).

For instance, Black queer students challenge cultural politics rooted in heterosexist and heterogendered ideologies through the ways they dress (Ford, 2015; Mobley & Johnson, 2019; Patton, 2014; Patton & Simmons, 2008). Patton and Simmons (2008) found that some Black lesbians at HBCUs frequently experienced ostracization on campus because their physical appearance was viewed as traditionally masculine. Black queer men at Morehouse College were subjected to the Morehouse Appropriate Attire Policy, which required them to wear traditional men's clothing at college events (Mobley & Johnson, 2019; Patton, 2014). The policy was designed to discourage and diminish the existence of Black queer men who wore feminine presenting attire and reinforce heterogendered conceptualizations of Black men. Instead of subscribing to binary gender norms, HBCU stakeholders should learn from their Black queer and trans* students so that they can expand the diversity of Blackness on their campuses. As Mobley & Hall (2020) note, "at HBCUs, Blackness has been perpetually (re)imagined and given space to be performed in its infinite possibilities" (p. 498). Queer and trans* students at HBCUs continue this tradition by resisting and transgressing oppressive cultural politics. Quaring student identities creates transformative opportunities for HBCUs to become more significant sites of inclusive Black liberation. To further operationalize this tenet, HBCUs need a collective mission shared throughout multiple organizational structures.

Tenet Two: Quaring Organizational Structures

Recent scholarship has focused on the role HBCU administrators can play in ushering in organizational change that is inclusive of Black queer and trans* identities (Johnson, 2021a, 2021b; 2023) Lewis & Ericksen, 2016; Mobley & Hall, 2020; Nguyen et al., 2018). The quaring of organizational structures at HBCUs refers to how administrators can work to ensure that all institutional units share responsibility for developing and implementing initiatives for queer and trans* student inclusion (Johnson, 2021a, 2021b; 2023). Because HBCUs have been known to work collaboratively with stakeholders across multiple institutional units to ensure student success, the ideal of employing collaborative leadership tactics in the service of queer and trans* students aligns with current organizational practices at HBCUs. There have been numerous calls for HBCU leaders to establish and implement queer and trans* resource centers on their campuses (e.g., Jones et al., 2020). While queer and trans* student resource centers have the potential to shape inclusion efforts for students in these populations significantly, we know that students exist in multiple institutional spaces beyond resource centers (Vaccaro, 2012). Therefore, institutional leaders at HBCUs must consider how they can charge various units on campus with the task of becoming inclusive of queer and trans* students.

Johnson (2021a, 2021b) has proposed the Model for Transformational Inclusion at HBCUs (MTI at HBCUs), a framework that seeks to assist HBCU stakeholders in facilitating transformative change that is inclusive of the varied experiences Black queer and trans* students encounter. This framework outlines three domains that HBCU administrators can operationalize to enact organizational change. Here I will focus only on the first domain of the MTI at HBCUs framework: the network of transformational agents, also known as the "who" domain. This domain includes the people (e.g., senior institutional leaders, faculty, administrators/staff, external organizations) responsible for spearheading and galvanizing inclusion efforts on their campuses. Johnson highlights how senior leaders and midlevel student affairs administrators (e.g., presidents, vice presidents of student affairs, directors of student life and residence life) can use the organizational change strategy of collaborative leadership to institutionalize inclusion efforts in support of Black queer and trans* students. For example, the administrators at a public HBCU in Johnson's study discussed how the president used his positional power to mobilize queer and trans* student inclusion efforts by requiring institutional leaders and faculty to become trained through their Safe Zone training program. He also established a queer and trans* student advisory board that consisted of multiple institutional leaders (e.g., academic deans of the colleges, the vice president for academic affairs, leaders within student life functional areas). Johnson found that in some cases, it was midlevel administrators who led the charge to make their campuses more inclusive for queer and trans* students. They developed and implemented inclusion efforts (e.g., establishment of trans* residence halls and gender-neutral restrooms) and channeled inclusion efforts up to senior-level administrators when they needed additional support for their work.

Collaborative leadership must extend beyond institutional boundaries. The HBCUs involved in Johnson's study leveraged the resources of queer and trans* advocacy organizations at the local, state, and national levels. For example, a private HBCU in Johnson's study solicited the help of several local and state organizations to help connect queer and trans* students to queer and trans* student leadership development and community-building opportunities and clothing resources for trans* students. Midlevel administrators at a public HBCU applied for and received grant funding from national queer and trans* advocacy organizations to provide external training opportunities for faculty interested in learning about how to be inclusive of queer and trans* students. Leaders at HBCUs will need to be industrious about addressing the needs of queer and trans* students. Developing meaningful partnerships with external organizations that advocate for and work to empower queer and trans* individuals is one way that HBCUs can strategically draw on resources to facilitate organizational change that is focused on the inclusion of queer and trans* students.

I close this tenet by offering a word of caution. Quaring organizational structures at HBCUs is an intentional act that leaders must honor and continuously reflect on. It requires willing and strong senior leadership, an appropriate allocation of human and financial resources, and constant (re)evaluation and establishment of institutional structures needed to sustain inclusion efforts (Kezar & Eckel, 2002; Johnson, 2021a). Without the support and strategic engagement of institutional leaders in the quaring of organizational structures, inclusion efforts may never be realized.

Tenet Three: Quaring Student Policies and Practices

Queer and trans* HBCU students deserve to be seen, heard, and represented in the institutional fabric of their respective campuses. Another way that HBCUs can ensure that they are becoming inclusive and liberatory spaces for Black queer and trans* students is through the quaring of student policies and practices (Mobley et al., 2019). In this tenet, I elucidate how inclusion efforts need to acknowledge the tensions and assets these students bring to HBCU campuses and urge HBCU stakeholders to see queer and trans* students as powerful individuals who can excel and thrive in HBCU campus environments if their institutions give them the right tools. I demand that HBCU institutional members depart from deficit framings of queer and trans* students that label them as the "other," "weak," and in need of institutional support. Instead, through a lens of empowerment and advocacy, I call for the inclusion of queer and trans* students through policies and programs that see these students as a part of the diversity that is represented in Blackness.

HBCUs will need to reckon with policies and practices that relegate queer and trans* students to the margins of their institutions. The third domain of Johnson's (2021a) MTI at HBCUs framework, "quared levels of empowerment and advocacy," suggests three equally important layers of institutional support for queer and trans* students: (1) quared student policies; (2) quared student practices, programs, and services; and (3) quared institution-wide educational trainings and or campaigns. Quared student policies are the foundation that HBCUs can work from to ensure that their campuses have inclusive and liberatory spaces for queer and trans* students. Johnson's (2021a) research shows that the absence of institutional policies that affirm and account for the complexities of Black queer and trans* HBCU students is often harmful to them. Midlevel administrators at the public HBCU in the study reported instances in which trans* students who were in the university band were subjected to policies about wearing uniforms and housing when the band traveled that were rooted in the gender binary. A trans* woman student at the HBCU was forced to wear a men's uniform and was assigned to a men's hotel accommodation. The university worked to rectify this situation by drafting a document outlining how band program administrators must provide accommodations for trans* students. Revisiting and revising policies rooted in the gender binary is essential for ensuring that a campus includes and embraces queer and trans* students.

Quared student programs and services should work to assist HBCU stakeholders in designing inclusion efforts that celebrate, empower, and advocate for queer and trans* students. HBCU administrators can acknowledge the contributions of Black queer and trans* students to their campus communities with events such as the Lavender Graduation ceremony. Administrators will need to consider how to ensure that programming is inclusive of the varied gender identities, gender expressions, "outness," and sexual identities of Black queer and trans* students. For example, a midlevel administrator at the private HBCU in Johnson's (2021a) study discussed including elements of queer and trans* issues in general campus programming on romantic relationships to include students who might not publicly identify as queer or trans*. Campus-wide programs such as Safe Zone trainings and Pronoun Pin Initiatives quare campus culture at the institutional level. At the public HBCU in Johnson's study, pins featuring each person's preferred pronouns engaged the entire campus in awareness of and discussing the importance of acknowledging and respecting a person's pronouns. The Safe Zone training provided opportunities for faculty and staff to gain knowledge about the queer and trans* community. Such training opportunities can be beneficial in helping multiple stakeholders do the internal work they need to do to be supportive of queer and trans* students.

Tenet Four: Quaring for Co-Conspirators

Quaring for co-conspirators is vital for HBCU stakeholders who continuously engage in self-reflection and in seeking knowledge about Black queer and trans* issues. Self-reflection often leads HBCU stakeholders to use their privileges (e.g., as cisgender and heterosexual people) to advance and expand inclusion efforts for queer and trans* students. David Johns, the executive director of the National Black Justice Coalition, says that if someone puts in the work, they can be invited in to understand the lived experiences of (Black) queer and trans* individuals (Moulite, 2020). I ask HBCU stakeholders: What are you currently doing to be invited into understanding and advocating for the lives of your Black queer and trans* students? As they reflect on this question, I hope that all HBCU stakeholders will examine their prejudices and complicities in upholding queer and trans* oppression. I will be clear here: being a co-conspirator is challenging work. It is labor intensive and requires individuals to constantly challenge themselves to learn more as they work to foster inclusive and liberatory HBCUs and work alongside the queer and trans* community.

This tenet is opposed to performative or self-glorifying allyship (Love, 2019). The privileges cisgender and heterosexual individuals hold contribute to the current marginalization of queer and trans* individuals. Therefore, I unapologetically reject the notion that Black queer and trans* liberation needs the allyship of Black cisgender and heterosexual persons. Instead, I summon co-conspirators outside of the queer and trans* community to strategically deploy their social and cultural capital to dismantle oppressive forces, potentially leading to institutional change at HBCUs. Like Love's (2019) assertion, I believe that true allyship works "toward something that is mutually beneficial and supportive to all parties involved" (p. 117). I call for co-conspirators (Love, 2019) who:

1. Understand their link to systems of privilege and oppression while unlearning the behaviors and practices that enable those systems.
2. Form authentic relationships of solidarity and mutuality.
3. Transparently acknowledge and confront power imbalances to forge genuine relationships.
4. Ground social change work in partnership, humility, and accountability.
5. Pursue an internal voyage that embodies silence, mediation, inner wisdom, and deep joy, which is intimately related to the external work of social change.

I ask potential and current co-conspirators at HBCUs to consider how they can practice self-reflection understand their privileges, and comprehend how they can dismantle systems that perpetuate queer and trans* student ostracism. I invite HBCU stakeholders to form organic and meaningful relationships of solidarity and mutuality that allow for the honest acknowledgment and confrontation of power inequalities. Black queer and trans* student liberation and inclusion are dependent on willing individuals who use their privileges to call for the holistic, uninhibited participation of students in these populations.

CONCLUSION

This manifesto provides four considerations for HBCU stakeholders who seek to make their institutions liberatory and inclusive spaces for Black queer and trans* students. First, HBCU stakeholders must seek to understand the intersectional and complex identities Black queer and trans* students hold. Secondly, HBCU administrators need to strategically work across multiple departmental units to ensure that the inclusion of queer and trans* students is engrained within every facet of their institutions. Third, inclusive institutional practices and policies should be framed through a lens of empowerment and advocacy to acknowledge the tensions and assets queer and trans* students enter HBCU environments with. Fourth, HBCU stakeholders must join the fight to advance and expand the liberation and inclusion of Black queer and trans* students as co-conspirators. HBCUs have tremendous potential to model how various societal institutions can enact liberation and inclusion. It is up to members of HBCU campuses to lead that change.

NOTES

1. The term "quare" was coined by Johnson's (2005) (homophobic) grandmother who pronounced "queer" as "quare" to describe persons in the queer and trans* community.
2. Coming out refers to one's public acknowledgment of their queer or trans* identity.

3. Othermothering is referred to as a tenet of care that some HBCU faculty and staff employ to look after students. This parental strategy has received critiques as it sometimes is invasive and hypercritical of students' life decisions (Njoku et al., 2017).
4. Black respectability politics refers to a strategy Black communities use to maintain and negotiate their existence in American society by subscribing to sexual conservatism, patriarchal family structures, and intellectual achievement (Higginbotham, 1993; White, 2001).
5. McCune (2014) defines passing as Black men performing a heterosexual presentation of their masculinity in order to survive in and navigate various spaces.
6. Johnson (2005) argued that quare theory is a theory embedded in the racialized bodies, real-life occurrences, and intellectual perspectives of Black queer and trans* individuals.

REFERENCES

Anderson, J. D. (1988). *The education of Blacks in the South, 1860–1935*. University of North Carolina Press.

Barmore, L. K. O. (2019). *Experiences of African American lesbians who attended a historically Black college or university* [Doctoral dissertation]. Walden University. ProQuest Dissertations and Theses Global.

Brockenbrough, E. (2013). Introduction to the special issue: Queers of color and anti-oppressive knowledge production. *Curriculum Inquiry, 43*, 426–440. https://doi.org/10.1111/curi.12023

Ferguson, R. A. (2004). *Aberrations in Black: Toward a queer of color of critique*. University of Minnesota Press.

Ford, O., III (2015). From navigation to negotiation: An examination of the lived experiences of Black gay male alumni of historically Black colleges and universities. *Journal of Homosexuality, 62*(3), 353–373. https://doi.org/10.1080/00918369.2014.972814

Higginbotham, E. B. (1993). *Righteous discontent: The women's movement in the Black Baptist church, 1880–1920*. Harvard University Press.

Johnson, E. P. (2005). Quare studies, or almost everything I know about queer studies I learned from my grandmother. In E. P. Johnson & M. G. Henderson (Eds.), *Black queer studies* (pp. 124–157). Duke University Press.

Johnson, E. P., & Henderson, M. G. (2005). Introduction: Queering Black studies/"quaring" queer studies. In E. P. Johnson & M. G. Henderson (Eds.), *Black queer studies* (pp. 1–17). Duke University Press.

Johnson, J. T. (2021a). *Quaring HBCUs: A case study investigating and theorizing queer and trans* student inclusion at two historically Black colleges and universities* [Doctoral dissertation]. Iowa State University. ProQuest and Theses Global.

———. (2021b). The category is . . . transformational inclusion: A conceptual framework for (re)imagining the inclusion of Black queer and trans* students attending HBCUs. In G. B. Crosby, K. A. White, M. A. Chanay, & A. Hilton (Eds.), *Reimagining historically Black colleges and universities*. Emerald Publishing Limited. https://doi.org/10.1108/978-1-80043-664-020211014

Jones, B., Lo, P., Wilkerson, A., Xu, A., Hall, L., Cooper, K., Gonzalez, S. A., & Gasman, M. (2020) *Modeling Inclusion: HBCUs and LGBTQ+ support*. The Rutgers Center for Minority Serving Institutions and Human Rights Campaign Foundation. https://cmsi.gse.rutgers.edu/sites/default/files/CMSI%20and%20HRC%20LGBTQ%2B%20Brief.pdf

Kezar, A., & Eckel, P. (2002). Examining the institutional transformation process: The importance of sensemaking, interrelated strategies, and balance. *Research in Higher Education, 43*(3), 295–328. https://doi.org/10.1023/A:1014889001242

King, A. (2020, May 1). The mean girl of Morehouse returns. *Level*. https://level.medium.com/the-mean-girl-of-morehouse-returns-280934648c3

Lewis, M. W., & Ericksen, K. S. (2016). Improving the climate for LGBTQ students at an Historically Black University. *Journal of LGBT Youth, 13*(3), 249–269.

Love, B. L. (2019). *We want to do more than survive: Abolitionist teaching and the pursuit of educational freedom*. Beacon Press.

Marquez, R., & Brockenbrough, E. (2013). Queer youth v. the state of California: Interrogating legal discourses on the rights of queer students of color. *Curriculum Inquiry, 43*(4), 461–482. https://doi.org/10.1111/curi.12021

McCune, J. Q., Jr. (2014). *Sexual discretion: Black masculinity and the politics of passing*. The University of Chicago Press.

Means, D. R. (2014). *Demonized no more: The spiritual journeys and spaces of Black gay male college students at predominantly white institutions* [Doctoral dissertation]. North Carolina State University. ProQuest and Global Theses.

Means, D. R., & Jaeger, A. J. (2013). Black in the rainbow: "Quaring" the Black gay male student experience at historically Black universities. *Journal of African American Males in Education (JAAME), 4*(2), 124–140.

Mobley, S. D., Jr. (2017). Seeking sanctuary: (Re)Claiming the power of historically Black colleges and universities as places of Black refuge. *International Journal of Qualitative Studies in Education, 30*(10), 1036–1041. https://doi.org/10.1080/09518398.2017.1312593

Mobley, S. D., Jr., & Hall, L. (2020). (Re)Defining queer and trans* student retention and success at historically Black colleges and universities. *Journal of College Student Retention: Research, Theory & Practice, 21*(4), 497–519. https://doi.org/10.1177/1521025119895512

Mobley, S. D., Jr., & Johnson, J. M. (2015). The role of HBCUs in addressing the unique needs of LGBT students. *New Directions for Higher Education, 2015*(170), 79–89.

———. (2019). "No pumps allowed": The "problem" with gender expression and the Morehouse College "Appropriate Attire Policy." *Journal of Homosexuality, 66*(7), 867–895. https://doi.org/10.1080/00918369.2018.1486063

Mobley, S. D., Jr., McNally, T., & Moore, G. (2019). (Re)Centering the narrative: Revealing the potential for HBCUs to be liberatory environments for queer students. In E. M. Zamani-Gallaher, D. D. Choudhuri, & J. L. Taylor (Eds.), *Rethinking LGBTQIA students and collegiate contexts: Identity, policies, and campus climate* (pp. 99–119). Routledge.

Moulite, Jessica. (2020, September 18). Why some Black LGBTQIA+ folks are done "coming out." *The Root*. https://www.theroot.com/why-some-black-lgbtqia-folks-are-done-coming-out-1840507460.

Muñoz, J. E. (1999). *Disidentifications: Queers of color and the performance of politics* (Vol. 2). University of Minnesota Press.

Nguyen, T., Castro Samayoa, A., Gasman, M., & Mobley, S., Jr. (2018). Challenging respectability: Student health directors providing services to lesbian and gay students at historically Black colleges and universities. *Teachers College Record, 120*(2), 1–44.

Njoku, N., Butler, M., & Beatty, C. C. (2017). Reimagining the historically Black college and university (HBCU) environment: Exposing race secrets and the binding chains of respectability and othermothering. *International Journal of Qualitative Studies in Education, 30*(8), 783–799. https://doi.org/10.1080/09518398.2017.1350297

Patton, L. D. (2011). Perspectives on identity, disclosure, and the campus environment among African American gay and bisexual men at one historically Black college. *Journal of College Student Development, 52*(1), 77–100. doi:10.1353/csd.2011.0001

———. (2014). Preserving respectability or blatant disrespect? A critical discourse analysis of the Morehouse appropriate attire policy and implications for intersectional approaches to examining campus policies. *International Journal of Qualitative Studies in Education, 27*(6), 724–746. https://doi.org/10.1080/09518398.2014.901576

———. (2016). Disrupting postsecondary prose: Toward a critical race theory of higher education. *Urban Education, 51,* 315–342. https://doi.org/10.1177/0042085915602542

Patton, L. D., Blockett, R. A., & McGowan, B. L. (2020). Complexities and contradictions: Black lesbian, gay, bisexual, and queer students' lived realities across three urban HBCU contexts. *Urban Education, 58*(6), 1355–1382. https://doi.org/10.1177/0042085920959128

Patton, L. D., & Simmons, S. L. (2008). Exploring complexities of multiple identities of lesbians in a Black college environment. *Negro Educational Review, 59*(3–4), 197–215.

Squire, D. D., & Mobley, S. D., Jr. (2015). Negotiating race and sexual orientation in the college choice process of Black gay males. *The Urban Review, 47*(3), 466–491. https://doi.org/10.1007/s11256-014-0316-3

Vaccaro, A. (2012). Campus microclimates for LGBT faculty, staff, and students: An exploration of the intersections of social identity and campus roles. *Journal of Student Affairs Research and Practice, 49*(4), 429–446. https://doi.org/10.1515/jsarp-2012-6473

White, E. F. (2001). *Dark continent of our bodies: Black feminism and the politics of respectability.* Temple University Press.

Williams, S. (2018, June 21). It's time for HBCUs to address homophobia and transphobia on their campuses. *The Nation.* https://www.thenation.com/article/archive/time-hbcus-address-homophobia-transphobia-campuses/

11 • OUTSIDER WITHIN

The Experiences of Queer Black Women College Athletes at Historically Black Colleges and Universities

CHRISTA J. PORTER AND
AKILAH R. CARTER-FRANCIQUE

Higher education institutions are characterized by hegemonic discourses and legacies of exclusion rooted in patriarchy and white supremacy (Bruening et al., 2005; Howard-Hamilton, 2003; Hurtado et al., 1998, 1999). Historically, Black people "have been told by white people what to do, how to do it, and in general, what constitutes reality" (Stratta, 1995, p. 53). Because white people have created and managed the narratives concerning sociocultural relations and behavior (e.g., who and what is deemed valuable in athletics/sports), people outside of or in opposition to that narrative are relegated to the margins (Ferguson & Satterfield, 2017; Patton & Haynes, 2018). Specifically, Black women college athletes are "often ascribed roles and expectations and forced to fit within the discourses primarily centered on their Black male and/or white female peers" (Cooper et al., 2017, p. 130).

The conflation of Black women's experiences with those of Black men (concerning race) and white women (concerning gender) in sport is not only problematic, it also perpetuates invisibility and marginalization (Cooper et al., 2017). This conflated narrative does not consider the relationships among intersecting and multiple marginalized identities that are unique to Black women beyond race and gender (e.g., gender identity and expression, sexual identity, and socioeconomic status) at various types of institutions (hooks, 1981; Porter & Maddox, 2014). This chapter uses a critical discourse analysis of intersectionality to illuminate how power and inequality shape the representation of queer Black women college athletes at HBCUs. The literature on Black women college athletes describes how they live at the intersections of marginalization on the basis of race, gender, and social class and are consequently rendered silent and invisible. However, the literature that highlights the multiplicative sexual identity intersections that queerness creates is scant. We offer strategies and resources for holistically supporting the well-being and academic and athletic development of queer Black women college athletes (Carter-Francique, 2013; Carter-Francique et al., 2017; Carter-Francique & Richardson, 2015; Hawkins et al., 2015). In this chapter, we use "queer" as an umbrella term for the various representations of sexual identity and gender identity based usages in academic literature and how participants in academic studies identified themselves. It is not our intention to conflate biological sex, gender, and/or sexual identity; we acknowledge the differences among the terms.

INTERSECTIONALITY: BLACK, QUEER, AND OTHERED

Identification as a Black lesbian, bisexual, queer, genderqueer, or having an "othered" sexual identity and/or gender identity involves the use of a critical framework that centers lived experiences within the confines of oppressive systems. Intersectionality theory acknowledges the fullness of the experiences of historically marginalized populations in all their complexity. While it was Crenshaw (1989) who coined the term intersectionality to describe the social categorization marginalized populations (specifically Black women) experience because of oppression, discrimination, and social inequalities, Black women and women of color scholars discussed the effects of these structural inequalities before there was an identifiable framework (e.g., Anzaldúa, 1987; Combahee River Collective, 1982).

Crenshaw's (1991, 1993) framing of intersectionality acknowledged the many realities that Black women experience simultaneously at multiple levels, including the structural level, the political level, and the representational level. The structural level of intersectionality involves the ways dominant power structures (e.g., race, gender, social class, sexual identity) create differential treatment and experiences for minoritized people and groups. The political intersectionality level relates to how policies for practices for such as hiring and firing and sexual harassment marginalize issues and/or position one identity over another and thus fail to acknowledge the fullness of the discrimination. The representational level of intersectionality concerns how historical and contemporary productions of images present marginalized people and groups in negative ways and how any critique of such images can further derogate and/or objectify people or groups. These three levels operate to shape how people who live within the intersections are affected by discrimination.

Crenshaw's analytical framework of three levels of intersectionality (structural, political, and representational) works well with the three characteristics of what Collins (1986) identified as outsider within status when examining the experiences of queer Black women college athletes: Black women's self-definition and self-evaluation, the interlocking nature of oppressions, and the importance of Black women's culture. Because of their understanding of the power structures and the differential structural treatment they have experienced (Bruening, 2005; Bruening et al., 2005; Carter, 2008; Foster, 2003; Howard-Hamilton, 1993; Vertinsky & Captain, 1998), Black women can, and in some cases are forced to, create and develop personal (re)definitions of what it means to be a Black woman athlete in their sport (Carter-Francique et al., 2017).

The institutional systems and practices that hinder and/or perpetuate Black women's marginalization are an example of interlocking forms of political oppression. Juxtaposing the hegemonic standards, constructions, and expectations of women (e.g., beauty, femininity, behavior) with lived realities of women in sport (e.g., how they are represented in the media) illuminates the importance of Black women's queer culture. An examination of the literature can begin to situate the realities of queer Black women college athletes and their sexual identity and gender identities in institutions of higher education.

A METHOD OF INCLUSION

While a body of scholarship exists on the experiences of Black women college athletes, there is scant literature on queer Black women and their unique experiences at HBCUs. Critical discourse analysis (Fairclough, 1989, 1992) provides a vehicle for examining how a topic is narrated in the literature in relation to power. Using Fairclough's (1989) dimensions of analysis, we focused on queer Black women college athletes, how researchers and institutional policies and practices presented their experiences (e.g., in written or verbal form), and the contexts within which their experiences were governed (e.g., socially and historically). We paid particular attention to how the experiences of Black women college athletes were constructed and interpreted in the language researchers used (Everett & Croom, 2017). We drew on Crenshaw's analytical framework of structural, political, and representational levels of intersectionality in our analysis of these women's experiences.

Data Collection and Analysis

We searched for relevant literature using all available databases and peer-reviewed journals (e.g., EBSCO, ERIC, APA PsycInfo). We used search terms that included woman (or female), Black (or African American), queer, lesbian, gay, bisexual, college (or university), athlete (or athletes), and USA (or United States). We reviewed each of the available titles and abstracts and excluded literature that explored health challenges and alcohol and/or drug use by college athletes. We also excluded articles that examined other groups besides Black women (e.g., literature that compared Black women to white women or Black men or athletes of color). Our process yielded twenty-five articles. Few of them discussed the experiences of queer Black women athletes at HBCUs and even fewer explored the intersections of race, gender, and sexual identity. We interpreted the experiences of queer Black women athletes using three analytical categories: othering as the outsider within, invisibility, and (lack of) support structures.

FINDINGS: LIVING AS THE OBJECTIFIED OTHER

Black women college athletes are the objectified other. This definitive statement is supported by historical accounts and treatments that placed their experiences and achievements on the margins (Cahn, 1994; Bruening, 2005; Bruening et al., 2005; Carter, 2008; Carter & Hart, 2010; Carter & Hawkins, 2011; Corbett & Johnson, 2000; Howard-Hamilton, 1993; Smith, 2000; Vertinsky & Captain, 1998; Withycombe, 2011). In the literature we reviewed, scholars described the ability of Black women athletes to persevere despite experiences shaped by racism, sexism, classism, and systemic processes that render(ed) them voiceless and invisible (Bruening, 2005; Cooper et al., 2017; Green et al., 1981; Smith, 2000; Vertinsky & Captain, 1998). Specific types of marginalization include mobilizations of negative stereotypes and myths (Ruggiero & Lattin, 2008; Withycombe, 2011); racism, sexism, and heterosexism (Bernhard, 2014; Carter & Hawkins, 2011; Newhall & Buzuvis, 2008); negative portrayals of identity formation processes (Carter, 2008); limited and derogatory media portrayals (Bruening et al., 2005; Foster, 2003); responses to performances of hyperfemininity (Ferguson & Satterfield, 2017); academic engagement (Cooper et al., 2016); and development through sport and society (Carter-Francique et al., 2017).

Othering as Outsider Within

Images of Black women in the media have portrayed them as "defective females who want to be or act like men and are sexually promiscuous" (Green, 1994, p. 398). Collins (1990), who examined such images, underscored how white men perpetuate harmful narratives about Black women (e.g., Jezebel and Mammy) in order to control them. White people other Black women college athletes when they categorize them in ways that differentiate them from white women and Black men. This type of objectified marginalization shows up in the form of assigning Black women college athletes an outsider within status (Collins, 1986, p. S14) and comes "complete with the contradiction that they have earned admittance to the sporting world, but they are not fully welcomed there" (Bruening et al., 2005, p. 83). In the broader society and in the world of sports, Black women athletes' lack of whiteness and maleness means that they are automatically devalued (Collins, 1990; Smith 1992, 2000). This often leaves Black women to navigate their sports careers with limited support (e.g., from mentors, counseling, or programs and services earmarked for athletes; Carter & Hart, 2010; Carter-Francique, 2014; Person et al., 2001).

As Ferguson and Satterfield (2017) have noted, "the hegemonic discourses about women in general, and sports in particular, are rooted in white men's social construction of femininity and beauty. The racist dichotomy of accepted beauty and femininity, juxtaposed with how the white dominant cultural group positions Black women, still exists and is uniquely manifested in the world of sports" (pp. 116–117). In other words, these constructions of beauty, femininity, and what women athletes "should" and "should not" represent contrast with the stereotypical and historical images ascribed to Black women (Ferguson & Satterfield, 2017; Satterfield & Croft, 2015; Smith, 2000). Black women athletes whose bodies are strong and muscular contradict dominant narratives of femininity (Cahn, 1994; Roth & Basow, 2004), and the level of stigmatization increases when Black women athletes expand and deconstruct gender norms by appearing masculine (Griffin, 1992; Krane, 2001; Vertinsky & Captain, 1998).

Queer Black women athletes are often seen as masculinized, thus calling "into question society's definition of women [and femininity] at its deepest level" (Collins, 1990, p. 94). There is no monolithic experience of queerness or of being a Black woman collegiate athlete, but controlling images exacerbate feelings of otherness in queer Black women. Even though some research has been done on Black lesbian and/or queer identity(ies), it is crucial to explore and acknowledge the diverse ways Black queer women athletes identify and experience the intersections of marginalization based on race (racism), gender (genderism), and sexual identity (heterosexism).

Ross's (2006) master's thesis examined how two Black queer college athletes (one bisexual and one lesbian) negotiated the intersections of their racial identity, sexual orientation, and gender identity as NCAA Division I athletes. Although both women shared a pride in their role as athletes and were aware of the privilege they enjoyed as athletes, the study revealed several differences between them. These included the degree to which they disassociated with their racial identity (preferencing a student-athlete identity), performance as masculine versus not wanting to be associated with a gender-identity label, and degrees of comfort with expressions of sexual identity. These differences are characteristic of the varied experiences of Black queer women athletes with respect to their socialization into sport, their perspectives on gender expression, and how they view the intersections of their identities in terms of race, gender, and sexuality.

Invisibility

The dearth of literature on queer Black women athletes perpetuates both their invisibility in public scholarship and the erasure of awareness of identity intersections in the media and in federal policy. Newhall and Buzuvis (2008) examined the intersections of race, gender, and sexual identity and the law in relation to the experiences of Jennifer Harris, a Black former women's basketball player at Pennsylvania State University, and her coach, Maureen "Rene" Portland. The case

Harris vs. Portland (2006) presents all three levels of Crenshaw's intersectional analysis (e.g., structural, political, and representational). Portland, who was infamous for her anti-lesbian policy, dismissed Harris from the team at the end of her sophomore season, citing poor performance. Harris then filed a lawsuit alleging that Portland had discriminated against her based on her sexual orientation and her race. Specifically, Portland terminated Harris because she refused Portland's demands that she change "her image to be more feminine and [that she] stop wearing cornrows" (*Harris vs. Portland*, 2006, p. 23). Harris experienced invisibility (e.g., based on white standards of femininity) and consistent othering as an outsider within. This case is a good example of how the media fails to recognize intersectionality. As Newhall and Buzuvis (2008) note, "Harris's claims of discrimination based on sexual orientation were pondered, discussed, and often validated in the media, whereas the allegations of racial discrimination were largely ignored or summarily dismissed as implausible" (p. 346).

McDonald and Birrell (1999) emphasize that the tendency to overlook the complexity of intersectional identity in higher education is problematic because it perpetuates erasure. While Title IX of the Education Amendments of 1972 has provided increased opportunities for the participation of [white] women (Carpenter & Acosta, 2005; Carter-Francique & Richardson, 2015; Smith, 2000; Theune, 2016), the policy failed to address discrimination at the intersection of sex and sexual identity and "contributed to the public framing of Harris's case in a way that erased the racial nature of the discrimination" (Newhall & Buzuvis, 2008, p. 361). This invisibility of the experiences and identities of queer Black women athletes perpetuates both their relegation to the margins and their othering as outsiders within and the corresponding erasure of their lived realities (Newhall & Buzuvis, 2008).

(Lack of) Support Structures

Several authors have discussed the influence of family members and faculty engagement on the academic and career trajectories of Black women college athletes and the roles coaches and athletic advisors can play in their success in sport (Carter & Hart, 2010; Carter-Francique, 2014; Cooper et al., 2017; Person et al., 2001). Black women have identified ways they have been able to, and have been encouraged to, employ various forms of cultural capital (Yosso, 2005) as resources for navigating societal norms (e.g., familial, resistant, aspirational, social, and navigational; Cooper et al., 2017). HBCUs have been nurturing and essential environments for Black women college athletes because they represent not only "institutions of scholastic education, but education and development for life by creating a sense of community through the university personnel [, including] the athletic coaches and their team" (Carter-Francique & Richardson, 2015, p. 66).

While the climate at HBCUs has reflected supportive spaces, promoted academic success, and racial uplift for Black women athletes (Carter-Francique &

Richardson, 2015; Cooper & Cooper, 2015; Hawkins et al., 2015), these environments have not been immune to patriarchal and hegemonic views about gender (in)equity and to perpetuating ideals of what Black women college athletes should represent (e.g., through providing unequal funding of women's sports, unequal facilities, and insufficient team accommodations; Carter-Francique & Richardson, 2015; Theune, 2016). For example, the number of scholarships for Black women college athletes who participate in basketball or track and field at HBCUs has decreased due to an increase in non-Black women receiving these funds for tennis, soccer, and golf (Theune, 2016). These sports have been added to meet Title IX requirements; however, they have ultimately locked Black women out of these opportunities. Theune (2016) describes this change: "Although many schools are demonstrating their commitment to females by adding growth sports and providing athletics scholarships to attract participation, unfortunately these practices do not address race inequity. Even HBCUs have been forced to disregard the intersectionality of race and gender in the lives of Black females and to shift toward more diverse athletes and sports programs beyond the traditional 'Black' sports of basketball and track and field" (p. 67).

These inequitable funding practices and structures create differential treatment and experiences for Black women college athletes (e.g., structural intersectionality). While there are critical masses of Black women athletes at HBCUs, historical and contemporary images and standards continue to marginalize their experiences (e.g., representational intersectionality). Particularly when a queer Black women athlete's gender identity, sexual identity, and/or queerness falls outside the expected norm of femininity, her marginalization and isolation are exacerbated.

IMPLICATIONS FOR PRACTICE

Our interpretations of the three narrative constructions of the experiences of Black women college athletes that follow—outsider within, being invisible, and experiencing lack of social support—are consistent with the historical and contemporary literature on Black women athletes. Employing Crenshaw's intersectionality theory, our analyses illuminate how power and inequality influence the experiences and representation of queer Black women college athletes at HBCUs. Intersectionality illuminates the simultaneity of multiple systems of oppression and the constant work queer Black women college athletes must do to manage the interplay of these systems.

Structural Implications

An understanding of intersectionality gives administrators and coaches tools they need to see, hear, and advocate for queer Black women college athletes. Using the dimension of structural intersectionality illuminates how their experiences have an additional layer of complexity because of hegemonic ideologies (e.g., white supremacy, patriarchy) and binary rhetoric (e.g., white/Black, man/woman, queer/heterosexual). Acknowledging the multiplicity of systems of oppression and intersections of identities interrupts and challenges the perpetuation of heteronormative, racist, and gendered standards in sport. Those who want to eradicate stereotypes and social stigmas about queer Black women college athletes must have a working understanding of intersectionality.

In 1996, the Women's Sports Foundation (2018) launched the It Takes a Team campaign to support queer athletes and educate coaches, athletes, parents, and interested people and groups. The *It Takes a Team* DVD is a comprehensive toolkit that consists of PowerPoint slides, a set of definitions, and personal narratives that describe the issues and challenges queer athletes experience. While this educational tool is dated, it is a good resource for Black queer women athletes and those who support them. The DVD is co-narrated by tennis great Zina Garrison and includes narratives from two Black lesbian athletes who were college basketball players. They describe how the role of race adds a layer of complexity that often hinders Black women athletes from revealing their sexual identities to their teammates and coaches. HBCU administrators and coaches must acknowledge and respect the diversity among queer Black women athletes and provide the systems of support that are needed to combat hegemonic standards of what Black women should represent (Carter-Francique & Richardson, 2015; Theune, 2016). Those seeking to better support queer Black women athletes should learn the varied ways individuals may come out or disclose their sexual identity and/or gender identity. They should also disrupt rhetoric, slurs, and discrimination on and off the court/playing fields and in locker rooms among the team and coaching staff.

Political Implications

The experiences of queer Black women college athletes challenge the policies and best practices espoused by the NCAA. More specifically, their intersected identities challenge the single-axis framing of the college athlete experience. The book *Champions of Respect: Inclusion of LGBTQ Student-Athletes and Staff in NCAA Programs*, which was created through the support of an NCAA inclusion initiative (Morrison, 2012), presents many best practices for supporting queer college athletes. These include providing education at the department level at member institutions through workshops and videos, self-education, learning about sensitive language use, and cultivating allyship. While the book recognizes the compound effects of race and class with sexual identity, and of gender with sexual identity, it does not acknowledge the many variations and nuances of these relationships. When coaches, teammates, classmates, faculty, support staff, and administrators understand how race, gender, and social class interact with sexual identity for Black women athletes—and we could easily add sport as an identity—the potential exists to increase the inclusion of queer Black women college athletes and improve team dynamics.

More recently, Barbour et al. (2014) examined the experiences of gay and lesbian college athletes in order to identify some best practices for recruiting and retaining them. Although most of the participants were Black and women, the article provided no recommendations based on the race and gender of the study participants. Instead, the researchers offered broad-based recommendations for higher education staff, athletic department administrators, and coaches (e.g., using inclusive language and endorsing policies related to nondiscrimination and discrimination). While these recommendations promote inclusive efforts, they fail to fully appreciate the significance of the intersecting identities that queer Black women college athletes navigate.

Representational Implications

Representational intersectionality relates to how the media portrays and covers the "other," or those situated outside the dominant narrative(s). Extant literature revealed a dearth of research examining the media portrayal of Black women athletes (Carter-Francique & Richardson, 2015 Eastman & Billings, 2001); however, scholars who have explored the topic have discussed the myths, stereotypes, and gendered ideologies the media perpetuates (Bruening et al., 2005; Carter-Francique, 2020; Kane & Greendorfer, 1994). Their findings suggest that Black women athletes are subjected to negative racial stereotypes when they are depicted and discussed on television. For example, Eastman and Billings (2001) found that white women basketball players received more television commentary than Black women basketball players even though white women players are fewer in number than Black women. While commentary that expressed gender bias was limited, commentary that promoted racial bias was common. Television commentators tended to tap into racial myths about Black women's naturally superior athletic ability, but when they talked about white women athletes, then tended to focus on their mental skill. The greater finding from this study was that most of the announcers were white men and women. Lapchick and colleagues (2018) analyzed the racial and gender demographics of the Associated Press Sports Editors and gave the organization a grade of D+ for its lack of diversity and its hiring practices. The (mis)representation of Black women others them as outsiders within sport, illustrating how critical it is to understand the intersectionality of representation and outsider within status (Collins, 1986; Crenshaw, 1991, 1993). Administrators must engage professional journalists, media commentators/announcers, mass media professional, and communication students in equity and inclusion training, as they are the people who are responsible for (re)presenting these Black women athletes.

Conducting a Needs Assessment

Acquiring an understanding of the unique and nuanced experiences of queer Black women collegiate athletes is an essential step that must happen in efforts to provide appropriate support for these students. While HBCU administrators and coaches need not necessarily treat queer Black women athletes differently, they must ensure that all policies, practices, and decisions take into account the intersectional identities and experiences of these students (Morrison, 2012). Before making decisions concerning (in)equitable scholarship funding, programs, and services, institutions and athletic departments should conduct a campus climate assessment for queer students in order to evaluate student needs, determine what the campus/athletic department is doing well, and learn which areas still need improvement. Making sure students, and perhaps alumni, are involved in the creation and dissemination of assessments, programs, and services is a representation of collaborative efforts and an affirmation that their unique experiences matter.

CONSIDERATIONS FOR RESEARCH

While scholars have examined the experiences of Black women college athletes, there is a gap in the literature concerning the intersections of gender identity and sexual identity across institutional types. However, we acknowledge that the influences of structural, political, and representational intersectionality may prevent queer Black women athletes from (a) identifying themselves as potential participants for empirical studies, (b) accepting invitations to participate in studies for/with researchers who have not or do not intend to establish rapport, and (c) outing themselves because they fear having their identities (mis)represented, and/or their experiences (mis)understood. Accordingly, creating a safe space (e.g., as trusting and authentic as possible) when recruiting and engaging with Black women athletes with varying sexual identities and gender identities for academic studies is important.

Researchers must employ critical theories and methodologies such as intersectionality that center the experiences of Black women athletes (Carter-Francique, 2017). Few et al. (2003) emphasized that researchers must empower students to tell their truth(s) by adopting research practices that "(a) [contextualize the] research, (b) [contextualize ourselves] in the research process, (c) [monitor] our symbolic power in the representation process, (d) [triangulate] multiple sources, and (e) [care] for our informants in the research process" (p. 209). Researchers must approach their processes with intentionality and reflexivity and avoid perpetuating the same hegemonic systems that relegate queer Black women athletes to the margins and deem them invisible.

CONCLUSION

While HBCUs provide essential environments for racial and cultural identity development, administrators and coaches must identify and disrupt hegemonic and patriarchal standards and expectations of how and what Black women athletes should (re)present within sport and society. Through analyses that incorporate the intersectionality of structural, political, and representational systems, administrators, coaches, faculty, and staff can better examine and support the unique experiences of queer Black women athletes on HBCU campuses. Efforts should specifically acknowledge queer Black women athletes' constructions of their own experiences as significant and foster environments that support the academic work, athletic career, social identities, and developmental experiences of queer Black women athletes throughout their college and post college endeavors.

REFERENCES

Anzaldúa, G. (1987). *Borderlands/la frontera: The new Mestiza*. Lute Press.

Barbour, C. L., Roberts, G., & Windover, R. (2014). *Recruiting and retaining LGBT athletes: Lessons from the population* [Doctoral dissertation, master's thesis]. New Albany: Indiana University Southeast. https://cardinalscholar.bsu.edu/server/api/core/bitstreams/ab7e633a-8e60-4dd2-aeb3-501feb208b50/content

Bernhard, L. M. (2014). "Nowhere for me to go": Black female student-athlete experiences on a predominantly white campus. *Journal for the Study of Sports and Athletes in Education*, 8(2), 67–76.

Bruening, J. E. (2005). Gender and racial analysis in sport: Are all the women white and all the Blacks men? *Quest*, 57(3), 330–349.

Bruening, J. E., Armstrong, K. L., & Pastore, D. L. (2005). Listening to the voices: The experiences of African American female student athletes. *Research Quarterly for Exercise and Sport*, 76(1), 82–100.

Cahn, S. K. (1994). *Coming on strong: Gender and sexuality in twentieth-century women's sport*. The Free Press.

Carpenter, L., & Acosta, R. V. (2005). *Title IX*. Human Kinetics.

Carter, A. R. (2008). *Negotiating identities: Examining African American female collegiate athlete experiences in predominantly white institutions* [Doctoral dissertation]. University of Georgia.

Carter, A. R., & Hart, A. (2010). Perspectives of mentoring: The Black female student-athlete. *Sport Management Review*, 13(4), 382–394.

Carter, A. R., & Hawkins, B. J. (2011). Coping strategies among African American female collegiate athletes' in the predominantly white institution. In K. Hylton, A. Pilkington, P. Warmington, and S. Housee (Eds.), *Atlantic Crossings: International Dialogues in Critical Race Theory* (pp. 61–92). Sociology, Anthropology, Politics (C-SAP), The Higher Education Academy Network.

Carter-Francique, A. R. (2013). Black female collegiate athletes' experiences in a culturally relevant leadership program. *The National Journal of Urban Education & Practice*, 7(2), 87–106.

———. (2014). An ethic of care: Black female college athletes and development. In J. L. Conyers (Ed.), *Race in American sports: Essays* (pp. 35–58). McFarland Company, Inc.

———. (2017). Theoretical considerations in the examination of African American girls and women in sport. In A. Ratna & S. F. Samie (Eds.), *Race, gender, and sport: The politics of ethnic 'other' girls and women* (pp. 63–84). Routledge.

———. (2020). Intersectionality and the influence of stereotypes for Black sportswomen in college sport. In V. L. Farmer & E. S. W. Farmer (Eds.), *Critical race theory in the academy* (pp. 453–480). Information Age Publishing.

Carter-Francique, A. R., Dortch, D., & Carter-Phiri, K. (2017). Black female college athletes' perception of power in sport and society. *Journal for the Study of Sports and Athletes in Education, 11*(1), 18–45.

Carter-Francique, A. R., & Richardson, F. M. (2015). Black female athlete experiences at historically Black colleges and universities. In B. Hawkins, J. N. Cooper, A. R. Carter- Francique, & J. K. Cavil (Eds.), *The athletic experience at historically Black colleges and universities (HBCUs): Past, present, & persistence* (pp. 61–83). Rowman & Littlefield.

———. (2016). Controlling media, controlling access: The role of sport media on Black women's sport participation. *Race, Gender & Class, 23*(1–2), 7–33.

Collins, P. H. (1986). Learning from the outsider within: The sociological significance of Black feminist thought. *Social Problems, 33*, S14–S22.

———. (1990). *Black feminist thought: Knowledge, consciousness, and the politics of empowerment*. Routledge.

Combahee River Collective (1982). A Black feminist statement: The Combahee River Collective. In G. T. Hull, P. Bell-Scott, and B. Smith (Eds.), *All the women are white, all the Blacks are men, but some of us are brave: Black women's studies* (pp. 13–22). The Feminist Press.

Cooper, J. N., & Cooper, J. E. (2015). Success in the shadows: (Counter) narratives of achievement from Black scholar athletes at a historically Black college/university (HBCU). *Journal for the Study of Sports and Athletes in Education, 9*(3), 145–171.

Cooper, J. N., Cooper, J. E., & Baker, A. R. (2016). An anti-deficit perspective on Black female scholar-athletes' achievement experiences at a Division I historically white institution (HWI). *Journal for the Study of Sports and Athletes in Education, 10*(2), 109–131.

Cooper, J. N., Porter, C. J., & Davis, T. J. (2017). Success through community cultural wealth: Reflections from Black female college athletes at a historically Black college/university (HBCU) and a historically white institution (HWI). *Journal of Intercollegiate Sport, 10*, 129–156.

Corbett, D., & Johnson, W. (2000). The African American female in collegiate sport: Sexism and racism. In D. D. Brooks & R. C. Althouse (Eds.), *Racism in college athletics: The African American athlete's experience* (pp. 199–225). Fitness Information Technology.

Crenshaw, K. W. (1989). Demarginalizing the intersection of race and sex: A Black feminist critique of antidiscrimination doctrine. *University of Chicago Legal Forum, 1989*(1), 139–168.

———. (1991). Mapping the margins: Intersectionality, identity politics and violence against women of color. *Stanford Law Review, 43*(6), 1241–1299.

———. (1993). Race, gender, and violence against women. In M. Minow (Ed.), *Family matters: Readings on family lives and the law* (pp. 230–232).

Eastman, A. C., & Billings, S. (2001). Biased voices of sports: Racial and gender stereotyping in college basketball announcing. *Howard Journal of Communication, 12*(4), 183–201.

Everett, K. D., & Croom, N. N. (2017). From discourse to practice: Making discourses about Black undergraduate womyn visible in higher education journals and student affairs practice. In L. D. Patton and N. N. Croom (Eds.), *Critical perspectives on Black women and college success* (pp. 75–87). Routledge.

Fairclough, N. (1989). *Language and power*. Longman.

———. (1992). *Discourse and social change*. Polity Press.

Ferguson, T., & Satterfield, J. W., Jr. (2017). Black women athletes and the performance of hyper-femininity. In L. D. Patton & N. N. Croom (Eds.), *Critical perspectives on Black women and college success* (pp. 115–126). Routledge.

Few, A. L., Stephens, D. P., & Rouse-Arnett, M. (2003). Sister-to-sister talk: Transcending boundaries and challenges in qualitative research with Black women. *Family Relations, 52*(3), 205–215.

Foster, K. M. (2003). Panopticonics: The control and surveillance of black female athletes in a collegiate athletic program. *Anthropology & Education Quarterly, 34*(3), 300–323.

Greene, B. (1994). Lesbian women of color: Triple jeopardy. In L. Diaz and B. Greene (Eds.), *Women of color: Integrating ethnic and gender identities in psychotherapy* (pp. 389–427). The Guilford Press.

Green, T., Oglesby, C., Alexander, A., & Franke, N. (1981). *Black women in sport*. American Alliance of Health and Physical Education Recreation and Dance Publications.

Griffin, P. (1992). Changing the game: Homophobia, sexism, and lesbians in sport. *Quest, 44*, 251–265.

Harris v. Portland, Amended Complaint. (2006, May 26). Filed in the United States District Court for the Middle District of Pennsylvania.

Hawkins, B., Cooper, J. N., Carter-Francique, A. R., & Cavil, J. K. (Eds.). (2015). *The athletic experience at historically Black colleges and universities (HBCUs): Past, present, & persistence*. Rowman & Littlefield.

hooks, b. (1981). *Ain't I a woman?* South End Press.

Howard-Hamilton, M. (1993). African American female athletes: Issues, implications, and imperatives for educators. *NASPA Journal, 30*(2), 153–159.

———. (2003). Theoretical frameworks for African American women. *New Directions for Student Services, 104*, 19–27.

Hurtado, S., Milem, J. F., Clayton-Pedersen, A., & Allen, W. R. (1998). Enhancing campus climates for racial/ethnic diversity through education policy and practice. *Review of Higher Education, 21*(3), 279–302.

———. (1999). *Enacting diverse learning environments: Improving campus climate for racial/ethnic diversity in higher education*. Jossey-Bass.

Kane, M. J. & Greendorfer, S. L. (1994). The media's role in accommodating and resisting stereotyped images of women in sport. In P. J. Creedon (Ed.), *Women, media and sport: Challenging gender values* (pp. 28–44). Sage Publications.

Krane, V. (2001). We can be athletic and feminine, but do we want to? Challenging hegemonic femininity in women's sport. *Quest, 53*(1), 115–133.

Lapchick, R., Bloom, A., Marfatia, S., Balasundaram, B., Bello-Malabu, A., Cotta, T., Morrison, E., Mueller, M., Mulcahy, M., Sylverain, S., Currie, T., & Chase, T. (2018, May 2). *Associated Press Sports Editors (APSE) Racial and Gender Report Card*. http://nebula.wsimg.com/e1801a8b96d97c40f57cf3bf7cd478a3?AccessKeyId=DAC3A56D8FB782449D2A&disposition=0&alloworigin=1

McDonald, M., & Birrell, S. (1999). Reading sport critically: A methodology for interrogating sport. *Journal of Sociology of Sport, 16*, 283–300.

Morrison, K. (Ed.). (2012). *Champions of respect: Inclusion of LGBTQ student-athletes and staff in NCAA programs*. http://www.ncaapublications.com/productdownloads/CRLGBTQ.pdf

Newhall, K. E., & Buzuvis, E. E. (2008). (e)Racing Jennifer Harris: Sexuality and race, law and discourse in Harris v. Portland. *Journal of Sport and Social Issues, 32*(4), 345–368.

Patton, L. D., & Haynes, C. (2018). Hidden in plain sight: The Black women's blueprint for institutional transformation in higher education. *Teachers College Record, 120*, 1–18.

Person, D. R., Benson-Quaziena, M., & Rogers, A. M. (2001). Female student athletes and student athletes of color. *New Directions for Student Services, 93*, 55–64.

Porter, C. J., & Maddox, C. E. (2014). Using critical race theory and intersectionality to explore a Black lesbian's life in college: An analysis of Skye's narrative. *NASAP Journal, 15*(2), 25–40.

Ross, J. R. (2006). *Triple threat: My journey as a Black lesbian athlete in search of additional Black lesbian student-athletes*. [Master's thesis]. University of Tennessee. TRACE: Tennessee

Research and Creative Exchange. https://trace.tennessee.edu/cgi/viewcontent.cgi?article=3130&context=utk_gradthes

Roth, A., & Basow, S. A. (2004). Femininity, sports, and feminism: Developing a theory of physical liberation. *Journal of Sport & Social Issues, 28*(3), 245–265.

Ruggiero, T. E., & Lattin, K. S. (2008). Intercollegiate female coaches' use of verbally aggressive communication toward African American female athletes. *The Howard Journal of Communications, 19,* 105–124.

Satterfield, J. W., & Croft, C. J. (2015). The athletic casting call: Factors contributing to the social construction of the Black male college athlete. In R. A. Bennett III, S. R. Hodge, D. L. Graham, and J. L. Moore III (Eds.), *Black males and intercollegiate athletics: An exploration of problems and solutions* (pp. 21–43). Emerald Group Publishing Limited.

Smith, Y. (1992). Women of color in society and sport. *Quest, 44*(2), 228–250.

———. (2000). Sociohistorical influences of African American elite sportswomen. In D. Brooks and R. Althouse (Eds.), *Racism in college athletics: The African American athlete experience* (2nd ed., pp. 173–197). Fitness Information Technology, Inc.

Stratta, T. M. (1995). Cultural inclusiveness in sport: Recommendations from African American women college athletes. *Journal of Physical Education, Recreation & Dance, 66*(7), 52–56.

Theune, F. (2016). The shrinking presence of Black female student-athletes at historically Black colleges and universities. *Sociology of Sport Journal, 33,* 66–74.

Vertinsky, P., & Captain, G. (1998). More myth than history: American culture and representations of the black female's athletic ability. *Journal of Sport History, 25*(3), 532–561.

Withycombe, J. L. (2011). Intersecting selves: African American female athletes' experiences of sport. *Sociology of Sport Journal, 28*(4), 478–493.

Women's Sports Foundation. (2018). *About It Takes a Team.* Women's Sports Foundation: For Athletes. https://www.womenssportsfoundation.org/athletes/for-athletes/know-your-rights/coach-and-athletic-director-resources/it-takes-a-team/

Yosso, T. J. (2005). Whose culture has capital? A critical race theory discussion of community cultural wealth. *Race Ethnicity and Education, 8*(1), 69–91.

12 · QUEERING THE YARD

LGBTQ Advocacy, Experiences, and Socialization at Two Public HBCUs

MICHELE K. LEWIS AND
ISIAH MARSHALL JR.

> I didn't really know how to interact. I knew the slang from social media and tv but not face-to face interaction. We were side eyeing and figuring each other out.

The developing sexual identities of young people have been facilitated by internet usage in today's technologically advanced society (Harper et al., 2015). Thus, when college students appear on today's HBCU campuses, some may already have a solid queer identity that was established in middle school or high school, as indicated by the quote above from a Black queer student at a southeastern HCBU who was interviewed for this project.

HBCUs are contexts in which queer students have historically experimented with and expressed their attractional identities. This has been eloquently revealed through ethnographic research (Johnson, 2011). Yet without consistent formalized opportunities for engagement, students may have experiences like the one mentioned above. They may come to the HBCU with an intact queer identity yet may lack experiences with open, face-to-face substantive interactions with other members of the Black queer community.

Some aspects of Black diversity (i.e., LGBT rights) have not been mainstreamed and celebrated throughout HBCU history. An example is the rule against men wearing women's attire that became part of the student dress code at Morehouse College in 2009 (see Mobley & Johnson, 2019; Patton, 2014). Administrators, faculty, staff, students, and alumni may not have a good understanding of how the sociocultural environments of HBCUs shape the development of Black queer identities. Black queer students have reported less than optimal episodes of inclusivity and mainstreamed acceptance (Lewis & Marshall, 2012;

Mobley & Johnson, 2015). This chapter will offer administrators at HBCUs useful strategies for making curricular and co-curricular engagement more inclusive of LGBT populations using the framework liberation psychology.

We conducted interviews with six individuals who were attending or working at two HCBUs in the Southeast. These individuals were recruited to participate based on the following characteristics: (1) they self-identified as Black and queer, (2) they were currently enrolled at one of these HBCUs, or (3) they were employed in an administrative capacity at one of these two schools. This chapter begins with a review and discussion of the theoretical framework of liberation psychology as a way of interpreting the experiences of Black queer people on HBCU campuses. After that, we will discuss defined spaces as a method of supporting relationships among members of LGBT populations on campus. We will also discuss how curriculum enhancement can expose non-LGBT persons to Black queer trailblazers in various academic disciplines (i.e., Bayard Rustin in political science/activism and E. Lynn Harris in Black American literature). Finally, we suggest ways an administration can use financial and relational resources such as campus space and media, to address and support queer issues in the context of the HBCU experience.

LIBERATION PSYCHOLOGY

Rooted in Latin American experiences of oppressed and marginalized persons, liberation psychology advocates for change in the minds of both oppressors and the oppressed in order to bring about healing of entire communities (Martín-Baró, 1996). Brazilian educator and philosopher Paulo Freire (1972) referred to these mental changes as conscientization, a process that has the effect of motivating oppressed persons to deconstruct their lives, including taking into consideration events that were significant in their history. In African-centered psychology, it has been written that the healing of people of African descent requires a deconstruction, reconstruction, and construction of the spirit (Nobles, 1973). In addition, Black queer writers have discussed the significance of affirming the spirits of Black queer people (James & Moore, 2006).

Conscientization begins a process of self-liberation and self-healing that influences the minds and actions of both the oppressed and the oppressors within a community. This has relevance for HBCUs, where internalized oppression and colonized thinking may be unconsciously prevalent in beliefs based in Christianity, since many HBCUs were founded by religious denominations and may still have financial and other ties to religious organizations. This religious ethos may negatively influence the perceptions of queer students at HBCUs. For example, a queer male staff member at an HBCU remarked about his undergraduate experiences attending an HBCU affiliated with the African Methodist Episcopal Zion Church. He reported that "there was this fear of me not wanting to express who I really was, because of the religious piece of it." In this case, he did not report that he had a bad experience during his undergraduate years, but he did not want to disrespect the institution, Christianity, and his great-grandmother by being something other than what was "expected for a Black male to be." Lingering religious-based attitudes among Black professors, staff, and administrators may be relevant for identifying which HBCUs promote more visible and consistent queer events and educational offerings.

Both Fayetteville State University (in North Carolina) and Bowie State University (in Maryland) have been featured in the media for their celebration of queer history. However, a close reading of an NBC News article (Simon, 2017) reveals that all of the professors and queer activist/guest speakers mentioned in the article are white. Some might ask what difference that makes if the students are gaining exposure to information about being queer or are affirmed in their identity. But representation does matter. Mobley & Hall (2020) note that, "HBCU students should also be able to 'see' themselves in their professors as well. If HBCUs were to promote cultures where their [Black queer and trans*] faculty members could be "out" and serve as "possibility models" for their students, this would lead to vital reciprocal mentorship relationships" (pp. 509–510). Is it beneficial to send a message that affirmation of queer identities and history at HBCUs is possible only when white faculty, staff, and administrators bring this awareness? Does this create the impression that HBCU institutional acceptance of queering the yard is primarily made possible only by whitening the yard? These notions should be interrogated.

Martín-Baró (1996) argues that theories should not be used to define the problems of a community; instead, the problems of the community should provide the basis for formulating theories and taking actions. For Black HBCU communities, the effects of slavery and its aftermath, heterosexism, and sexism have resulted in a type of conscientization. These social ills have led to the development of creative solutions to the stress and challenges of oppression via the establishment of communities of resistance and thereby to liberation (Shulman & Watkins, 2010).

Because of social conditions and the interpersonal experiences of people of African descent, Black people's identities at HBCUs have been shaped by social units even during the modern individualistic era of history (Sampson, 1989). This contradicts what is described as a major change in the modern era: the development of people as autonomous self-contained beings (Sampson, 1989). Because of social conditions and marginalization, Black people have always self-selected their own spaces of liberatory social interaction and resistance, and these spaces and actions have shaped and represented their identities and communities (Lewis, 2014; Livingston, 1996; Stringfellow, 2011).

A Black queer male staff member who was interviewed for this chapter spoke of his experiences of resistance in the face of marginalization decades ago as an undergraduate at an HBCU: "Although in the minority, some gay students had power. I remember walking behind one of them and there was a football tree [campus space] where the football players were gathered. [An] effeminate [gay] guy was walking [in] the area and the group of football players grew louder with taunts directed at the guy. So the guy, who dressed feminine, got to the tree and pointed out a player and said. 'I know you not over there joking with them because you already know who I am' . . . and the tree got quiet. . . . I said, that dude has power." He also shared this reflection about his days as an HBCU undergraduate: "As a student, all of my suitemates/neighbors were gay; my roommate was a heterosexual football player. The gay guys would have their house music going before they went to the club. One day some other guys threw trash at the doors of the gay guys and urinated on the trash. The football player addressed the situation and said to the guys, 'Y'all need to leave these guys alone and let them be.'"

This interviewee recalled his roommate stating that some of the guys were taking showers at 2–3 A.M. every night and that some of these heterosexual-identified guys may have been fooling around with other queer guys on campus. He alluded to rendezvous by asking "Who takes showers every night at that time?" The interviewee felt that it was "big of the football player" to be vocal to the whole floor, thereby acting as an ally.

Based on interviews with staff and students, it seems there have always been allies. Yet some patterns remain regarding open allyship and closeted queer behavior. Staff persons we interviewed mentioned the ongoing existence of "undercover guys who mess around with gay or bi men, while presenting and confessing heterosexuality" at their HBCUs. While this behavior is not exclusive to HBCU contexts, it raises the question of what Black faculty, staff, and administration in higher education can do to create more comfort for all students who choose to attend an HBCU (Mobley, 2017). HBCUs will likely have to make continuous changes according to what is happening technologically, multiculturally, interculturally, and internationally. Black queer individuals must be viewed as a cultural group that is able to shape and be shaped in the global society and on the HBCU landscape of the twenty-first century (Mobley & Johnson, 2015).

DEFINED SPACES

Jegna Matching Program

Navigating these social interactions and transformations may be challenging for Black queer students. A Black queer male student who was interviewed for this chapter shared sentiments consistent with previous research that faculty at HBCUs need sensitivity training. Administrators should take the lead in ensuring that this happens (Lewis & Ericksen, 2016). HBCUs may consider developing a jegna program that matches entering queer students with a queer faculty member, staff member, or administrator who is comfortably out on campus. However, this cannot be the sole criteria for the jegna (pl. jegnoch). In keeping with the historical tradition of being a jegna, the definition of and qualifications for acting in this capacity must be detailed.

In African Amharic culture, jegna is a title of distinction. The word jegna has been translated into English as hero; warrior; soldier, courage; strength; protection of our culture, land, and people; and elder. Queer HBCU faculty, staff, and administrators who participate in a matching program for Black queer students on campus must be educated about the following special characteristics of jegnoch:

- A history of being tested in struggle or battle
- Possessing extraordinary and unusual fearlessness
- A history of demonstrating determination and courage in protecting his/her people, land, and culture
- A history of demonstrating diligence and dedication to their people
- A history of producing exceptionally high-quality work
- A history of demonstrating dedication to protecting, defending, nurturing, and aiding the development of their young by advancing their people, place, and culture

The Association of Black Psychologists (n.d.) describes jegnoch as people who are "still growing, still [learners], still with potential, and whose [lives continue] to have within [them] promise for and connection to the future" (para. 3). After becoming fully educated about the historical and cultural significance of being a jegna, individuals who want to become a jegna should understand that a jegna is deserving of honor and respect as they carry out their role of synthesizing wisdom from across their years of living; the goal is to pass this along for the benefit of future generations.

Every year, HBCUs have about a week of activities for their incoming students. A jegna matching program may be a good way to demonstrate to queer students that HBCUs mainstream queer students instead of relegating them to a "don't ask, don't tell" type of silenced status. Likewise, this would help mainstream the presence of queer faculty, staff, and administrators on HBCU campuses. The jegna activities for the incoming students might include a meet-and-greet reception for those who are matched and a luncheon later in the semester. Ideally, the luncheon would include a presentation from an invited speaker to inform attendees about the historical significance of successful Black queer-identified persons from various academic disciplines and professions (i.e., Alain Locke, Barbara Jordan).

Several interviewees regarded this recommendation for a matching program as a good idea and said it was something they would welcome on their campus.

We do understand, however, that some students do not come to their awareness of queer identity until farther along in their college career. Thus, it may not occur to some entering students to indicate their queer identity on their application.

Self-Selected Spaces and Mainstreaming of a Liberated Queer Identity

Black sexual minorities have a history of self-selecting and consciously creating practices in response to oppression (Arnold & Bailey, 2009; Conner & Sparks, 2004; Lewis & Marshall, 2012). Interviews with Black queer HBCU students and administrators revealed examples of self-selected spaces and settings such as band, modeling troupes, and gospel choirs. Black queer students at HBCUs are like Black persons throughout the Americas; people can be socially shaped to create and exhibit nuanced intercultural identities and practices while on a quest for liberatory existence (Shulman & Watkins, 2010).

As Freire (1972) discussed, after a person has been conscientized, experiencing oppression may prompt a change of mind regarding critical consciousness and may motivate the person to work for change as opposed to entering a depressed state of inactivity. In Black queer spaces, one can witness collective sociocultural, transnational, and spiritual influences on people (Conner & Sparks, 2004). African-centered Black personality assessment asserts that African influences are strong enough to remain an influence on the minds, spirits, and interpersonal behaviors of displaced Africans. Black psychologists refer to this as a type of African self-consciousness (Conner & Sparks, 2004; Kambon & Bowen-Reid, 2010). Our suggestion to faculty, staff, and administrators within HBCU contexts is to accept that Black students who are gender-nonconforming or are queer may represent cultural carryovers from various African cultures (Holloway, 2005; Murray & Roscoe, 1998; Okpewho et al., 2001; Somé, 2000; Watzlawik, 2012; Coleman, 2016).

At one time in the history of HBCUs, having university-sanctioned student organizations, courses, and programming about Black queer people would have been unheard of. But Sampson (1989) argues that group or communal influences are significant for the development of a person. Black queer students at HBCUs have always maintained self-selected spaces in which they consciously subvert the dominant culture to freely express their cultural practices and identity. For these students, their connection to the unit or group in the form of an extended self (Nobles, 1973) is key to addressing their needs, the same as it is for heterosexual and cisgender students. This suggests that it would be beneficial for the human development of Black queer students to have a formally recognized mainstreamed community of the extended self on the campuses of HBCUs.

Information obtained from our interviews support the theme of a need to mainstream queer student existence at HBCUs. Winston-Salem State University has had varying degrees of momentum over the years with its queer student organization,

Prism. Jackson State University has a successful queer student organization, Spectrum. While today it is not surprising for an HBCU to have an official queer student organization, such organizations vary significantly in how consistently and visibly active they are on campus. In addition, a theme in our interviews was that the existence of an HBCU student organization for queer students does not mean that the students, the organization, or education about queer history and culture are also mainstreamed at the HBCU.

A queer Black female student who had transferred to another HBCU from Spelman College told us about her experience as a queer student at Spelman.

> If there were an active and visible queer student organization at [my current HBCU], I would like for it to be like how Afrekete was at Spelman. They had open mic [nights], poetry slams ... At [the HBCU I attend now], people seem to mind their own business. At Spelman, they said they protected and cared, but they didn't. We [members of Afrekete] would find derogatory notes left around where we were writing affirming things. I felt that we were not accepted there. I felt that I was always being put into a box there. One of my roommates said that I made her feel uncomfortable, even though we didn't even talk. All my lesbian friends would come into the room too, so maybe that was it. Both of our dads are preachers. I could tell that she felt uncomfortable around me. When we would see each other around campus, we wouldn't speak to each other. But they [Spelman] are so concerned about bad publicity and ruining the brand. Respectability politics and branding of HBCUs is major.

A Black queer male staff member we interviewed stated that "teaching and providing knowledge of LGBT issues is not a priority [at my institution.] ... [It is] not on their plate or [in their] realm of thinking. ... They are unaware that there are faculty who can teach the courses or students that want to take them."

When we asked a Black queer male student at another HBCU if there were places on campus where he did not feel as comfortable being himself, he replied, "Schoolwide functions like gym jams, [auditorium] events, cookouts—I don't feel like these events are for the gay community/students. You can tell by the music, because it is more male-dominance music. If we were to go there and try to dance to Beyonce, it would not be accepted." Black queer students who have experiences similar to this student's find their own ways of locating community. The social units that shape students' identities currently include social media and other online apps for connecting that may not include connecting on campus.

Developing a Black Queer Inclusive Curriculum at HBCUs

Winston-Salem State University has offered courses that include queer studies in its Department of Psychological Science and its Sociology Department. For example, seniors in psychology have the option of enrolling in a topical seminar focused on international queer issues. The professor for the seminar identifies as an openly queer Black man on campus. This same professor has hosted a Black transwoman as guest speaker for a large Introduction to Psychological Sciences course he taught; she was very well received by the students. The same guest speaker was well received again when she was invited back to campus by a professor of psychology for the department's Human Sexuality course. The psychology department has also offered a liberal learning seminar for first-year students that is taught by a Black openly queer female professor. The course, Black Issues in LGBT Psychology, has been popular and students have evaluated it positively. Finally, a Black queer student who was interviewed for this chapter had this to say about a sociology course taught by a heterosexual white cisgender female professor: "I've had five classes so far and there were openly queer people in the classes. There were trans students and queer students in the sex, gender, and feminist thought class. That class was really interesting!"

Ironically, although this student reported having a positive experience in the sociology course, she said that she was nervous about being interviewed because she is only used to talking to friends about queerness, not professors. She said that it seemed weird to be talking to a professor about "something like this." These comments relate to what a staff person we interviewed told us: "Students are probably not out in their classrooms.... Comments from social media... [indicate that they feel] that they are not safe regarding sexual orientation.... Race come[s] first and then sexual identity."

There is much to be added to the curriculums of HBCUs. The work of Crenshaw et al. (1996) on intersectionality can be incorporated in educational workshops and seminars at HBCUs. For example, Black gender-nonconforming individuals are often perceived as a threat or an embarrassment, as we learned in our interview with a Black queer male student: "When I have dressed more traditionally, a bit more masculine, I have been better received in the offices. But when I wore a cutoff shirt and booty shorts one time, it was literally called a 'costume' by a staff person. When we wear our 'scandalous outfits', they try to make it more about 'the business world.' I know the places and environments where I am supposed to wear certain clothes! They feed into respectability politics so much! They sit in the windows and rip anybody to shreds who doesn't fit their moral dress code."

CONCLUSION

As the framework of liberation psychology indicates, changes in the minds of both oppressors and the oppressed may bring about healing for communities. A deeper and intentional examination of ballroom cultures, modeling troupes, gospel and university choirs, marching bands, and drum majoring is warranted. These are a few of the spaces where it seems that conscientization is likely to begin among members of the LGBT population at HBCUs. These spaces allow for broad and deep interpersonal exchanges in alternative spaces of resistance.

HBCUs must continue to focus on becoming less ethnocentric in terms of US-based and Eurocentric-based miseducation about Black people (Woodson, 1933). Black people throughout the diaspora have demonstrated that their sense of self is connected to social units. The culture and educational offerings at HBCUs can be enriched by explorations of trans-Atlantic identities and practices and a global understanding of Black people's (including queer Black people's) continuous pursuit of freedom from oppression.

Administrators should openly and honestly evaluate their campuses by initiating surveys and conducting listening groups with LGBT students, faculty, and staff and other marginalized populations on campus. This provides the space for marginalized voices to be heard, not merely tolerated. Such practices align with liberation psychology's centering of conscientization.

Now is the time that HBCUs must honestly come to terms with homophobia and miseducation about LGBT students, faculty, staff, and communities. Ideally, administrators, faculty, and staff will explore attitudes and learn effective ways to dismantle their personal bias so they can better assist LGBT students, faculty, families, and staff. HBCUs must increasingly examine and revise campus policies on discrimination to ensure that LGBT students, faculty, staff, and their allies feel supported, represented, and protected as they work and learn on the campuses of HBCUs. In 2012, Bowie State University opened the first LGBTQIA Resource Center at an HBCU. The goal was to increase awareness of sexual orientation and gender identity and reduce discrimination based on those issues. The center collaborates with faculty, staff, and students to develop effective programs that promote knowledge and awareness. This should combat miseducation and may lead to what liberation psychologists call deconstruction.

HBCUs, especially state-governed institutions, have experienced massive budget reductions in recent times. Many HBCU administrators have had to slash mission-critical programming and positions at a time when institutions must deal with students who are challenged with anxiety, depression, and suicidal ideation due to family issues, financial issues, the global pandemic, and sexual identity issues. The Center for Excellence in Behavioral Health at Morehouse College in conjunction with the Substance Abuse and Mental Health Services Administration has awarded mini-grants to assist HBCUs in addressing mental health and sexuality issues. These mini-grants are the impetus for HBCU campuses to apply for larger grants with SAMHSA and other agencies. For example, in the summer of 2018, North Carolina Central University was awarded $306,000 to provide mental health education to students, targeting LGBT community members, disabled individuals, and veterans. The administrators and staff on that campus had clearly identified the need for such services for their students. These administrative decisions help advance healing in the vein of liberation psychology and can serve as models for other HBCUs.

HBCUs must reach out to LGBT alumni and friends to form partnerships that benefit the universities. These partnerships should seek to identify areas where the universities need to improve in terms of on-campus activities and could help HBCUs forge relations with community organizations that serve LGBT people of color. At Howard University, as a mechanism for reaching alumni and current students during homecoming festivities, the Lavender Fund Renaissance Reception, a university-supported event, focuses on inclusion, scholarship, and activism (Kelly, 2019). The reception honors Howard University undergraduates who are committed to improving their communities and the quality of life for LGBT persons. Formalized annual events like this align with the framework of liberation psychology because they normalize inclusivity, scholarship, and activism in the HBCU family. Homecoming is significant in HBCU culture, and having a university-supported lavender reception sends the message that members of the LGBT community are welcomed members of the HBCU family.

Now that more attention is being paid now to HBCUs in the contexts of global Black Lives Matter activism and increased philanthropic support, it is time for HBCU administrators and staff to move from sending messages about inclusivity for some to actively working to include all members of their campus. Ambassadors of all sexual and gender identities are needed to champion the cause of liberation at all HBCUs.

REFERENCES

Arnold, E. A., & Bailey, M. M. (2009). Constructing home and family: How the ballroom community supports GLBTQ youth in the face of HIV/AIDS. *Journal of Gay and Lesbian Social Services, 21*(2–3), 171–188. https://doi.org/10.1080/10538720902772006

Association of Black Psychologists. (n.d.). *What is Jegnaship?* https://www.abpsi.org/jegnaship/

Coleman, K. (2016). The difference safe spaces make: The obstacles and rewards of fostering support for the LGBT community at HBCUs. *Sage Open, 6*(2) 1–12. https://doi.org/10.1177%2F2158244016647423

Conner, R. P., & Sparks, D. H. (2004). *Queering creole spiritual traditions: Lesbian, gay, bisexual, and transgender participation in African-inspired traditions in the Americas.* Harrington Park Press. https://doi.org/10.1525/nr.2005.8.3.135

Crenshaw, K., Gotanda, N., Peller, G., & Thomas, K. (1996). *Critical race theory.* The New Press.

Freire, P. (1972). *Pedagogy of the oppressed.* Penguin Books. https://doi.org/10.1007/978-1-4614-5583-7_610

Harper, G. W., Serrano, P. A., Bruce, D., & Bauermeister, J. A. (2015). The internet's multiple roles in facilitating the sexual orientation identity development of gay and bisexual male adolescents. *American Journal of Men's Health, 10*(5), 359–376. https://doi.org/10.1177/1557988314566227

Holloway, J. E. (2005). *Africanisms in American culture*. Indiana University Press.
James, G. W., & Moore, L. C. (2006). *Spirited: Affirming the soul and black gay/lesbian identity*. Redbone Press.
Johnson, E. P. (2011). *Sweet tea: Black gay men of the South*. The University of North Carolina Press.
Kambon, K. K., & Bowen-Reid, T. (2010). Theories of African-American personality: Classification, basic constructs, and empirical predictions/assessment. *The Journal of Pan African Studies*, 3(8), 83–108.
Kelly, S. (October 18, 2019). *Four Howard students receive Lavender Fund Scholarship during Fifth Annual Renaissance Reception*. The Dig. https://thedig.howard.edu/all-stories/four-howard-students-receive-lavender-fund-scholarship-during-fifth-annual-renaissance-reception
Lewis, M. K. (2014). Liberatory practices amid lingering oppression [Review of *Butch queens up in pumps: Gender, performance, and ballroom culture in Detroit*]. *PsycCRITIQUES*, 59(11). http://dx.doi.org/10.1037/a0035745
Lewis, M. K., & Marshall, I. (2012). *LGBT psychology: Research perspectives and people of African descent*. Springer Science.
Lewis, M. W., & Ericksen, K. S. (2016). Improving the climate for LGBTQ students at an historically Black university. *Journal of LGBT Youth*, 13(3), 249–269. https://doi.org/10.1080/19361653.2016.1185761
Livingston, J. (Director). (1991). *Paris is burning* [Film]. Off White Productions.
Martín-Baró, I. (1996). *Writings for a liberation psychology*. Harvard University Press. https://doi.org/10.1525/9780520949454-027
Mobley, S. D., Jr. (2017). Seeking sanctuary: (Re)Claiming the power of historically Black colleges and universities as places of Black refuge. *International Journal of Qualitative Studies in Education*, 30(10), 1036–1041. https://doi.org/10.1080/09518398.2017.1312593
Mobley, S. D., Jr., & Hall, L. (2020). (Re)Defining queer and trans* student retention and success at Historically Black Colleges and Universities. *Journal of College Student Retention: Research, Theory & Practice*, 21(4), 497–519.
Mobley, S. D., Jr., & Johnson, J. M. (2019). "No pumps allowed": The "problem" with gender expression and the Morehouse College "Appropriate Attire Policy." *Journal of Homosexuality*, 66(7), 867–895.
Mobley, S. D., Jr., & Johnson, J. M. (2015). The role of HBCUs in addressing the unique needs of LGBT students. *New Directions for Higher Education*, 170, 79–89. https://doi.org/10.1002/he.20133
Murray, S. O., & Roscoe, W. (1998). *Boy-wives and female husbands: Studies in African homosexualities*. Palgrave.
Nobles, W. W. (1973). Psychological research and the black self-concept: A critical review. *Journal of Social Issues*, 29(1), 11–31. https://psycnet.apa.org/doi/10.1111/j.1540-4560.1973.tb00055.x
Okpewho, I., Davies, C. B., & Mazrui, A. A. (2001). *The African Diaspora: African origins and New World identities*. Indiana University Press.
Patton, L. D. (2014). Preserving respectability or blatant disrespect? A critical discourse analysis of the Morehouse Appropriate Attire Policy and implications for intersectional approaches to examining campus policies. *International Journal of Qualitative Studies*, 27(6), 724–746. doi:10.1080/09518398.2014.901576
Sampson, E. E. (1989). The challenge of social change for psychology: Globalization and psychology's theory of the person. *American Psychologist*, 44(6), 914–921. https://psycnet.apa.org/doi/10.1037/0003-066X.44.6.914

Shulman, H., & Watkins, M. (2010). *Toward psychologies of liberation: Critical theory and practice in psychology and the human sciences.* Palgrave Macmillan.

Simon, M. D. (2017, October 17). Historically Black colleges celebrate LGBTQ history. NBC News. https://www.nbcnews.com/feature/nbc-out/historically-black-colleges-celebrate-lgbtq-history- n815971

Somé, S. (2000). *The spirit of intimacy.* William Morrow.

Stringfellow, R. (2011). Soul work: Developing a Black LGBT liberation theology. In D. Boisvert & J. E. Johnson (Eds.), *Queer Religion* (vol. 1, pp. 113–126). Praeger.

Watzlawik, M. (2012). Cultural identity markers and identity as a whole: Some alternative solutions. *Culture and Psychology, 18*(2), 253–260. http://dx.doi.org/10.1177/1354067X11434843

Woodson, C. G. (1972). *The mis-education of the Negro.* Africa World Press. (Original work published 1933)

13 • RESEARCHING ALONGSIDE, FOR, AND BY BLACK, GAY, LESBIAN, BISEXUAL, TRANSGENDER, AND QUEER COMMUNITIES AT HBCUs

A Reflection

LORI D. PATTON, NADREA R. NJOKU, AND JENNIFER M. JOHNSON

As this book has illustrated, Black gay, lesbian, bisexual, transgender, and queer (GLBTQ) communities not only exist at HBCUs but also contribute to their greatness. In fact, HBCUs would not be where they are today without the presence of these communities in terms of leadership, creativity, innovation, and the overall campus culture and identity. We have each witnessed through our own unique experiences and research endeavors how significant GLBTQ communities are and their capacity to ensure that HBCUs thrive as open and engaging environments for all students. We found that our individual motivations for embarking on research about, with, and for HBCUs was sharpened through the acknowledgment of our identities and personal experiences within this context. These experiences allowed us to build the types of relationships needed to gain access to these spaces, and to remain committed to moving beyond scholarship for scholarship's sake, and to think critically about the ways HBCU leaders can shape policy and practice to embrace GLBTQ community members. In order to guide how this action could take place, we found it valuable to engage in a reflection of our experiences researching alongside and for Black gay, lesbian, bisexual, transgender and queer communities at HBCUs.

ENGAGEMENT IN THE FIELD

Nadrea Njoku, a graduate of Xavier University in New Orleans, is an avid advocate for HBCUs. Her robust experiences at Xavier prepared her for graduate work and allowed her to witness and participate in the cultivation of Black womanhood among the women at Xavier. In her dissertation, "Woman in the Making: The Impact of the Constructed Campus Environment of Xavier University of Louisiana on the Construction of Black Womanhood," she contended that "[HBCUs] should map their institutional proximity to racism, sexism, classism, and homophobia" and that they "should also distance themselves from a commonly held belief that because they are predominantly Black institutions they do not participate in, nor have issues with inclusivity" (Njoku, 2017, p. 203). In this quote she acknowledged the need for HBCUs, her beloved Xavier included, to dig deeper to witness the presence, beauty, and humanity of Black lesbian students by examining how these institutional spaces marginalize students based on respectability politics and homophobia. In their chapter titled "Constructions of Black Womanhood at HBCUs," Nadrea and Lori Patton looked at "the performance of heteronormative femininities in the construction of Black womanhood among Black undergraduate women in HBCU contexts" (Njoku & Patton, 2017, p. 146). They presented examples from their independent projects on Black women collegians and lesbian, gay, and bisexual students at HBCUs to reveal how Black women push back against conservative institutional structures and resist "traditional prescriptions of Black womanhood" (Njoku & Patton, 2017, p. 154) that made them feel as if their bodies were policed or under surveillance at some HBCUs. As noted above and in her coauthored article "Reimagining the Historically Black College and University (HBCU) Environment: Exposing Race Secrets and the Binding Chains of Respectability and Othermothering" (Njoku et al., 2017), Nadrea approaches scholarship on HBCUs with "critical love" that she hopes will move HBCUs along the continuum of inclusion and transformation but maintain the mission-driven purpose for which they were founded. She continues this approach in her work as lead researcher for the Frederick D. Patterson Research Institute at the United Negro College Fund.

Lori Patton approached her work on lesbian, gay, and bisexual students as an early career scholar. Realizing that the research on GLBTQ populations was situated at predominantly white institutions, she asked why the scholarship in this area had not centered HBCU environments. During her graduate studies, she participated in a close-knit community that included HBCU graduates who spoke highly of their experiences, but conversations regarding GLBTQ students rarely if ever emerged. With this information, she applied for and received a grant from the American Psychological Foundation to begin a study on lesbian, gay, and bisexual students at HBCUs. She spent the subsequent years contributing publications that shifted the narrative on Black lesbian, gay, and bisexual identity development, particularly the politics of GLBTQ identity disclosure at HBCUs (Patton, 2011), negotiating multiple identities in the coming-in (rather than the coming-out) process (Patton & Simmons, 2008), understanding GLBTQ millennial students (Patton et al., 2011; Patton & Chang, 2011), and, more recently, the contradictions and complexities embedded in the culture of urban HBCU environments (Patton et al., 2020).

Jennifer Johnson enters this work through collaborative efforts to explore how and why students choose to attend HBCUs. She is a former employee of an HBCU and over time developed an increased interest in exploring the intersections of race, gender, and sexuality at HBCUs to bring these experiences to the forefront of research literature and practice. She has focused on the gendered experiences of Black women (Johnson, 2017; Williams & Johnson, 2019) and Black men (Johnson & McGowan, 2017), and on Black students' motivations for and experiences attending HBCUs (Johnson, 2019; Johnson & Jackson, 2024). Through her scholarship, she has learned that GLBTQ identities can and have shaped students' college choices, particularly Black students desiring to attend HBCUs. Yet too often, scholars interested in college choice focus on race as students' primary motivating factor without considering the intersectional nature of how identities influence students' decisions to attend a Black college and their experiences therein.

AMPLIFYING THE EXPERIENCES OF GLBTQ COMMUNITIES AT HBCUS

Over the years, we, along with coeditor Steve D. Mobley Jr., have individually and collectively worked to amplify the experiences of GLBTQ communities at HBCUs through our research, scholarship, and service. One shared area of concern was the importance of unpacking and critiquing the relationship between institutional policies and structures and the experiences of GLBTQ community members on campus (Mobley & Hall, 2020; Mobley & Johnson, 2015). Both Jennifer and Lori through their scholarship have examined institutional policies at HBCUs and the meaning such policies signal to GLBTQ students. For example, in separate publications, they examined the Morehouse Appropriate Attire Policy via critical discourse analysis (Mobley & Johnson, 2019; Patton, 2014). As an analytical strategy, critical discourse analysis allows researchers to explore "how language as a cultural tool mediates relationships of power and privilege in social interactions, institutions, and bodies of language" (Mobley & Johnson, 2019, p. 876). In "Preserving Respectability or Blatant Disrespect: A Critical Discourse Analysis of the Morehouse Appropriate Attire Policy and Implications for Intersectional Approaches to Examining Campus Policies," Patton (2014) used critical discourse analysis to unpack the policy, noting that "African American men [were] relegated to a space solely predicated upon race instead of an intersectional space where issues affecting Black men from a number of perspectives [could] be embraced. The Appropriate Attire policy [limited] the pertinent discussions that could occur at Morehouse and instead [reinscribed] heterosexism, homophobia, and patriarchy" (p. 741). In "'No Pumps Allowed': The 'Problem' with Gender Expression and the Morehouse College 'Appropriate Attire Policy," Jennifer and Steve examined media discourses surrounding the policy. They wrote, "We understand that Morehouse College is a unique higher educational context; it is the only historically Black men's college in the country. However, the Morehouse community can and should take the lead in bringing about change on their campus so that they may provide an example to other HBCUs and higher education as a whole" (Mobley & Johnson, 2019, p. 24).

LESSONS LEARNED

Our scholarship has not only resulted in publications that would carve out a space for exploring GLBTQ experiences for years to come, it has also revealed several important lessons across our work. Our collective works as scholars and the chapters of this book illustrate that GLBTQ students create their own networks and support systems, oftentimes without institutional acknowledgment and support. Through these networks we have observed the unfolding of nuanced experiences. For example, although the GLBTQ students who participated in our research felt affirmed in their Blackness and expectations of excellence, their sexual and gender identities remained on the margins. Perhaps most important, we noticed that these students did not regret their decision to attend their HBCU and despite some challenging experiences, they were more than prepared to successfully graduate and pursue their careers. Further, they felt validated at their HBCU in ways that have been fleeting at a predominantly white institution.

Based on these lessons and others, those interested in studying Black GLBTQ communities at HBCUs should acknowledge first and foremost that Blackness is not monolithic. In fact, HBCUs boast the most dynamic representations of Blackness, representations that encompass diversity of race, class, gender, religion, nationality, and sexuality. Thus, conducting this work requires letting go of preconceived notions of who attends HBCUs and what students' experiences consist of in those spaces. With this information, "HBCUs must work toward creating a more inclusive and supportive campus environment ... not only for [GLBTQ] students but for students and staff seeking to express themselves on campus without fear of retribution" (Mobley & Johnson, 2015, p. 82).

Second, Black GLBTQ students, just like any population of students, will always be light years ahead of institutional change. In fact, they are the influencers of that change. By this, we mean that while some HBCUs are viewed as having conservative environments, this characteristic is also reflected in most postsecondary institutions. Colleges and universities writ large are strongly resistant to substantive change. Patton (2011) has noted that "the reality is that few institutions have disseminated enough information to adequately educate members of the academic community about the experiences and needs of gay and bisexual students" (p. 78). Where HBCUs are concerned, the changes related to recognizing, validating, and supporting Black GLBTQ students is now happening and will continue to make progress due to the work and labor that their students have been engaged in for decades. The rise of student activism across HBCU campuses is evidence that students are advocating for change. Black queer and trans* HBCU students are "demanding for HBCUs to openly embrace free and bold Blackness that is not stifled by antiquated notions" (Mobley et al., 2021, p. 25). The strategies HBCU leaders use to respond to these demands will have lasting ramifications.

Third, researchers interested in GLBTQ populations should not assume that by the nature of their identities, they need or even want support. Nor should they assume that the mere presence of support programs and resources will attract GLBTQ populations or meet their needs. As Patton et al. (2020) explain, "For some, the presence of an organization would signal hypervisibility, which would be unwarranted if the goal was to make LGBQ students feel welcomed. For others, the presence of support services was at least appreciated and recognized even if the students were not involved" (p. 18). Institutions should not look to build a "one size fits all" approach to cultivating spaces of support. Rather, they should be open to students and staff creating and modifying their own communities with the support of rather than "approval" from the institution. Conversely, institutional leaders should be mindful of the costs associated with "queer student labor," or the expectation that GLBTQ students will lead change efforts while pursuing their college degree (Mobley et al., 2021). This arose in Nadrea's (Njoku, 2017) work around Black womanhood with HBCU alumnae. A participant said of her continuum of experiences at HBCUs—first as a student and now as a tenure-track faculty member—that there is often a lone queer faculty member who shoulders the responsibility of mothering all the GLBTQ students. That participant's experiences as a student were devoid of any examples of womanhood as she searched for answers as a queer and questioning young adult. As a faculty member, she was then clear that her self-care could not also include mothering a campus full of students seeking support; additional resources and staff were needed to scale the services required to create inclusive spaces.

Fourth, research related to Black GLBTQ groups must be done in community with *and* alongside them to center their voices in a collective desire to transform our HBCUs. So many histories of HBCU alumni have been lost due to the othering and erasure of the GLBTQ identity of the members of these groups. They have rich, illustrative stories and perspectives that are critical to the production of scholarship. They also have the capacity to write, engage in research design, data collection, and so forth and where appropriate should have opportunities to write themselves into existence during the research process.

Last, but not least, in order for HBCUs to align with their founding missions, it is important for those in leadership and administrative roles to not only engage in decisions informed by the scholarship presented in this book and similar scholarship offered by other scholars but also to be thoughtful about and committed to disrupting "heteronormativity, stringent gender roles, and ... white supremacy" (Njoku et al., 2017, p. 783).

CONCLUSION

What is clear across our collective work is that we are scholars who deeply value HBCUs, and part of valuing them is a desire to see them thrive, particularly in terms of GLBTQ populations. James Baldwin said, "I love America more than any other country in the world and, exactly for this reason, I insist on the right to criticize her perpetually" (Baldwin, 2017, p. 10). Similarly, we love HBCUs more than any other type of postsecondary institution and it is for that reason that we remain committed to the act of critiquing, questioning, and calling them to account in research and practice. Our hope is that this type of love will ensure the presence and representation of GLBTQ students, faculty, and leaders at HBCUs as well as policies, practices, and campus cultures that promote respect and humanity. Whether research is available to inform practice (or not), it is entirely possible for HBCUs to create services, outreach, and any other resources necessary to support GLBTQ students, hire GLBTQ administrators and leaders, and implement policies that regard GLBTQ people as whole and worthy humans.

REFERENCES

Baldwin, J. (2017). *Notes of a native son.* Penguin Classics.

Johnson, J. M. (2017). Social norms, gender imbalance, perception of risk, and the sexual behaviors of African American women at historically Black Colleges and universities. *Journal of African American Studies, 21*(2), 203–215. https://doi.org/10.1007/s12111-017-9354-8

———. (2019). Pride or prejudice? Motivations for choosing Black colleges. *Journal of Student Affairs Research and Practice, 56*(4), 409–422. https://doi.org/10.1080/19496591.2019.1614936

Johnson, J. M., & Jackson, E. R. (2024). The HBCU advantage: Reimagining social capital among students attending Black colleges. *Frontiers in Education, 9*(1344073). https://doi.org/10.3389/feduc.2024.1344073

Johnson, J. M., & McGowan, B. L. (2017). Untold stories: The gendered experiences of high-achieving African American alumni of historically Black colleges and universities. *Journal of African American Males in Education, 8*(1), 23–44.

Mobley, S. D., Jr. (2017). Seeking sanctuary: (Re)claiming the power of historically Black colleges and universities as places of Black refuge. *International Journal of Qualitative Studies in Education, 30*(10), 1036–1041. https://10.1080/09518398.2017.1312593

Mobley, S. D., Jr., & Hall, L. (2020). (Re) Defining queer and trans* student retention and "success" at historically Black colleges and universities. *Journal of College Student Retention: Research, Theory & Practice, 21*(4), 497–519. https://doi.org/10.1177/1521025119895512

Mobley, S. D., Jr., & Johnson, J. M. (2015). The role of HBCUs in addressing the unique needs of LGBT students. *New Directions for Higher Education 2015*(170), 79–89. https://doi.org/10.1002/he.20133

———. (2019). No pumps allowed": The "problem" with gender expression and the Morehouse College "Appropriate Attire Policy." *Journal of Homosexuality, 66*(7), 867–895. https://doi.org/10.1080/00918369.2018.1486063

Mobley, S. D., Jr., Johnson, R. W., Sewell, C. J. P., Johnson, J. M., & Neely, A. J. (2021). "We are not victims": Unmasking queer and trans* student activism at HBCUs. *About Campus: Enriching the Student Learning Experience, 26*(3), 24–28. https://doi.org/10.1177/1086482220953221

Njoku, N. R. (2017). *Woman in the making: The impact of the constructed campus environment of Xavier University of Louisiana on the construction of Black womanhood*. [Doctoral dissertation]. Indiana University. ProQuest Dissertations & Theses Global.

Njoku, N. R., Butler, M., & Beatty, C. C. (2017). Reimagining the historically Black college and university (HBCU) environment: Exposing race secrets and the binding chains of respectability and othermothering, *International Journal of Qualitative Studies in Education, 30*(8), 783–799. https://doi.org/10.1080/09518398.2017.1350297

Njoku, N. R., & Patton, L. D. (2017). Explorations of respectability and resistance in constructions of Black womanhood at HBCUs. In L. D. Patton & N. N. Croom (Eds.), *Critical perspectives on Black women and college success* (pp. 31–43). Routledge.

Patton, L. D. (2011). Perspectives on identity, disclosure and the campus environment among African American gay and bisexual men at one historically Black college. *Journal of College Student Development, 52*(1), 77–100. https://doi.org/10.1353/csd.2011.0001

———. (2014). Preserving respectability or blatant disrespect? A critical discourse analysis of the Morehouse College appropriate attire policy and implications for conducting intersectional research. *International Journal of Qualitative Studies in Education, 27*(6), 724–746. https://doi.org/10.1080/09518398.2014.901576

Patton, L. D., Blockett, R. A., & McGowan, B. (2020). Complexities and contradictions: Black lesbian, gay, bisexual, and queer students' lived realities across three urban private HBCU contexts. *Urban Education*, https://doi.org/10.1177/0042085920959128

Patton, L. D., & Chang, S. (2011). Crossroads and intersections: Exploring LGBTQ identity development among millennial college students. In F. A. Bonner, A. Marbley, & M. F. Howard Hamilton (Eds.), *Diverse millennial students in college* (pp. 193–212). Stylus Publishing.

Patton, L. D., Kortegast, C., & Barela, G. (2011). Policies, practices, and current perspectives on working with LGBTQ millennial college students. In F. A. Bonner, A. Marbley, & M. F. Howard Hamilton (Eds.), *Diverse millennial students in college* (pp. 175–192). Stylus Publishing.

Patton, L. D., & Simmons, S. L. (2008). Exploring complexities of multiple identities of lesbians in a Black college environment. *Negro Educational Review, 59*(3–4), 197–215. https://doi.org/10.1057/9781137480415_14

Williams, M. S., & Johnson, J. M. (2019). Predicting the quality of Black women collegian's relationships with faculty at a public historically Black university. *Journal of Diversity in Higher Education, 12*(2), 115–125. https://doi.org/10.1037/dhe0000077

ACKNOWLEDGMENTS

Dr. Steve D. Mobley Jr.:
I would first like to acknowledge my mother, Cheryl D. Bonner-Mobley (September 9, 1957–March 5, 2015). She TRULY was THE first person who loved me for all of me! My mommy gave me ALL of the room to express myself and just "be" without judgment! I have to give her credit; my mother raised a free Black queer and questioning child in the 1980s and 1990s who loved to sing, dance, and jump double dutch. This could not have been easy, and I think of her every day. Next, I have to thank my amazing coeditors, Drs. Nadrea R. Njoku, Jennifer M. Johnson, and Lori D. Patton. This project would not have been possible without any of you. You each have stood with me very step of the way and I shall be forever thankful. I also must thank Dr. Beverly Guy-Sheftall for her tireless fortitude, love, and labor on the behalf of Black queer and trans* HBCU communities that has she illuminated in the foreword of this book. I also must acknowledge and thank every HBCU president, senior-level administrator, faculty, and staff member who believes in the liberation of every HBCU Black queer and trans* stakeholder. Also, I would be remiss if I did not thank each author who is featured in this work. This is TRULY a project that is "for us and by us," as Solange Knowles sang in her song "F.U.B.U." This is *one for us!* Finally, I must thank my village—my ancestors, friends, family, fraternity brothers, and loved ones who have been there for me every step of the way as I embarked on the journey of embarking on this project. Thank you!

Dr. Nadrea Njoku:
I would like to acknowledge the women and fems at Xavier University of Louisiana who navigated at the margins of campus to wrestle cultural capital in an environment that placed value on hyperfemininity and heteronormativity yet continually articulating who they intended to be with purpose and without apology. These students were a part of the experiences I drew on as a young student affairs professional that drove me to center Black women in my scholarship. I'd also like to thank my coeditors for their support and collaboration throughout the book process.

Dr. Jennifer Johnson:
I acknowledge the labor and love that went into the conceptualization of this book. We appreciate the perspectives, lived experiences, and scholarly insights that unfold in each chapter. I also give thanks to the tireless efforts of my coeditors and my graduate assistant, Amani Rush, for their dedication to completing this important project.

Dr. Lori D. Patton:

I am incredibly grateful to see this book come to fruition and acknowledge the hard work, passion, and dedication of my coeditors in doing much of the heavy lifting and allowing me to mentor, coach, support, and contribute along the way. This book is particularly special because when I came to understand the need for such a book, I knew it would be best led by Dr. Steve D. Mobley Jr. When I approached him about partnering, he boldly took the reins and guided this project to completion. I recall the challenges of engaging this work earlier in my career and acknowledge Iowa State University, the American Psychological Foundation, and the Student Affairs Administrators in Higher Education (NASPA) for funding my research to explore and place on center stage the voices and experiences of LGB students at HBCUs, particularly when funding opportunities were limited. I acknowledge the queer and trans* students across several HBCUs who allowed space for me in their lives and made time to share their stories and experiences. I acknowledge the many queer and trans* family members, friends, colleagues, and advisees who not only encouraged and challenged me but also pushed my thinking and understanding in my personal and professional life. Thank you to all of our contributors as well as the institutional leaders committed to listening to queer and trans* communities. I offer a special acknowledgment to my graduate assistant and future PhD, Michelle Leao, the APA whisperer, for editing and formatting support.

NOTES ON CONTRIBUTORS

STEVE D. MOBLEY JR., PhD, is an associate professor of higher education and student affairs in the Department of Advanced Studies, Leadership, and Policy at Morgan State University. His scholarship focuses on the contemporary placement of historically Black colleges and universities, especially the understudied facets of HBCU communities related to race, social class, and student sexuality. He earned his BA in communication and culture from Howard University. He completed his master's in higher education management at the University of Pennsylvania and his PhD in higher education at the University of Maryland, College Park. In 2021, he was a College Student Educators International (ACPA) Emerging Scholar, and in 2022, he was a Diverse: Issues in Higher Education Emerging Scholar. He has published in *Teachers College Record*, *The Journal of Higher Education*, *The Journal of Homosexuality*, *The Urban Review*, and the *International Journal of Qualitative Studies in Education*.

NADREA R. NJOKU, PhD, is the assistant vice-president of the Frederick D. Patterson Research Institute at the United Negro College Fund. Her research foci include African American women in higher education, historically Black colleges and universities, gender, and student development theory. Her scholarship is centered in a critical race and feminist framework that is devoted to disrupting issues of race and gender in the postsecondary education context. Her recent and forthcoming publications explore topics that include the constructed campus environments of HBCUs and their impact on students' developing ideas of gender performance, the multiple constructions of Black womanhood in the postsecondary context, and the use of sister circles and interpersonal relationships in supporting Black women in graduate school. Dr. Njoku is a graduate of Xavier University of Louisiana and holds a master's degree and a doctorate from Indiana University.

JENNIFER M. JOHNSON, PhD, is an associate professor of higher education in the Department of Policy, Organizational & Leadership Studies at Temple University. Her research areas include pre-college access programs; historically Black colleges and universities; students in science, technology, engineering, and math (STEM); and high-achieving students of color. This scholarship explores the ways race, gender, and class intersect to shape the educational experiences of students across diverse institutional contexts. She has presented at several national conferences, including the Association for the Study of Higher Education and the American Educational Research Association. Dr. Johnson holds a bachelor of science degree in biology and psychology from Syracuse

University, a master's degree in elementary education from Chestnut Hill College, and a master's degree in higher education management from the University of Pennsylvania. She earned her PhD in higher education from the University of Maryland, College Park.

LORI D. PATTON, PhD, is chair of the Department of Educational Studies and professor of higher education and student affairs at The Ohio State University. She is best known for her important cross-cutting scholarship on Black communities in higher education with a focus on women and girls, critical race theory, campus diversity initiatives, and college student development. Dr. Patton's scholarship has been funded by grants from the Spencer Foundation, the Lumina Foundation, the American Psychological Foundation and an array of other entities. She is a fellow of the American Educational Research Association and a member of the National Academy of Education.

MAKOLA M. ABDULLAH, PhD, is the fourteenth president of Virginia State University. Through dynamic leadership, he has positioned VSU for continued growth focusing on six strategic areas: student opportunity/access, academic excellence, student holistic experiences, the land-grant mission, brand, and financial/operational effectiveness. Dr. Abdullah is active on numerous boards and committees including the Council of 1890 Presidents for the Association of Public and Land-grant Universities, the Southern Association of Colleges and Schools Commission on Colleges, and the Council of Presidents for the State Council of Higher Education for Virginia. He earned an undergraduate degree from Howard University and master's and doctorate degrees in civil engineering from Northwestern University.

AKILAH R. CARTER-FRANCIQUE, PhD, is dean for the School of Education, Health and Human Services at Benedict College. A former college athlete in track and field, she conducts research that examines the intersection of sport, society, and social justice, including issues of diversity, social movements, and the dynamics of social change and development. Carter-Francique served as the 2018–2019 president of the North American Society for the Sociology of Sport, and she is the co-editor of *The Athletic Experience at Historically Black Colleges and Universities: Past, Present, and Persistence* and *Black Athletic Sporting Experiences in the United States: Critical Race Theory*.

FELECIA COMMODORE, PhD, is an associate professor of higher education in the College of Education at the University of Illinois Urbana-Champagne in the Department of Education Policy, Organization and Leadership. Felecia's research focuses on leadership, governance, and administrative practices with a particular focus on HBCUs and Minority Serving Institutions. Her research interests also include how leadership is exercised, constructed, and viewed in various communities and the relationship of Black women to leadership. She is the lead author of *Black Women College Students: A Guide to Student Success in*

Higher Education. She earned her PhD in higher education from the University of Pennsylvania's Graduate School of Education.

CHRISTOPHER N. CROSS, PhD, is a biomedical engineer, anatomist, neuroscientist, population geneticist, cancer biologist, LGBTQ+ advocate, and entrepreneur. His passion lies in using scientific research to understand and address the etiology of population health disparities. He leads Cross River Strategies, a U.S.-based boutique consulting firm that uses community engagement and scientific research to power health equity strategies and services across biotech, pharma, and academic institutions. As a former member of the board of trustees at Howard University, he championed development efforts to establish the Lavender Fund, the first university-wide fund-raiser to support LGBT+ students at any HBCU. To date, the fund has awarded scholarships to seventeen students in disciplines that include medicine, law, and dentistry. Dr. Cross completed his bachelor's degree at the Georgia Institute of Technology and his master's degree and PhD at Howard University. He was a postdoctoral fellow at Yale University.

K. T. EWING, PhD, is an associate professor of History in the Department of Gender and Race Studies at The University of Alabama. As an alum of Xavier University of Louisiana and a third-generation HBCU graduate, they are dedicated to preserving Black cultural and intellectual spaces. Their research interests include Black history, women and gender studies, and the influence of blues culture in American society. She has writings published in *The Black Scholar, Black Perspectives, Transformations in Africana Studies, and Black Female Sexualities*. Her current book project, *Remember My Name: Alberta Hunter and the Two-Faced Archive*, examines the life of Alberta Hunter, a twentieth-century blues and cabaret singer from Memphis, Tennessee.

LETIZIA GAMBRELL-BOONE, EdD, earned her doctorate in higher education administration from The George Washington University in 2002. A proud two-time alumna of Hampton University, she began her career in higher education there in 1992 and continued her career in a variety of student success and administrative positions. Before joining the senior leadership team at Salve Regina University as vice president for student affairs, Dr. Gambrell-Boone was the vice president of student success and engagement at Virginia State University. She writes and presents on diversity and inclusion, change management, authenticity, leadership, organizational culture, and student development.

ASHLEY GRAY, PhD, is senior consultant and founder of ALG Consulting. She also served as a senior research analyst for the American Council on Education. She is a scholar, practitioner, and activist with a passion for creating equity within higher education. Dr. Gray is the first graduate of the higher education leadership and policy studies doctoral program at Howard University. She also holds an MEd in higher education administration from the University of

Missouri–St. Louis and a BA in African American Studies from Saint Louis University.

LESLIE HALL, PhD, is the director of the Historically Black Colleges and Universities Program of the Human Rights Campaign Foundation, the largest LGBTQ civil rights organization in the world. At the Human Rights Campaign, Leslie works with HBCU presidents and administrators toward the goal of achieving full LGBTQ equality and inclusion for LGBTQ students. A frequent speaker and panelist, Leslie has been highlighted in *Black Enterprise*, *Blavity*, the *Washington Post*, *Reuters*, among other places. Leslie holds a bachelor's degree in sociology from Bowie State University and a master of social work degree from Howard University and recently earned his PhD in Higher Education Leadership and Policy Studies at Howard University. Leslie's research agenda is focused on the pathways to the presidency for LGBTQ HBCU administrators, leadership development for LGBTQ student leaders, and fund-raising among LGBTQ populations of color. He devotes his professional work and scholarship toward the liberation of Black and Brown LGBTQ people.

DARRYL B. HOLLOMAN, PhD, serves as vice president for student affairs at Spelman College, a historically Black college for women located in Atlanta, Georgia. He has worked in higher education for over twenty-seven years and has an extensive portfolio that includes experiences in student affairs practice, higher education governance, and faculty life. Dr. Holloman has served on the faculty at Rutgers University–Newark, the University of Arkansas at Little Rock, Columbus State University, Georgia State University, and Spelman College. Dr. Holloman has several articles and book chapters to his credit. His research examines social and cultural inequities in school settings.

JARREL T. JOHNSON, PhD, is an assistant professor of higher education at the University of Utah. Previously, Dr. Johnson served as a student affairs practitioner who promoted access to college and the success of students from diverse backgrounds at Cornell University, Morehouse College, and Iowa State University. His research examines how the social identities of institutional stakeholders influence their time in higher education environments and the role higher education institutions play in shaping equitable policies and practices. Dr. Johnson holds a BA in English from Shaw University, an MEd from Mercer University, and a PhD in higher education administration from Iowa State University.

MICHELE K. LEWIS, PhD, is professor of psychological sciences at Winston-Salem State University and a member of the Association of Black Psychologists and the Society for Black Brain and Behavioral Scientists. She is a frequently an invited speaker at historically Black colleges and university. Dr. Lewis co-authored *LGBT Psychology: Research Perspectives and People of African Descent*. Her latest book is *Our Biosocial Brains: The Cultural Neuroscience of Bias, Power, and Injustice*.

She has written several book chapters, reviews, and articles that center people of African descent. She was a 2017–2018 research fellow at the Center of Socioeconomic Economic Mobility through Education.

DARYL LOWE, JD, is the associate vice president for student affairs at Spelman College. Prior to his appointment, he served as the assistant vice president and dean of students at Valdosta State University. He was the first African American to hold the latter post at Valdosta. Lowe is very passionate about the student experience and student development and is considered a thought leader on issues related to Title IX, student conduct, and equity. Lowe graduated from Morehouse College with a BA in philosophy. He later earned his doctor of jurisprudence degree from the University of Massachusetts School of Law at Dartmouth.

DIANA LU, PhD, is a molecular biologist and project management professional with over sixteen years of experience in clinical research, molecular biology, biochemistry, and genetics and adjacent fields. In her current leadership role as a principal with Cross River Strategies, Dr. Lu serves as senior consultant working with a wide variety of medical institutions, nongovernmental organizations, and biotechnology corporations. Dr. Lu previously worked as a freelance editor and writing coach for clients in STEM fields, in which capacity she earned funding from agencies including the National Science Foundation and the Ford Foundation. From 2014 until 2016, Dr. Lu served in a variety of cross-disciplinary leadership roles through Partners Healthcare Inc. and Harvard Medical School, including managing the financial structure of a bioengineering research group and overseeing operations in a research center composed of engineers, computer scientists, and clinicians. Dr. Lu completed their bachelor's degree at University of California, Berkeley and their PhD at the Massachusetts Institute of Technology.

ISIAH MARSHALL, JR., PhD, is dean and professor at the Ethelyn R. Strong School of Social Work at Norfolk State University. Prior to these roles he was associate dean of the School of Social Work at Jackson State University in Jackson, Mississippi. Dr. Marshall's research interests and publications have highlighted gerontology, qualitative research, and LGBTQ people of color. He is dedicated to advocacy for and service to historically black colleges and universities.

TRINICE MCNALLY, MS, is a feminist, a nationally recognized transformative leader, a student affairs professional, a community organizer, a cultural worker, and a priestess in the Yoruba tradition. As a queer Black immigrant first-generation HBCU college graduate, she founded the first Gay-Straight Alliance at a Florida HBCU at Bethune-Cookman University in 2012. This student organizing work set the foundation of her lifetime commitment to ensuring that HBCUs foster intersectional learning environments that center the experiences of historically marginalized students through policy, programming, and academic curricula. Trinice has extensive experience in higher education, student affairs, and Black queer feminist organizing. She has served as the coordinator of the LGBTA Resource Center at North Carolina Central University. She currently serves as the founding director of the Center for Diversity, Inclusion and Multicultural Affairs at the University of the District of Columbia, which is committed to providing a safe and welcoming environment for diverse student populations, specifically LGBTQ+/nonbinary international (status and nonstatus holders) and first-generation students. She is most passionate about developing strategies and initiatives and curating spaces that enable historically marginalized populations to transform and thrive through programmatic, advocacy, and political education efforts through education, arts, and culture.

TOBIAS RAPHAEL MORGAN, PhD, is a higher education student affairs professional who has been nourished by a passion for student development. His background is rich with positive experiences in student engagement and instruction and in insights toward building bridges between students and the community. Dr. Morgan earned a doctor of philosophy in higher education from Morgan State University in May 2020. He currently serves as dean of students at Shaw University. Combining his passion of higher education with fraternity and sorority life, Dr. Morgan's research specifically focuses on gender, race, sexuality, and Black Greek-letter Organizations.

CHEVELLE MOSS-SAVAGE, LPC, MHS, HS-BCP, CGCS, is a licensed psychotherapist and founder of HEAL LLC. She holds a master's degree in human services clinical counseling from Lincoln University. Moss-Savage is also a certified grief counseling specialist and a human services-board certified practitioner. Chevelle is an international thought leader who has been recognized for her amazing work to further social justice and equity for LGBTQIA+ and Black and Brown folx. Although she is a licensed clinician and a diversity and inclusion consultant, she is also versed in promoting cross-intersectional awareness through trainings that seek to eradicate stigmas related to mental health, ability status, faith traditions, or LGBTQIA+ identities.

YÉMAYA DIAVIAN POPE is an educator, storyteller, and Black woman of trans* experience who resides in Atlanta, Georgia. She is an alumna of Morehouse College in Atlanta, Georgia, where she earned a BA in sociology. She is the first trans* female on record to graduate from Morehouse College in the school's more than 150-year history. Yémaya was also the first full-time female student on the Morehouse student record since the 1930s, which, as a graduate, makes her the first institutionally documented Morehouse Woman in over 80 years. Yémaya also holds a master's in education from Marshall University, and is currently preparing herself to attend law school to earn a JD. Most recently, Yémaya published her memoir titled *Natural Woman: A Memoir Anthology*, and established House of Diavian, an interior designing company. Above all, Yémaya's focus is on the institution of family and one day fulfilling the roles of wife and mother.

CHRISTA J. PORTER, PhD is associate dean for graduate education and associate professor of higher education administration at Kent State University. She critically examines policies and practices that influence the development and trajectory of Black women in higher education, college student development; and research and praxis in higher education and student affairs. She was recognized by the American College Personnel Association as an Emerging Scholar in 2017. Dr. Porter's work has appeared in various refereed education journals and academic books. She also coedited *Case Studies for Student Development Theory: Advancing Social Justice and Inclusion in Higher Education*.

W. RUSSELL ROBINSON, PhD, is associate professor and chair of the Department of Communications at Alabama State University. His research interests include social media and social movements, representations of Black masculinity in popular culture, and hip-hop cultural studies. His recent chapter depicting the use of Instagram and the Black Lives Matter movement is in *From Tahrir Square to Ferguson: Social Networks as Facilitators of Social Movements*. Dr. Robinson has appeared on Al Jazeera English, The Stream, and Diverse: Issues in Higher Education, where he discussed the impact of social media in connection with the Pulse nightclub attack. Additionally, he has appeared in the *Wall Street Journal*, and *Ebony*. He is currently editing a volume about Black masculinity in the twenty-first century as well as serving as guest coeditor of a special issue of the *Howard Journal of Communication* on Prince Rogers Nelson and transcending race.

BEVERLY GUY-SHEFTALL, PhD, is founding director of the Women's Research and Resource Center (since 1981) and Anna Julia Cooper Professor of Women's Studies at Spelman College. Guy-Sheftall has published a number of texts in African American and women's studies, including the first anthology on Black women's literature, *Sturdy Black Bridges: Visions of Black Women in Literature*, which she coedited with Roseann P. Bell and Bettye Parker Smith; *Words of Fire: An Anthology of African American Feminist Thought*; and *Traps: African American Men on Gender and Sexuality*, an anthology she coedited with Rudolph P. Byrd. Guy-Sheftall is the recipient of numerous fellowships and awards, among them a National Kellogg Fellowship, a Woodrow Wilson Fellowship Women's Studies Fellowship, and Spelman's Presidential Faculty Award for outstanding scholarship. She has been involved with the national women's studies movement since its inception and provided leadership for the establishment of the first women's studies major at a historically Black college. Beyond the academy, she has been involved in a number of advocacy organizations, including serving on the boards of the National Black Women's Health Project, the National Council for Research on Women, and the National Coalition of 100 Black Women. In her role as director of Spelman's Women's Center, she has been involved with the development of student activism around misogynist images of Black women in hip-hop as well as a broad range of social justice issues, including reproductive rights and violence against women. She teaches women's studies courses, including feminist theory and global Black feminisms.

BONNIE TAYLOR, EdD, is a leadership consultant with Vantage Leadership Consulting. Prior to joining Vantage Leadership Consulting, she served as the assistant vice president and dean of students at Spelman College. Dr. Taylor previously served communities at the Georgia Institute of Technology as associate dean of students and at Georgia State University as the director of student integrity and coordinator for student conduct. She has nearly twenty years of progressive experience in student affairs and is a member of American School Counselor Association (ASCA), National Association of Student Personnel Administrators (NASPA), and Southern Association for College Student Affairs (SACSA). Dr. Taylor holds a BA in speech communication from Muskingum University, an MA in business administration from King University, and a EdD in educational leadership from East Tennessee State University.

JENNIFER M. WILLIAMS, MA, is director of the Women's Center, associate director of diversity and inclusion, and program coordinator of the LGBTA Resource Center at North Carolina Central University. She is an educator, artist, clinician, and social entrepreneur. Williams has made a profession of being the change she wants to see in the world. Prior to joining the NCCU family in January 2013, Williams enjoyed appointments in radio broadcasting, education, and health and education journalism.

KATHRYN C. WYMER, PhD, is professor of English at North Carolina Central University, where she also teaches in the Women's and Gender Studies program. She has published on partnering with students as researchers in *The International Journal for the Scholarship of Teaching and Learning*, and following the passage of HB2 in North Carolina, she began to partner specifically with LGBTQ students on campus to promote equality and visibility. Following a 2016 advocacy piece in *The Chronicle of Higher Education*, she developed NCCU's first course in LGBTQ literature with a grant funded by the Franklin Humanities Institute's Mellon Humanities Futures initiative. As a co-recipient with Dr. W. Russell Robinson of an NCCU Academic Innovation Grant to research the HBCU experiences of queer and trans people of color, she is currently engaged in research and advocacy with particular interests in supporting transgender individuals. She is the author of *Introduction to Digital Humanities*. Her work has also appeared in publications such as *The Journal of Gender Studies*, *Punk & Post-Punk*, *The Journal of Effective Teaching in Higher Education*, and *The Chronicle of Higher Education*.

INDEX

Note: Page numbers followed by *f* or *t* indicate figures or tables, respectively.

Abdullah, Makola M., 88–89
academic affairs, student affairs working with, 126, 128–129, 132–134
Academic Innovation Grant, 126, 132
Academy of Art University, 134
administrators, 7, 115, 192; at Bethune-Cookman University, 51; Black queer and trans* students impacted by, 162, 164–165; campus culture developed by, 141; guide for, 150–151; professional development for, 118; quare and trans* students calling out, 110; queer spaces supported by, 89; student affairs, 96–97, 100; tolerance assumed by, 116–117. *See also* board of trustees
Adodi (safe space organization), 41
advancement offices, of historically Black colleges and universities, 6
advisor, fraternity, 114–115
Advisory Board for LGBTQIA+ Inclusion, of Virginia State University, 90–91
African Methodist Episcopal Zion Church, 185
AIDS epidemic, 109
Alabama State University, 113
Allen, W. R., 111–112
Alliance Group, The (T.A.G.), 59, 60
All the Women Are White (Crenshaw), 17, 28
allyship, privileges and, 165–166
alumni, lesbian, gay, bisexual, transgender, queer or questioning, intersex, and asexual or allied, 134
A&M College, 113
American Missionary Association, 111
American Psychological Foundation, 197
Appropriate Attire Policy, Morehouse, 162, 198–199
Armstrong, Samuel Chapman, 35
Associated Press Sports Editors, 178
Association for the Study of African American Life and History, 24, 39
Association of Black Psychologists, 188
athletes, Black queer women college. *See* Black queer women college athletes

Atlanta (Georgia), 36, 141
Atlanta University Center, 36
Audre Lorde Black Lesbian Feminist Project, 58

Baldwin, James, 32, 41, 127, 201
ballroom culture, 33
Barbour, C. L., 178
beauty, femininity and, 174
Beginning College Survey of Student Engagement, 91
belonging, sense of, 84, 86–87
Bessie (film), 16
"Best Practices for Social and Cultural Networks Necessary to Foster Safe Learning Environments for LGBTQ Students at HBCUs" (McNally), 52
Bethune, Mary McLeod, 49, 54, 74
Bethune-Cookman University (B-CU), 49–53
Beyond Respectability (Cooper), 26
biannual campus-wide identity seminars, 44
Big Freedia (music ambassador), 27
Billings, S., 178
Birrell, S., 175
Black education, Christianity influenced by, 111
Black gay, lesbian, bisexual, transgender, and queer communities, 196–199
Black History Month, 22–23, 39
Black identity, Black queer and trans* students balancing queer identity and, 160
Black Is . . . Black Ain't (film), 23
Black land-grant institutions, 111
Black Lives Matter movement, 15, 60, 193
Blackness: focus on defining, 22; historically Black colleges and universities centering, 157; Mobley on, 162
Black queer and trans* communities, lesbian, gay, bisexual, transgender, queer or questioning communities marginalizing, 109
Black queer and trans* students, 166; administrators impacting, 162, 164–165; Black identity and queer identity balanced

213

214   Index

Black queer and trans* students (*continued*) by, 160; coming out rejected by, 161. *See also* queer and trans* students; trans* students
Black queer communities, heterocisnormative norms impacting, 86
Black queer identity, building a sense of, 23
Black queer inclusive curriculum, 190–191
Black queer male staff members, 186–187, 190
Black queer men, and identity choices, 160–162
Black queer people, in queer studies marginalizing, 29
Black queer scholars, the academy and, 28
Black queer students: campus environments undermining, 157–158; dress of, 161–162; at historically Black colleges and universities, 15–16; isolation of, 101
Black queer women college athletes, 7, 170–171, 180; literature lacking on, 172, 174–175, 179; NCAA challenged by, 177; as objectified other, 172; representation of, 176
Black students, systemic oppression faced by, 98
Black trans* students, historically Black colleges and universities miseducating, 34
Black trans *womx[x]yn, historically Black colleges and universities miseducating, 4, 32, 38, 42
Black womanhood, 197, 200
Black women, 26; in higher education, 35; marginalization of, 171–172; media portrayals of, 174; television commentators marginalizing, 178
Black womx[x]yn: curriculum not centering, 41; at historically Black colleges and universities, 35–38; as teachers, 35
board of trustees, 5, 151; committees by, 146; composition of, 73–75; decision-making by, 73–75; diversity of, 74–75; external relationships of, 76; for Howard University, 144; institutional culture influenced by, 72; institutions impacted by, 77; queer and trans* students supported by, 80–81; role of, 71–72, 77–78; values influencing, 75
Bowie State University, 55, 70, 110, 186; Howard University contrasted with, 141; Lesbian, Gay, Bisexual, Transgender, Queer, Intersex, and Allies Resource Center at, 99–100; Queer Culture course offered at, 128

Brother Outsider (documentary film), 23
Brown, Ariana, 133
Bryant, Taylor, 60
budget reductions, at historically Black colleges and universities, 192
Buzuvis, E. E., 174–175
Byrd, K., 42, 99, 112–113

Caffrey, Margaret, 24
Campbell, Mary Schmidt, 95–96
Camp Pride (leadership academy), 87
campus climate, 90–91, 102; quare student leadership influencing, 112; queer, 68–69; at University of Missouri-Columbia, 71
Campus Climate Index for LGBTQ Inclusion, 90–91
campus culture, 98; administrators developing, 141; conservatism influencing, 50, 72–73; lesbian, gay, bisexual, transgender, queer/questioning, intersex and asexual/agender students protected by, 91; religious affiliations shaping, 111
campus environments: Black queer students undermined by, 157–158; conservatism of, 69; respectability politics in, 115; scholarship exposing, 157–158; trans*-inclusionary spaces lacked in, 41
campus involvement, gender expression negotiated with, 114
capitalism, Hampton model exemplifying, 35
Carella, Kristen, 132, 137n1
Carter, Mandy, 125
Center for Diversity, Inclusion and Multicultural Affairs, at University of the District of Columbia, 5, 58–60
Center for Excellence in Behavioral Health, at Morehouse College, 192
Center for Revolutionary Scientific Thought (CReST), 143
Champions of Respect (book), 177
Cheyney University, 15, 85
Chicago, Judy, 59
Chickering, A. W., 135
Chocolate Cities Symposium, 27
Christianity, 86–87, 111
cisgender students, trans* students in conflict with, 34
#citeblackwomen, 28
Civil Rights Movement, 22–23, 140

Clance, P. R., 114
Clarke, Cheryl, 28
classrooms, inclusive, 25–26
clearing, 36
Clifton, L., 58
climate, campus. *See* campus climate
Clinton College, 120
"closet," the, conservatism creating, 69–71
co-conspirators, quaring for, 165–166
collaborations, organizing and partnership, 56; collaborative leadership, 162
Collected Poems of Audre Lorde, The (Lorde), 21
colleges. *See specific colleges*
college services, 76, 87, 89, 102, 103
Collins, A. C., 35, 171, 173
Combahee River Collective Statement, 24
coming out, 107, 161, 166n2
committees, and board of trustees, 146
Commodore, Felecia, 69
communities. *See specific communities*
compartmentalizing, by queer students, 22
"complementary pathway," "pervasive pathway" contrasted with, 126
Congressional Science Fellow, 144
conservatism, 81n1, 111–112, 140; campus culture influenced by, 50, 72–73; of campus environments, 69; the closet created by, 69–71; queer and trans* stakeholders impacted by, 86–87. *See also* religious affiliations
Conway, James, 24
Cooper, B. C., 26
cooperative inquiry, 52
Counseling Services department, at Bethune-Cookman University, 51–52
course development, 129–131
courses, queer studies, 128–132
Cox, Laverne, 128–129
Creating Open Lives Organizing for Real Success (COLORS), 55, 129
Crenshaw, Kimberlé, 17, 171, 172, 176, 191
Cross, Christopher N., 139, 145f
culture: ballroom, 33; hetero-cis normative, 98–99; heteronormative, 69–70; institutional, 72; popular, 27; queer, 102–103, 128; queer students doubting, 101–102. *See also* campus culture
curriculum, 61–62; Black queer inclusive, 190–191; Black womx[x]yn not centered in, 41; instruction reform and, 44; lesbian, gay, bisexual, transgender, queer or questioning, intersex, and asexual or allied content incorporated into, 127–128; queering, 126–129

Dinner Party, The (art installation), 59
direct services, for queer students 104
discrimination: Black women athletes and, 177–178; on campus, 88, 112, 116, 147, 192; creation of HBCUs in response to, 84, 85; gender based, 41, 43; intersectionality and, 171–172, 175
disidentification, concept of, 159
diversity, of board of trustees, 74–75
Diversity Speaks (support group), 87
Dominant Overly Motivated Studs (DOMS), 56
double consciousness theory (Du Bois), 16
Douglass School, 39
Doxey, Tia Marie, 54
dress, of Black queer students, 161–162
dress codes: at Morehouse College, 162, 184; one-on-one discussions shifted to from, 117; queer population targeted by, 38
dressing professionally, historically Black colleges and universities teaching, 18–20
Du Bois, W.E.B., 16
Dunye, Cheryl, 23

Eastman, A. C., 178
Education Amendments (1972), 175
education awareness, recommendations for, 104–105
education research, historically Black colleges and universities misrepresented in, 1
enrollment, trans* intentionality and, 43
environments, campus. *See* campus environments
Evans, S. Y., 35

"Facilitating Campus Climates of Pluralism, Inclusivity and Progressive Change at HBCUs" (Guy-Sheftall), 99
Fairclough, N., 172
family, as social institution, 33–34
Fayetteville State University, 55, 186
federal government, Howard University funded by, 141

femininity, beauty and, 174
feminism, second-wave, 59
Ferguson, T., 174
fictive kin, kinship ties contrasted with, 34
financial reserves, lesbian, gay, bisexual, transgender, queer or questioning+ students dedicated, 61
fiscal resources, recommendations for, 105–106
Florida A&M University, 116
Ford, Obie, 109–110, 160
Ford, T. C., 19
"for us, by us" (FUBU) project, 1
fraternity advisors, 114–115
Frederick, Simone, 139, 149
Frederick, Wayne A. I., 139, 147–149
Frederick D. Patterson Research Institute, at United Negro College Fund, 197
Free Application for Federal Student Aid (FAFSA), trans* students outed by, 43
Freedmen's Bureau, 111, 140
Freire, Paulo, 185, 189
funding, queer and trans* stakeholders and, 61

Gaither, Zenobia, 20
Gamson, Zina F., 117, 135
Gasman, Marybeth, 35, 37
gay, lesbian, bisexual, transgender, and queer communities, Black, 196–199
gay rights movement, 25, 109
Gay-Straight Alliance, 5, 51–53
Gender and Sexual Diversities Resource Center, at Bowie State University, 70
gender diversity and inclusion liaison, development of, 43
gender expression, and campus involvement, 114
gender pronouns, correct use of, 119
general education requirement, pro-trans*, 45
Generation Z, 16
Gilmore, Angela, 125
Givens, J. R., 45
"go back and get it" (*Sankofa*), 16, 28–29, 40
Gomez, Jewelle, 24–25
Graduate Association for African American History, 24
Graduate Student Alliance, Howard University, 143
Graduate Student Council, Howard University, 143
graduate trustees, 119, 139, 142–143, 145*f*
Green-Hayes, A., 112
groupthink, 74
guest lecturers, benefits of, 132
Guy-Sheftall, Beverly, 99

Hall, L., 33, 43–44, 54, 69, 86, 162
Hampton model, capitalism exemplified by, 35
Hampton University, 35, 110
Hansberry, Lorraine, 23
harassment, of queer students, 114–115
Harlem Renaissance, 148–149
Harris, Jennifer, 174–175
Harris, P. J., 115
Harris vs. Portland (court case), 175
HB2 (North Carolina law), 124, 125, 131
HBCU Initiative (Human Rights Campaign), 56–57, 88, 118
HBCU LGBTQ-Equality Initiative (National Black Justice Coalition), 58
HBCU Out Loud Day (Human Rights Campaign), 110
Hemphill, Essex, 60
hetero-cisnormative culture, at historically Black colleges and universities, 98–99
hetero-cisnormative norms, Black queer communities impacted by, 86
heteronormative culture, queer and trans* students marginalized by, 69–70
Hidden Figures (film), 33
Higginbotham, Evelyn Brooks, 115
higher education: Black women in, 35; intersectionality overlooked by, 175; patriarchy and white supremacy characterizing, 170
historically Black colleges and universities (HBCUs). *See specific topics*
historically white institutions (HWIs), 2, 34, 85
HIV, 56, 88, 120
Home Girls (Smith), 17
homophobia, at historically Black colleges and universities, 29, 115, 192
Howard University, 100, 118–120, 139–140, 150; board of trustees for, 144; Bowie State University contrasted with, 141; federal government funding, 141; Graduate Student Council at, 143; Lavender Fund at,

6, 78, 139, 147, 151, 193; LGBTQ+ Advisory Council of, 149, 152
Howard University International Lesbian, Gay, Bisexual, Transgender, Ally, and Alumni Association, 149–150, 152
Howard University LGBT Alumni Association, 149
Howard University Rainbow Alumni Association (HURAA), 150, 152
Hudson, Chanel, 38
Hull, G. T., 17
Human Rights Campaign, 119–120; HBCU Initiative, 56–57, 88, 118; HBCU Out Loud Day, 110; historically Black colleges and universities partnering with, 78
Hunter, Marcus, 27
Huntington, West Virginia, 38–39
Hurston, Zora Neale, 36
Hurtado, S., 100

identities. *See specific topics*
Imes, S., 114
imposter syndrome, 114, 145
inclusion, 5, 41, 43, 58–60, 89–91, 162–164; data collection and analysis on, 172–173; history of, 85–86; importance of, 86–87; method of, 172–173; at Virginia State University, 87–88, 90t
inclusive academic spaces, for queer students, 135–137
inclusive classroom, 25–26
institutional culture, board of trustees influencing, 72
integration concept, and HBCUs, 46
intersectionality, 26, 115, 171–172, 191; higher education overlooking, 175; representational, 178; trans*, 43
isolation, 20–21, 141
It Takes a Team campaign, 177

Jack, Laura, 146
Jackson, Edison O., 52
Jackson, Mary, 33
Jackson State University, 8, 190
Jaeger, A. J., 161
jegna matching program, 187–189
jegnoch, characteristics of, 188
Jewell, J. O., 111–112
Johns, David, 165

Johnson, E. Patrick, 29, 98, 109–110, 162–165, 166n1, 167n6
Johnson, Jarrel T., 159
Johnson, Jennifer, 198
Johnson, J. M., 28
Johnson, Katherine, 33
Johnson C. Smith University, 120
Jolly, David, 131

Kaleidoscope (residential community), 125
Kiamsha movement, 59
Kiburi Pride LGBTQ+ Scholarship, 60
King, Aliya S., 38
King, Martin Luther, Jr., 22–23
kings, class, 113, 114
kinship, historically Black colleges and universities lacking, 39
kinship ties, fictive kin contrasted with, 34
Kirby, Victoria, 57

Ladder, The (Hansberry), 23
land-grant institutions, Black, 111
Lapchick, R., 178
Lavelle, Lydia, 125
Lavender Ceremony, 88, 130–131
Lavender Fund, at Howard University, 6, 78, 139, 147, 151, 193
Lavender Liaisons program, at LGBTA Resource Center, 128
Lavender Report, The (document), 146
leadership: collaborative, 162; institutional, 45–46; queer and trans* stakeholders included in, 67–68; queer and trans* students supported by, 76–79. *See also* quare student leadership
lecture models, 128–129, 132–134
LePeau, L., 126
Lesbian, Gay, Bisexual, Transgender, Queer, Intersex, and Allies Resource Center, at Bowie State University, 99–100
lesbian, gay, bisexual, transgender, queer or questioning (LGBTQ): online resource centers, 42–43; quare student leadership advancing, 116; task force, 118
lesbian, gay, bisexual, transgender, queer or questioning (LGBTQ) communities: Black queer and trans* communities marginalized in, 109; organizational structures engaging with, 5

Index

lesbian, gay, bisexual, transgender, queer or questioning, intersex, and asexual or allied (LGBTQIA): alumni representation, 134; communities, 84

lesbian, gay, bisexual, transgender, queer or questioning, intersex, and asexual or allied (LGBTQIA) content: curriculum incorporating, 127–128; undergraduate academic coursework incorporating, 126; women's and gender studies focusing on, 129

lesbian, gay, bisexual, transgender, queer or questioning, intersex and asexual/agender+ (LGBTQIA+) students, 5, 50

lesbian, gay, bisexual, transgender, queer or questioning+ (LGBTQ+) students: campus culture protecting, 91; Counseling Services department supporting, 51–52; Creating Open Lives Organizing for Real Success led by, 55; financial reserves dedicated to, 61. *See also* queer and trans* students; trans* students

lesson plan model, 127–128

Lettman-Hicks, Sharon, 57

LGBTA Resource Center, at North Carolina Central University, 54, 125, 128–131, 135

LGBTQ+ Advisory Council, of Howard University, 149, 152

Liberated Threads (Ford), 19

Liberating Scholarly Writing (Nash), 3

liberation psychology, 185–187, 191–192

Lorde, Audre, 24, 58, 60; *The Collected Poems of Audre Lorde* by, 21; "Love Poem" by, 21; *Sister Outsider* by, 22, 53; "Transformation of Silence into Language and Action" by, 22, 53; *Zami* by, 21–22, 24

Love, Bettina, 29, 165–166

"Love Poem" (Lorde), 21

Lyceum Series, at North Carolina Central University, 129–130

March on Washington, 104

marginalization, of Black women, 171–172

Marshall University, 38

Martín-Baró, I., 186

McCune, J. Q., Jr., 167n5

McDonald, M., 175

McGwier, Marie, 137n1

McNally, Trinice, 52

"Mean Girls of Morehouse, The" (King, A.), 38

Means, D. R., 161

mental health and wellness, 44

Migration Matters (organization), 59

Miner, Myrtilla, 58

Mis-Education of the Negro, The (Woodson), 39, 44

"Miseducation of Yémaya, The" (Pope), 34, 38–42

missionary organizations, 111

Mister (title), 113, 114, 120

Mobley, S. D., Jr., 28, 43–44, 54, 86, 160; on Blackness, 162; on historically Black colleges and universities, 98, 100; on intersecting identities, 115; "No Pumps Allowed" by, 199; on "possibility models," 33; respectability politics discussed by, 69

Model for Transformational Inclusion at historically Black colleges and universities (MTI at HBCUs), 162–164

Monae, Janelle, 16

Morehouse Appropriate Attire Policy, 162, 198–199

#MorehouseCannotEraseMe, 110

Morehouse College, 4, 33, 36, 39, 70, 100; Black queer men at, 161–162; Center for Excellence in Behavioral Health at, 192; dress codes at, 162, 184; enrollment and persistence at, 40t; royal court at, 120; trans* admission gender policy at, 40–41

Morehouse-James Hall, 36, 37f

"Morehouse Women," 36

Morgan, M., 116–117, 120

Morgan, T. R., 109

Motivating Open-Minded Social Acceptance and Inspiring Change (MOSAIC), 70, 110

Muñoz, J. E., 159

NASA, 33

Nash, R. J., 3

National Black Justice Coalition, 56–58, 120

National Black Lesbian and Gay Leadership Forum, 125

National Pan-Hellenic Council, 115

National Women's Studies Association, 24

Natural Woman (Wesley), 41

NCAA, Black queer women college athletes challenging, 177

NCAA Division I, 174

New Black, The (documentary), 133

Newhall, K. E., 174–175
Niles, Joi, 51
Njoku, Nadrea, 99, 197, 198, 200
Noble, J. L., 35
"No Pumps Allowed" (Mobley and Johnson), 199
North Carolina Central University (NCCU), 55–56, 100; LGBTQ Resource Center at, 54, 125, 128–131, 135; Lyceum Series at, 129–130; Office of the Provost at, 133; queer students supported by, 6, 124, 126; queer studies courses at, 129, 131–132; School of Law at, 125; Student Affairs Division at, 136; women's and gender studies minor offered by, 129

Obama, Barack, 119
Obergefell v. Hodges (Supreme Court decision), 141, 142
objectified other, Black queer women college athletes as, 172
O'Neal, Keo Chaad, 95
organizational structures, lesbian, gay, bisexual, transgender, queer or questioning communities engaged with through, 5
organizational structures, quaring, 162–164
organizing, collaborations and partnership, 56
othermothering, 99, 159, 167n3
OutLAW (organization), 56
outsider within (status), 171
Owens, Aja, 23

Paris Is Burning (film), 23
Parks, Damian, 53
partnership, collaborations and organizing, 56
passing, McCune defining, 167n5
patriarchy, higher education characterized by white supremacy and, 170
Patton, Lori D., 161, 197–198, 200
Pennsylvania State University, 174–185
people of color, queer and trans, 132
"pervasive pathway," "complementary pathway" contrasted with, 126
Peters, Keadrick, 110
philanthropists, white, 140
policy: analysis of, 104; practices in relation to, 73; recommendations for, 42, 104. *See also* dress codes
Polychromes (organization), 56, 125

Pope, Yémaya Diavian, 34
popular culture, and reaching students, 27
Portland, Maureen "Rene," 174–175
"possibility models," 186
Potomac Institute for Policy Studies (think tank), 143
practices, 52; implications for, 176–179; institutional, 79; policy in relation to, 73; quaring, 164–165; recommendations for, 77–80, 102
praxis, research integrated into, 52–54
PrEPing Our Futures Tour, 58
"Preserving Respectability or Blatant Disrespect" (Patton), 198
presidents, queer and trans* students supported by, 80–81
Prism (organization), 190
privileges, allyship and, 165–166
professional aesthetics, and models for students, 19
professional development, for administrators, 118
Project Survival Through Education, Prevention, and Services (S.T.E.P.S.), 51
Pronoun Pin Initiatives, 165
pro-trans* general education requirement, 45
pro-trans* organizations, 42

QTPOC Research Experience (WGST 3610) (course), 132–133
quare and trans* students, administrators called out by, 110
quare student leadership, 110–111; campus climate influenced by, 112; disadvantages experienced by, 119; invisible, 113–114; lesbian, gay, bisexual, transgender, queer or questioning communities advanced by, 116; student affairs professionals not supporting, 117; support lacked for, 112–113, 117; visible, 116–117, 120
quare theory, 9n1, 29, 109–110, 158–159, 161, 167n6
queer (label), 109, 166n1
queer and trans* culture, at historically Black colleges and universities, 1–2
queer and trans people of color (QTPOC), 132
queer and trans* stakeholders: conservatism impacting, 86–87; funding and, 61; historically Black colleges and universities

queer and trans* stakeholders (*continued*) not including, 85; leadership including, 67–68

queer and trans* students, 71; board of trustees supporting, 80–81; heteronormative culture marginalizing, 69–70; historically Black colleges and universities and, 92–93, 104; leadership supporting, 76–79; presidents supporting, 80–81. *See also* Black queer and trans* students; trans* students

queer campus climates, historically Black colleges and universities and, 68–69

queer collegians, at historically Black colleges and universities, 101–102

queer communities: Black, 86; Black gay, lesbian, bisexual, transgender, and, 196–199; education of issues facing, 96–97; historically Black colleges and universities supporting, 99. *See also* lesbian, gay, bisexual, transgender, queer or questioning (LGBTQ) communities

queer culture, resources funding, 102–103

Queer Culture course, Bowie State University offering, 128

queer experiences, at historically Black colleges and universities, 98–101

queer faulty, queer students paired with, 187–188

queer identity: Black, 23, 160; Black queer and trans* students balancing Black identity and, 160; liberated, 189–190

queer inclusive curriculum, Black, 190–191

queer male staff members, Black, 186–187, 190

queer men, Black, 160–162

queer of color critique, 158, 159, 161

queer population, dress codes targeting, 38, 98, 117, 184

queer scholars, Black, 28

queer spaces, administrators supporting, 89

queer students. *See specific topics*

queer studies, Black queer people marginalized in, 29

queer studies courses, 128–132

queer women college athletes, Black. *See* Black queer women college athletes

racial demographics, of students, 68
racial-gender vindicationism, 45

"Rainbow blueprint," of Virginia State University, 89–91
Rainbow Soul (advocacy group), 87–88
Reason, P., 52
Reconstruction era, 68
"Reimagining the Historically Black College and University (HBCU) Environment" (Njoku and Patton), 197
religious affiliations, 140; campus culture shaped by, 111; queer students and, 106, 185; traditionalist norms and, 69
Renaissance Reception, 118–119, 139, 147–149, 193
representation, 137, 186; of Black queer women college athletes, 176; campus programming ensuring, 106; at historically Black colleges and universities, 54, 59, 61; of lesbian, gay, bisexual, transgender, queer or questioning, intersex, and asexual or allied alumni, 134
representational intersectionality, and the "other," 178
research, praxis integrating, 52–54
resource centers, lesbian, gay, bisexual, transgender, queer or questioning, 42–43
resource centers, sexuality and gender equity, 106
respectability politics, 198; in campus environments, 115; Mobley discussing, 69; as strategy, 167n4
Riggs, Marlon, 23
Riley, Patrick, 133
Roberson, Vanessa, 110
Robinson, W. Russell, 132
Robinson, Zandria F., 27
romantic partnerships, 20
Roque, Ashley, 133, 134
Ross, J. R., 174
royal courts, class, 113, 114, 120
Rustin, Bayard, 22–23, 104

Safe Zone Ally program, 87
Safe Zone trainings, 27, 91, 92, 125, 165
Sampson, E. E., 189
Sankofa ("go back and get it"), 16, 28–29, 40
Satterfield, J. W., Jr., 174
scholarship: campus environments exposed by, 157–158; queer students not addressed in, 101; trans* students lacking, 37–38; void

in, 2–3. *See also* Lorde, Audre; Mobley, S. D., Jr.
School of Law, at North Carolina Central University, 125
Second Morrill Act, 111
second-wave feminism, 59
self-selected spaces, 189–190
service learning, 45
services, college, 103
sexual identities, developing and experimenting with, 184
sexuality and gender equity resource centers, 106
sexual orientation, grappling with 50–51
Shaw University, 120
Shepard, Matthew, 97
Simmons, S. L., 161
Sister Outsider (Lorde), 22, 53
Smith, Barbara, 15, 17, 44, 45
Southern University, 113
Speaking OUT at NCCU (speaker series), 132
Special Topics (ENG 3040) (course), 129, 130, 131–132
Spectrum (organization), 190
Spelman College, 6, 70, 76, 95; Audre Lorde Black Lesbian Feminist Project at, 58; queer student experience at, 190; royal court at, 120; Women's Research and Resource Center at, 55, 99
Spivey, Mary, 36
Squire, D. D., 115, 160
staff members, Black queer male at HBCUs, 186–187, 190
St. Augustine's University, 120
Stranger Inside (film), 23
Strategies for Resistance, Resilience, and Hope (Summer Institute), 125
student affairs, 104; academic affairs working with, 126, 128–129, 132–134; queer students provided for by, 102; vice president of, 6, 96–97, 105
student affairs administrators, queer students advocated for by, 96–97, 100
Student Affairs Division, at North Carolina Central University, 136
student affairs professionals, quare student leadership not supported by, 117
student experience, and choice of college, 95–96

student identities, quaring, 160–162
student leadership, quare, 110–112, 116–117
Student Leadership Institute, at Tennessee State University, 118
student policies, quaring, 164–165
students, racial demographics of, 68
Substance Abuse and Mental Health Services Administration (SAMHSA), 51, 192
Suggs, E., 36
support structures, 175–176
"Swept Under the Rug?" (Gasman), 35
systemic oppression, Black students faced by, 98

#TakeBackHU protests, 147
Tarver, Terrence, 144
task forces, for lesbian, gay, bisexual, transgender, queer or questioning students, 118
teachers, Black womx[x]yn as, 35
television commentators, Black women marginalized by, 178
Tennessee State University, 24, 118
Thompson, Michelle, 53
Title IX, 105, 175
tolerance, administrators assuming, 116–117
traditionalist norms, religious affiliations and, 69
trans* admission gender policy, at Morehouse College, 40–41
"Transformation of Silence into Language and Action, The" (Lorde), 22, 53
trans*-inclusionary spaces, campus environments lacking, 41
trans* intersectionality, enrollment and, 43
trans* students, 3, 4; cisgender students in conflict with, 34; Free Application for Federal Student Aid outing, 43; scholarship lacked on, 37–38. *See also* Black queer and trans* students
trans* womx[x]yn, Black, 32
Traps (Byrd and Guy-Sheftall), 99
trustees, graduate, 119, 139, 142–143, 145*f*
Twi language, Ghanaian, 4, 16

Ubuntu Biography Project, 27–28
undergraduate academic coursework, lesbian, gay, bisexual, transgender, queer or questioning, intersex, and asexual or allied content incorporated into, 126

United Methodist Church, 50
United Negro College Fund, 197
universities. *See specific universities*
University Counseling Center, at Virginia State University, 87
University of Missouri-Columbia, 71
University of the District of Columbia, Center for Diversity, Inclusion and Multicultural Affairs, 5, 58–60

Vaughn, Dorothy, 33
vice president of student affairs, role of, 6, 96–97, 105
vindicationism, racial-gender, 45
Virginia State University (VSU), 5, 84; Advisory Board for LGBTQIA+ Inclusion, 90–91; inclusion at, 87–88, 90t; Lavender Ceremony at, 88; "Rainbow blueprint" of, 89–91; University Counseling Center at, 87

Walker, Alice, 127
Warmack, Dwaun, 51
Watermelon Woman, The (film), 23
Wesley, Jonathan, 41
West Virginia State University, 33, 40
white philanthropists, historically Black colleges and universities established by, 140
white supremacy, higher education characterized by patriarchy and, 170

Wholley, Jeshawn, 57
Why We Can't Wait (King, M.), 22–23
Williams, K. L., 2
Wilson, Frederica, 144
Winley, Lakesha, 54
Winston-Salem State University, 8, 189, 190–191
womanhood, Black, 197, 200
"Woman in the Making" (Njoku), 197
women, Black. *See* Black women
women college athletes, Black queer. *See* Black queer women college athletes
women's and gender studies (WGST), 129–130
Women's Research and Resource Center, at Spelman College, 55, 99
Women's Sports Foundation, 177
womx[x]yn: Black, 32, 35–38, 42; Black trans*, 4, 32, 38, 42; significance of spelling, 46n1
Woodruff Library, at Atlanta University Center, 36
Woodson, Carter G., 39, 42, 44, 45
World AIDS Day, 120
Wymer, Kathryn, 132

Xavier University, 15, 76, 197

"Yémaya," meaning of, 39, 46n2

Zami (Lorde), 21–22, 24